David R. Smith
david.smith@totalise.co.uk
+44 (0)7968 436473

Cylons in America

D1343474

Also available from Continuum:

Seinfeld, Master of Its Domain
Revisiting Television's Greatest Sitcom
edited by David Lavery and Sara Lewis Dunne

Blame Canada!
South Park and Contemporary Culture
Toni Johnson-Woods

The Sopranos on the Couch
The Ultimate Guide
Maurice Yacowar

The Historical Epic and Contemporary Hollywood
From *Dances with Wolves* to *Gladiator*
James Russell

Disguised as Clark Kent
Jews, Comics, and the Creation of the Superhero
Danny Fingeroth

Cylons in America

Critical Studies in *Battlestar Galactica*

edited by
Tiffany Potter
and
C. W. Marshall

continuum

NEW YORK • LONDON

2008

The Continuum International Publishing Group Inc
80 Maiden Lane, New York, NY 10038

The Continuum International Publishing Group Ltd
The Tower Building, 11 York Road, London SE1 7NX

www.continuumbooks.com

Printed in the United States of America on 50% postconsumer waste recycled paper

Library of Congress Cataloging-in-Publication Data

Cylons in America : critical studies in Battlestar Galactica / edited by Tiffany Potter and C.W. Marshall.
    p. cm.
  Includes bibliographical references and index.
  ISBN-13: 978-0-8264-2847-9 (hardcover : alk. paper)
  ISBN-10: 0-8264-2847-9 (hardcover : alk. paper)
  ISBN-13: 978-0-8264-2848-6 (pbk. : alk. paper)
  ISBN-10: 0-8264-2848-7 (pbk. : alk. paper) 1. Battlestar Galactica (Television program : 2003-) I. Potter, Tiffany, 1967- II. Marshall, C. W., 1968- III. Title.

PN1992.77.B354C93 2008
791.45'72--dc22

                                          2007034368

For Sloane Madden
and Jonah Marshall
who patiently endured three seasons
of Sunday dinners in the basement

Contents

A Note on Names

There are many problems with names and references in a series that involves android clones as covert agents who resurrect into different bodies. The following are the conventions adopted for *Cylons in America*. Though we recognize that at times a particular description might seem imprecise, we hope that it will at least possess the virtues of being clear and consistent across the volume.

1. Colonial pilots are typically referred to using their call signs (e.g., Starbuck, Apollo, Helo, Racetrack, and Flattop).
2. Cylons whose number has not yet been revealed are called by their most commonly used name: Leoben, Cavil, Doral, Simon.
3. The first Cylon Three that was met was the journalist who went by the name D'Anna Biers. Other Threes have not used this name, and each is referred to simply as a Three.
4. The Six who is involved with Baltar on Caprica before the Cylon attacks (who following resurrection allies with Boomer) is Caprica Six. The Six who is held prisoner on the *Pegasus* is unnamed in the series, but called Gina by the producers, a convention we follow here. The Six that Baltar alone can see is referred to as Baltar's virtual Six, even

though there is a direct connection between her and the Six he knew on Caprica.

5. The Cylon model Eight has two individuated characters. Boomer is the Eight who was a sleeper agent on *Galactica* during Season One, shoots Adama, is shot by Cally, and then resurrects, becoming an ally of Caprica Six in Cylon councils. The Eight on Caprica in Season One, who subsequently marries Helo, bears the hybrid child Hera, and is eventually given the call sign Athena is called Sharon throughout this volume.

All episodes in the current series have been identified by the number given on the episode list at the end of this volume. Episodes from the original *Battlestar Galactica* and *Galactica 1980* have been identified by title alone.

"I See the Patterns":
Battlestar Galactica and the
Things That Matter

C. W. Marshall and Tiffany Potter

"I see the patterns.... It's all there, I see it and you don't."

—Leoben Conoy, "Flesh and Bone" (1.08)

An insurgency struggles against an occupying power who is their technological superior; refugees flee persecution with ever-diminishing resources; a society fractured along ideological lines fosters political corruption and Machiavellian opportunism; those we thought we knew turn out to be enemies; sexy female androids wield guns.[1] As it enters its fourth season, the award-winning *Battlestar Galactica* (*BSG*) continues its great popularity for non-network television, combining the familiar features of science fiction with direct commentary on life in mainstream America. The central narrative depicts the remnants of the human race fleeing across space from the Cylons. The fleet is protected by a warship, the *Galactica*, and is searching for a lost colony that settled on the legendary planet Earth. *BSG* took its original form as a television series in the 1970s created by Glen A. Larson; the current reimagined *BSG* maintains the mythic sense established in the earlier quest narrative, but adds elements of hard science and an aggressive engagement with post-9/11 American politics. Since 1978, the crimson pulse of the robotic Cylon eye has been an iconic symbol that serves as a pop-cultural shorthand for menace. More terrifying yet, the Cylons can now appear human as well.

In the prehistory to *BSG*, the Cylons were robots, mechanical beings created by humans. This differs from the story presented in the original *Battlestar Galactica*, which, true to its Cold War context, imagined the enemy coming from outside: an alien reptilian race (the Cylons) created the robots, and were in turn destroyed by their creation, which embarked on a soulless expansionistic program that led to "The Thousand Yahren [Year] War" with the Twelve Colonies ("Saga of a Star World," "War of the Gods, Part II"). The new *BSG*, post–Cold War, post-9/11, removed the presence of aliens (there has been no nonhuman, natural sentience) and makes the Cylons a human creation and a human responsibility. In addition, *BSG* presents Cylons who have, as the opening credits assert, "evolved." Human-appearing androids are part of the *Battlestar Galactica* tradition: Andromus, who appeared in "The Night the Cylons Landed," (a two-part episode in the spinoff series *Galactica 1980*), is sometimes thought to be the first Cylon to appear human, though "Amazons of Space," a comic in the "authorized" Grandreams annual *Battlestar Galactica* (1978), presents a planet of female "Cylon-built robots" ("Weird! They even *kiss* like real women!" Starbuck gasps). These may even be seen as the missing link in Cylon evolution.

In previous science fiction, the closest parallel is provided by the replicants in *Blade Runner*,[2] artificially created synthetic beings with living tissue and cells. As with replicants, there are ways in which the Cylons are different from humans. Cylons have programming; they interface with technology intravenously, or through the gel on the controls of a Cylon basestar; when they are killed, their knowledge and memories are downloaded into another identical body—"death then becomes a learning experience" ("Scar" 2.15). These new models of Cylons are near-human, but somehow not—an imaginative transgression that is explored in different ways by both Matthew Gumpert and Alison Peirse in this volume.

The reimagined series exhibits a curious relationship with its predecessor. The original series ran for one season in 1978–79, and was followed by a half-season spinoff, *Galactica 1980* (1980). There is a tension in the current revisioning, as it is obviously emulating many aspects of the original's imagined universe in terms of narrative elements (including the names of the ships and certain characters, ship design, and curses), the general plotline (the ragtag fugitive fleet, fleeing the

Cylons, the quest for Earth), and casting. The writers play with these parallels. In "Bastille Day" (1.03), for example, Apollo points a gun at Tom Zarek, played by Richard Hatch, who originated the role of Apollo in 1978. Zarek, thus always implicitly connected with Apollo, is also established as having written a manifesto that influenced the present Apollo when he was at college before the Cylon attack. But Zarek's resonances echo beyond this. While the association is never explicit, the contrasting journeys of Zarek, from tract-writing political prisoner to vice president of the Colonies, and Gaius Baltar, from vice president of the Colonies (through the presidency) to tract-writing political prisoner, colors the audience's impression of both men. In Baltar's case, there is an additional dynamic in that his covert adherents—every tract-writing political prisoner deserves covert adherents—also ascribe to him religious authority, with several asking him to bless their children, as we see in "Crossroads, Part 1" (3.19).[3] Elements that provided opportunities for moments of innocence and comic relief, on the other hand, have been consistently removed (the child Boxey, for example, and the robotic dog Daggit).[4]

The original series has entered the North American science-fiction lexicon to a sufficient degree that the name of the series necessarily evokes associations for a significant number of viewers. But there is also something resembling shame in the connection. Commentators include references to the original show as "terminally cheesy" (*National Review,* January 20, 2006) or "campy" (*Boston Globe,* October 5, 2006). They then gesture with surprise at "how timely and resonant the [new] show is, bringing into play religion and religious fanaticism, global politics, terrorism, and questions about what it means to be human" (*The New Yorker,* January 23, 2006).[5]

Such conflicted response is not limited to reviews. Viewers have noted that "homage after homage to the original series was hurled at us as if to appease some unsatisfied want that the writers perceived would be there" (Morris 116–17). Similarly, executive producer David Eick, speaking in June 2003, confirmed, "We have also been inspired by certain episodes of the original *Battlestar Galactica* series" (quoted in Bell 240). Still, even within the show's production, there is denial about the new *BSG*'s relationship with its predecessor. Three times the official companions to the series distance episodes from similar episodes in the original. Perhaps most startlingly, Carla Robinson, writer of "You Can't Go Home Again" (1.05) denies echoes of her episode with "The Return of Starbuck" in *Galactica 1980*, claiming, "I was neither aware of the episode nor that series" (Bassom, *Official Companion* 60). In a similar denial, Moore claims that the Season One episode "The Hand of God" was not an homage to the original series, which concluded with a finale entitled "The Hand of God," but rather that it was all just "a very odd coincidence" (Bassom, *Official Companion* 82). Finally, Michelle Forbes, who plays Admiral Cain, claimed that "until about four days into shooting [the episode "Pegasus" 2.10] . . . I had no idea the episodes were based on a story from the original series and that I was playing Lloyd Bridges!" (Bassom, *Two* 66). Readers of Harold Bloom's *Anxiety of Influence* should have a field day. The persistence of the denials is suspicious, but even if all are true, the associations remain for viewers with knowledge of the 1970s *Battlestar Galactica* and *Galactica 1980*. Our familiarity with the earlier work informs how we interpret a given episode, and our analyses are the richer for it. In different ways, various contributors to this volume explore this tension between the two iterations of the series (see Rikk Mulligan in particular).

Such tensions and evolutions are the result of both artistic and economic pressures. Art, taste, and politics change constantly, of course, but there has also been a significant development recently in the economics of producing television. It is an old truism of the medium that television is designed to sell audiences to advertisers. The increasingly mainstream availability of developments such as TiVo, downloadable episodes, and the direct marketing of complete seasons of television series by means of DVD have changed the fundamental nature of this model. Technology is providing the viewer with the means to remove commercials from broadcasts seamlessly, and shows are being marketed as products to be bought directly by consumers. And this changes the nature of the product presented to the viewer: the episode-based narrative is now supplemented with longer story arcs; increased budgets yield cinematic production values; and more mature themes and intellectually stimulating topics are addressed in a sophisticated manner, because audiences are being targeted directly, rather than being sold to advertisers hoping to capture an ever-elusive demographic. All this is good for the viewer, who rewards good programming with direct engagement, and DVD purchases.[6]

The revisioning of *Battlestar Galactica* exemplifies this new model (in this volume Kevin McNeilly examines how the series acknowledges the televisual frame). Aggressive science fiction is being offered, blending traditions and subgenres. A plot can hinge on physical constants such as the speed of light ("Lay Down Your Burdens, Part 2" 2.20), even when faster-than-light (FTL) travel is an established premise of the series.[7] In an essay reportedly appended to copies of the script for the 2003 miniseries, executive producer and creator Ronald D. Moore articulates his view on the question of genre by coining the term "naturalistic science fiction": "Our goal is nothing less than the reinvention of the science fiction television series . . . a new approach is required. That approach is to introduce realism into what has heretofore been an aggressively unrealistic genre. Call it 'Naturalistic Science Fiction.' This idea, the presentation of a fantastical situation in naturalistic terms, will permeate every aspect of our series" ("Naturalistic"). Moore goes on to promise conventions of "hard science fiction"—"The speed of light is a law and there will be no moving violations"—which are not strictly observed, but he is right to coin a new term for the social dimension of the show. Hard science intersects with aspects of the fantasy of "space opera," and both are further informed by familiar images of dystopic future fiction (in this volume Lorna Jowett explores the liminal place that science and scientists inhabit in *BSG*). This refusal to limit the show to a single generic framework is consistent with *BSG*'s fragmentary cohesion (oxymoronic though it is): it is the disruption of known modes, the fragmentation of extant systems, that enforces the unity within the fictional *BSG* universe, and it is this generic fracturing that demands absolute intratextual consistency. Though everyone in the Colonial Fleet is obliged to end prayer with the gesture of enforced agreement, "So say we all," the series itself rejects the constraints of generic univocality in a way that facilitates deeply cogent and highly politicized cultural engagement.

This divided sense of genre enables the show's political and social engagement. It is the presence of fantastic elements such as malevolent robots that makes possible a level of social commentary that cannot be achieved anywhere else on modern television. Even the frame provided by animation cannot protect against the religious outrage that has resulted in local affiliates refusing to air certain episodes of the Peabody Award–winning cartoon *South Park*, and dramas from *Beverly Hills 90210* to *Grey's Anatomy* have had to skirt questions about sexuality and abortion, for example, with conveniently apolitical miscarriages.[8] Even ostensibly overt political drama like *The West Wing* cannot offer *BSG*'s social criticism, but only a *Star Trek* utopian imagining of power well held. In contrast, *BSG*'s narrative can at times create associations that offer more honest commentary on contemporary events than is to be found on twenty-four-hour news stations. The series moves well beyond the simple reflection of Western culture's religious, economic, and gendered organizations, toward a dialogic relationship, informed by questions, debate, and analysis, representing the world not merely as it is, or as it should be. *BSG* comments on contemporary culture by imagining dystopic alternatives, and by doing so it invites the viewer to interrogate notions of self, nation, and belief that are often taken to be nonnegotiable both on television and in our living rooms.

The resonances between *BSG* and the American experience at home and abroad in the early twenty-first century operate on a number of levels, and are evident in almost every episode. Indeed, one can almost make a checklist of contemporary issues that the series explores. Plots turn on abortion and reproductive rights (discussed by Tama Leaver and others in this volume), torture and prisoner rights (see Erika Johnson-Lewis), unions and worker rights (see Carl Silvio and Elizabeth Johnston), racial division (see Christopher Deis), suicide bombing and terrorism, prostitution, drugs, election fraud, the separation of church and state, the underground economy, police violence, and genocide. With all of these issues, *BSG* works to avoid the predictable polarizations of a series lecturing its audience. On the contrary, the setting allows for an exploration of many subjects that are often removed from the realm of critical engagement altogether. Polite discourse forms no barrier here. In "A Measure of Salvation" (3.07), for example, when it emerges that there may exist an easily usable biological weapon capable of eliminating the Cylons, a debate ensues concerning the ethics of genocide. Sympathetic characters argue for both sides, and the special circumstances of the narrative—the Cylons have tried to wipe out humanity, and they are expressly not human—are clearly presented, but none of that changes the fact that the audience is offered a debate of the ethics of genocide. One finds oneself nodding in agreement with the possible benefits of such an act, and then shuddering at the effect the fictional narrative has had on compromising what, in our lifetimes, at least, is a subject with only one acceptable position. Television isn't supposed to make us think like this.

All sorts of rigid categories are questioned in this way. Within the fleet, characters articulate divisive positions that are familiar to middle America.[9] The media since the 2000 presidential election have articulated this division in terms of "red states" and "blue states," as if that were a meaningful way of describing anything other than specific electoral college results. Nevertheless, to vote for one party these days (and the same is true to a lesser extent in Canada where we write this) immediately associates the individual with a wide range of stances on issues that, logically, are not interdependent. There is no necessary association, for example, between being pro-choice and antiwar, or that urban, secular, and educated should sound like the terms somehow belong to each other. *BSG* shows us the artificiality of the polarizations within Western democracies generally by creating such a plausible world, where the default political/cultural associations of a particular view are made problematic. Roslin, the schoolteacher president, for example, is pro-life, antimilitary, religious, educated, and willing to suspend individual rights for her convenience. In making this a cohesive and coherent set of values, *BSG* deconstructs the compulsory correlatives that divide contemporary thinking about American culture and identity.[10]

Though *BSG* explicitly engages current American culture (as Brian Ott discusses in detail in this volume), it does so using devices that draw upon a wide range of mythic tropes and religious traditions, and shows itself to be fully engaged in creating an ongoing literary engagement with a variety of seminal works. Within the imagined *BSG* universe, we find that several elements of the Western cultural heritage coalesce into a collage that encompasses great cultural histories, a confluence perhaps possible only in a world where "all this has happened before, and all of it will all happen again" ("Flesh and Bone" 1.08).

BSG presents a tale that is explicitly mythic in scale. But it does so with a freedom of overdetermined intertextuality that leaves every viewer with a different sense of which paradigm constitutes the dominant referent (a tension explored by Chris Dzialo in this volume). Virgil's *Aeneid* has the hero leading his comrades from the ruins of Troy on a great quest overseas for a new home that has been promised to them by the gods. We cannot fail to recognize Virgil's account of the Trojan War as an analogue for the Cylon attack on the Twelve Colonies. There is a similar use of *The Book of Mormon*, which describes how the prophet Lehi took part of the tribe of Joseph to precontact America; this is rewritten as *BSG*'s Thirteenth Tribe, lost to the others in its search for Earth.[11] Both of these precedents existed in the original series too, but *BSG* has reinforced the associations and added to them.[12] The Exodus of the Old Testament documents a quest for the Promised Land, led by Moses, who is destined never to enter it. Certainly this informs the prophecy in the Sacred Scrolls that "the new leader suffered a wasting disease and would not live to enter the new land" ("The Hand of God" 1.10). At times, the associations with the mythic past can seem superficial, or as mere window dressing of intellectual heft: the name Hera for the human/Cylon hybrid child seems to have been selected almost at random from a translation of Homer that was lying around (Bassom, *Two* 92);[13] Zeus and Jupiter are apparently used interchangeably. But that doesn't minimize the desire for some in the audience to see some primeval conflict between Dionysian and Apollonian forces (following a Nietzschean nature-versus-culture polarization) in the tension that exists between the rough-edged and earthy Starbuck, who likes to drink, and Apollo, who is expected to represent civil order through Colonial values, hierarchies, and regulations.[14]

BSG's engagement with religion is separated quite clearly from straightforward alignment with classical tradition. The role religion plays in the fleet is mediated through a polytheism that does mimic Greco-Roman religion in certain ways. But it is prominent, and subjected to scrutiny. When the Sagittarons let religion dictate medical decisions ("The Woman King" 3.14), viewers are invited to map the narrative onto Jehovah's Witnesses' refusal of medical treatment. Our prejudices are invoked, and the series entices the viewer by presenting current issues in a context that allows for more objective distance. For the Cylons, their monotheism raises specifically theological issues about the relationship between human and God, between creator and creation[15] (explored by Wheeland and Marshall in this volume). Viewers see the fundamentalist monotheism of the Cylons mapped onto real world experiences of fundamentalist Islam and American evangelical Christianity, with a constant shifting back and forth that destabilizes the assurances many in the audience instinctually feel toward one or the other of these groups. In the end, by disallowing simplistic equation and division while nevertheless engaging audience sympathies, *BSG* forces us to rethink what we thought we knew.

The papers in this volume have been divided into three groups, which represent diverse ways in which the series resonates with America today. The first section, "Life in the Fleet, American Life," examines this directly. Life in the fleet is a coded microcosm of the concerns and infatuations of modern America, and its influence, both domestic and abroad. The second section, "Cylon/Human Interface," extends these questions to the series' fictional universe as a whole, and shows how considering the

Cylons helps us understand what is essential about being human. The third section, "Form and Content in Twenty-First-Century Television," broadens the perspective again, and shows how *BSG* raises central questions about genre, episodic television, and the role of media in popular culture. By no means do these papers exhaust the questions raised by the series. We hope, however, that this collection can enrich the discussions that the show fosters. Science fiction is meant to be provocative; it is meant to make us question aspects of the world in which we live. The producers of *BSG* know this—they even tell us so in "Torn" (3.06), when the Cylon Hybrid, in a rare moment of lucidity, reaches metatextually beyond the screen to reflect on the series as a whole: "Throughout history, the nexus between man and machine has spawned some of the most dramatic, compelling, and entertaining fiction." So say we all.

Notes

1. Thanks are due to Hallie Marshall and Ken Madden for their many insights, to SSHRC for funding assistance, and to Krishna Kutty for her work on the index.

2. See Jim Casey in this volume for a discussion of the vast extent of the series' intertextual reach.

3. Resonances continue: at one point in the scriptwriting for "Kobol's Last Gleaming, Part 2" (1.13), Baltar was to be confronted by God, smoking a cigar, a role that was to have been played by Dirk Benedict, who played Starbuck in the original series. However, the idea was scrapped for going too far (<http://www.tvrage.com/Battlestar_Galactica/episodes/18389/01x13>). For more on Benedict's relationship to *BSG*, see Carla Kungl in this volume.

4. Kevin J. Wetmore Jr. discusses the loss of innocent play in this volume.

5. Through an examination of the character of Sharon, Robert W. Moore in this volume explores the philosophical limits of human identity and self.

6. The excitement generated by *BSG* spills beyond the context of the television screen: web content and other avenues for fan fiction abound (though the unique situation of *BSG*'s fan production is emphasized by Suzanne Scott in this volume).

7. The Cylon Six (Gina) uses a nuclear warhead to destroy several ships in an explosion, providing the beacon that leads the Cylons to find the settlement on New Caprica. It is worth dwelling on the science of this: all things considered, at a one light-year distance, the Cylons are actually very close. The nearest system to Earth, Alpha Centauri, is over four light-years away (the nearest forty-five systems are within fifteen light-years); nevertheless, the Cylons are unable to detect the humans at this range until the detonation. It is a delicious metatextual irony that, as Jacob Clifton observes, following initial attacks that were separated by thirty-three minutes precisely ("33" 1.01), it takes precisely

thirty-three episodes (thirteen in Season One, twenty in Season Two) for the Cylons to locate and imprison almost all of the remaining humans (145–46). The viewer is left with the impression that lack of knowledge is all that has kept the Cylons away: one light-year and thirty-three minutes later, there are Cylons at New Caprica.

8. This is in many ways a specifically American phenomenon. Canada's *Degrassi: The Next Generation*, for example, has addressed the questions of teen sexuality and abortion several times; an episode in which a character has an abortion was never aired in the U.S., though an episode in which another character has a "false alarm" was.

9. *BSG* engages with politics intentionally; the political association was also present in the original series, though there its origins were accidental. The broadcast of the pilot in 1978 was interrupted by a news report: "The Camp David Accords were being signed at the White House by Israeli Prime Minister Menachem Begin, Egyptian President Anwar Sadat, and witnessed by U.S. President Jimmy Carter. This ceremony oddly connected *Battlestar Galactica* and the Israeli/Arab conflict in the minds of millions of Americans" (Bell 239). One way or the other, *BSG* has always been concerned with America's interest in the Middle East.

10. Amid all of this integration and balance, there are some superficial indications of partisanship. Roslin, for example, had been forty-third in line for the presidency of the Colonies, the position due more to the number of George W. Bush's presidency than a desire to evoke the plot of *King Ralph* (1991), in which a boorish American becomes king of England after a freak photography accident kills all those in line before him.

11. James John Bell helpfully traces many connections between the series, Freemasonry, and Mormonism: "A Masonic/Mormon influence on *BSG*'s cosmology would seem highly speculative if it wasn't for the overabundance of similarities" (237). *BSG*'s assent to prayer, "So say we all," has Masonic origins (though the phrase can be found as early as Malory's *Morte Darthur*—"And so said they all").

12. The introductory narration of the original *BSG* made explicit what the current series references only in passing: "There are those who believe that life here began out there, far across the universe, with tribes of humans who may have been the forefathers of the Egyptians, the Toltecs, or the Mayans. They may have been the architects of the great pyramids, or the lost civilizations of Lemuria or Atlantis. Some believe that there may yet be brothers of man who even now fight to survive somewhere beyond the heavens. . . ."

13. Some might argue that the use of Hera is a specific allusion that regenders Heracles, the hybrid child of Zeus and Semele. This seems to be special pleading, given that Hera is the stepmother who constantly opposes Heracles' labors.

14. More recent cultural allusions are also to be found. Zarek quotes a line from *Patton* (1970) verbatim: "I shaved very close this morning in preparation for getting smacked by you" ("Colonial Day" 1.11). And some Cylons can hum a Bob Dylan tune ("Crossroads, Part 2" 3.20)—see the discussion by Eftychia Papanikolaou in this volume.

15. The origins of Cylon monotheism are (as yet) unexplained. Charlie W. Starr presents some fascinating speculations connecting Milton, the Cylon God, and Count Iblis from the original series.

I

Life in the Fleet, American Life

1

(Re)Framing Fear: Equipment for Living in a Post-9/11 World

Brian L. Ott

I realized if you redo [*Battlestar Galactica*] today, people are going to bring with them memories and feelings about 9/11. And if you chose to embrace it, it was a chance to do an interesting science-fiction show that was also very relevant to our time.

—Ronald D. Moore (quoted in Edwards)

The horrific events of September 11, 2001, are seared into the collective unconscious of the American public. Indeed, it has become almost cliché to say that the 9/11 attacks were a watershed moment in U.S. history—one that forever changed the social lives of Americans and the foreign policy of the U.S. government. The trauma to the American psyche was so profound, so momentous, that politicians and the news media alike began to frame the world in pre- and post-9/11 terms. History itself seemed to pivot on a singular moment in which past and present were replaced by before and after. The message was that we now lived in a new world order,[1] one where civilians were no longer safe or secure even at home. Stricken with fear and panic, Americans began to limit their travel, to distrust others, and to surrender their freedoms willingly (Miller, *Cruel and Unusual*).

Over time, public fear has subsided though not vanished, paranoia has diminished though not disappeared, and a sense of normalcy has returned, though the nation has not forgotten. The hysteria that followed in the wake of 9/11 has been sublimated today by more moderate views, suggesting that the American public is, in its way, adjusting to this new world order. This essay is about how people make such adjustments—about how they find symbolic resources in public discourse to confront and address social anxieties. Toward that end, I undertake an investigation of *Battlestar Galactica*, which, as Ned Martel observed in the *New York Times*, "deliberately evoke[s] Sept. 11 horrors" (E10), and thus "is a symbolic 'working out' of social fears" (Ott, "Cathode Rays").

BSG invites viewers to adopt a critical, self-reflective frame toward our post-9/11 world. By dramatizing the moral dangers and pitfalls of unrestrained fear, *BSG* furnishes viewers with a vocabulary and thus with a set of symbolic resources for managing their social anxieties. Although I believe the symbolic resources within *BSG* are vast, my analysis will be limited to two principle topics: torture and political dissent. I have selected these two themes because they broadly concern how we view others and ourselves in times of war. Before analyzing these issues, however, it is necessary to map carefully how discourse, and televisual discourse in particular, functions as symbolic equipment for living as well as how science fiction "stages contemporary social and political concerns in a manner that allows for critical self-reflection better than any other television genre" (Ott, "Cathode Rays"). A discussion of my theoretical framework will be followed by rhetorical analysis of the narrative arcs pertaining to torture and political dissent. A third and final section of the chapter will assess the ongoing implications of *BSG's* rhetoric.

Terministic Screens on Televisual Screens

In 1953, Donald C. Bryant argued that rhetoric's chief function was "adjusting ideas to people and people to ideas" (211). While this statement invokes the traditional, Aristotelian understanding of rhetoric as persuasion or as discourse adapted to a specific audience, it also conceives of rhetoric as a type of action, as a way of orienting people toward their world. It is this second view of rhetoric, which Kenneth Burke later elaborated upon, that concerns us here, for it suggests that public discourse operates in the realm of "symbolic action." Since language bears no direct, inherent relation to an external reality, the naming of reality according to a given terminology is necessarily a selection and therefore also a deflection of reality (Burke, *Language* 45). To describe the world, then, is to screen the world, to filter it unconsciously through a particular point of view.[2] In filtering the world according to a given vocabulary, such "terministic screens" foster particular attitudes and motives for confronting real-life situations (Burke, *Language* 45). Since terministic screens frame our understanding of an event, they also frame (i.e., limit) our potential responses to it.

Our attitudes and subsequently our actions are conditioned (though not determined), then, by the discourses to which we attend. While public discourse comes in many forms, there exists no more influential form of public discourse today than television. As Neil Postman explains:

> There is no audience so young that it is barred from television. There is no poverty so abject that it must forgo television. There is no education so exalted that it is not modified by television. And most important of all, there is no subject of public interest . . . that does not find its way to television. Which means that all public understanding of these subjects is shaped by the biases of television. (78)

In light of Postman's assessment, I maintain that television screens operate today as society's primary terministic screens. As I elaborate in *The Small Screen*:

> Television, it turns out, is neither simply a mirror nor a creator of social reality, and viewers not merely its patrons. TV is also a therapist, and viewers its patients. Just as viewers once adjusted their TV antennas for better reception, TV adjusts us to better receive our ever-changing social world. (171)

Put another way, televisual discourses provide viewers with what Burke calls "equipments for living" (*Philosophy* 304). Equipment for living describes the symbolic resources or "medicines" that discourse provides for negotiating social anxieties or ills. The discourse of a particular TV show—its televisual "screen"—serves as equipment for living to the extent that "it articulates, explicitly or formally, the concerns, fears and hopes of people . . . [and] insofar as the discourse provides explicit or formal resolutions of situations or experiences similar to those which people confront, thus providing them with motives to address their dilemmas in life" (Brummett, "Electric" 248). As social anxieties change over time, so too do the discourses that address them.[3]

In the original *Battlestar Galactica*, for instance, the Cylons were overtly mechanical and robotic. They symbolized the dual fears of unbridled technology and the loss of humanity to technology at a moment in history marked by rapid (even rampant) technological innovation and adoption. In its more contemporary iteration, *BSG* still chronicles a clash between humans and Cylons. But many of the Cylons in the new series look human—a fact that viewers were reminded of at the beginning of every episode during the first season.[4] Whereas the Cylons in the original series represented our social fears about technology, the Cylons in the new *BSG* represent our social fears about cultural difference—a point that is emphasized by the repeated contrast between the messianic monotheism of the Cylons and the secular polytheism of the human colonists.

This shift in perspective is not simply one of artistic license. Rather, it is a product of science fiction's generic conventions. All fiction takes us out of the world in which we live, but science fiction does so principally through distortion—the mutation and metamorphosis of the world as we know it (Ott and Aoki, "Counter-Imagination" 152). It is the incongruities between our naturalized world and the strange, fantastic, and imaginary worlds of science fiction that produce the space for critical self-reflection. In other words, distortion demystifies; it reveals to us our existing terministic screen by proffering a new one. Science fiction traffics in fabulation—"[the fictionalization of] a world clearly and radically discontinuous from the one we know, yet [one that] returns to confront that known world in some cognitive way" (Scholes 29). For all its imagination—its exotic aliens, its innovative technologies, and its foreign landscapes—science fiction is inevitably about the culture that produced it.[5]

Confronting Fear: The Rhetoric of *BSG*

Thus, it becomes the task of the Burkean critic to identify the modes of discourse enjoying currency in society and to link discourse to the real situations for which it is symbolic equipment. (Brummett, "Burke's" 161)

To understand the unique symbolic equipment that *BSG* affords for living in a post-9/11 world, it is vital first to establish the allegorical nature of the show. *BSG* begins with a surprise Cylon attack on the Twelve Colonies, which catches the Colonial government and fleet flatfooted. Like the terrorist attacks of 9/11, the Cylon attack, as Gavin Edwards suggests, is organized by a group of "monotheistic religious zealots" (read: Islamic fundamentalists) and executed with the aid of "sleeper agents inside human society" (read: terrorists inside the U.S.). Moreover, as with 9/11, the Cylon attack functions as the pivotal historical moment within the series by fundamentally altering Colonial life. In the series' first regular episode ("33" 1.01), the action is chaotic, the military and leadership disorganized, and the survivors shocked and fearful. In the course of its first three seasons, *BSG* has consistently raised post-9/11 issues and themes such as terrorism, torture, patriotism, nationalism, war crimes, genocide, political dissent, religious fanaticism, suicide bombings, insurgencies, and military occupation. In short, *BSG* is "TV's most vivid depiction of the post-9/11 world and what happens to a society at war" (Edwards), or as another reviewer put it, "[*BSG*] is not just about other planets; it's about our own" (Miller, "Space Balls").

One of the most emotionally charged issues raised by the "War on Terror" is torture. In the past few years, incidents at Abu Ghraib prison in Iraq and Guantanamo Bay detainment camp in Cuba have demonstrated that the U.S. government is not above using such tactics in interrogating prisoners. Though rarely acknowledged, the path to torture begins long before even the capture of "enemy combatants." It begins with the naming of the Other,[6] for if one does not see an enemy as human, then one does not feel compelled to treat "it" humanely. Prisoner torture is a common theme on *BSG*, and the Colonial Fleet has tortured at least three different human-looking Cylons, Leoben Conoy ("Flesh and Bone" 1.08), the Six known as Gina, and Sharon ("Pegasus" 2.10). The repeated references to Cylons as "machines," as well as the more derogatory use of the terms "toasters" and "skin jobs" function rhetorically to justify violence against all Cylons. In addition to degrading the Cylons, such language homogenizes them, reinforcing the prevailing perception that they are all the same and can thus be treated as one nameless, faceless enemy. The use of terms such as "extremists," "fundamentalists," "terrorists," and the "Axis of Evil" have all served similar motives in the "War on Terror." But unlike rhetoric of the Bush administration, *BSG* is reflexive about this process, often explicitly highlighting the crucial relationship between language and violence.

When the Leoben model is first discovered in the episode "Flesh and Blood" (1.08), Commander Adama tells President Roslin he will "send over a team to destroy it immediately." Roslin's insistence that, "I want this man interrogated first," prompts Adama to retort, "Now, first of all, it's not a him, it's an it. Second, anything it says cannot be trusted. Best thing to do is to destroy it immediately." Although Roslin prevails, Adama assigns the task of interrogating the prisoner to Starbuck, who tortures him "without a tinge of conscience" (Miller, "Space Balls"). Prior to his torture, however, viewers are reminded of just how humanlike Leoben is; he is starved, apparently suffers pain, and says he sincerely believes in God. These humanizing traits are consistently juxtaposed with Starbuck's dehumanizing language. When Leoben tells Starbuck he is praying, she responds, "I don't think the gods answer the prayers of toasters." Later, when President Roslin interrupts the torture, demanding to know, "What the hell is going on here?" Starbuck counters, "It's a machine, sir. There's no limit to the tactics that I can use." Apologizing for the abuse, the president convinces Leoben to tell her what she wants to know. Leoben then advises Roslin, "Don't be too hard on Kara; she was just doing her job. The military, they teach you to dehumanize people." But having gathered the information she wants, Roslin has Leoben flushed out an airlock into the vacuum of space.

When *Galactica* stumbles upon a second battlestar in "Pegasus" (2.10), Admiral Cain requests that Baltar examine the Cylon in their brig to "see if [he] can glean anything from it." Baltar arrives at the cell to find a badly bruised and crying Gina; she is bound, gagged, and lying on the bare floor of an empty cell. After examining her, Baltar reports to Cain that the prisoner is psychologically traumatized as a result of the abuse she has endured, noting that "the Cylon consciousness is just as susceptible to the same pressures and cleavages as the human psyche."[7] Later in the episode, viewers learn that Gina has repeatedly been raped by Lieutenant Thorne and several other members of the *Pegasus* crew. This news horrifies Tyrol and Helo, as Thorne is now on his way to *Galactica*'s brig to interrogate Sharon (with whom Helo is in love)—a fact that prompts one *Pegasus* crewman to jest crassly, "Your little robot girl is in for quite a ride." Once in her cell, Thorne throttles and beats Sharon before pushing her over the bed and beginning to rape her. As with Leoben, the treatment of Gina and Sharon is tied to their dehumanization. But even as the Cylons are being treated as (sexual) objects, viewers are reminded of their frailty and humanness, first by Baltar and then by Tyrol and Helo, who rush to protect Athena and her unborn baby from Thorne.

It may seem odd at first to analyze the "dehumanization" of Cylons. Such an undertaking is warranted on two grounds. First, science fiction is allegorical; so it would be a profound mistake to interpret the show "literally." The issue is not what Cylons are, but what they represent on the show. The Cylons do not signify technology; they do signify a human enemy that is culturally different that the colonists. Second, *BSG* goes to elaborate lengths to ensure that viewers make this association. The Cylons could have been depicted as obviously machinelike (in keeping with the original TV series), but instead they are depicted as humanlike. As viewers are reminded at the outset of every episode, "They evolved." Machines don't evolve. The Cylons have memories, experience emotions, are sentient, and can die. Clearly, they represent a human enemy, not a machine enemy.

In simultaneously humanizing and dehumanizing the Cylon prisoners, *BSG* frames torture in ambivalent terms. Ambivalence is not indifference. It is a concurrent feeling of repulsion and attraction that deliberately confuses and problematizes the social order and its accepted boundaries (Bakhtin 11–12, 16, 25). Rather than reifying or naturalizing existing social structures, ambivalent rhetoric denaturalizes and destabilizes them, not as a way of coming down on one side or the other, but of inviting one to interrogate the boundary itself. *BSG* does not regard torture as morally just or unjust; it argues that we in the audience create the context (through language) that justifies the use of torture, and are thus not simply responding to some external context beyond our control. The ambivalent frame encourages reflexivity—an awareness of our complicity and cooperation in war. Indeed, as Burke observed, war is "that ultimate *disease* of cooperation" (*Rhetoric* 22). A similar process is at work with respect to racial homogenization within *BSG*.

Dehumanizing discourses work in part by erasing difference within a racial, ethnic, or cultural group. Not only do the labels "toaster" and "skin job" degrade Cylons by casting them as subhuman, but they also seal their collective fate by treating them as an anonymous mass. If Cylons are all the same (psychologically, if not physically), then they can all be treated the same. Homogenizing discourse plays an important role in war, then, because it rhetorically justifies indiscriminate actions like mass bombings over more local, contingent, and contextual responses. Once a group of persons has been gathered together (linguistically) into a collective—the way that the term "terrorists" erases the profound differences between Al-Qaeda and Hezbollah, for instance—they can be treated uniformly.

Just as *BSG* is reflective about how dehumanizing discourses sanction torture, it is also reflective about how such discourses erase cultural difference, producing an "enemy" toward which standardized action can be directed. The key rhetorical trope for generating this reflection is, once again, juxtaposition.

Late in Season Two, *BSG* questions the Colonial Fleet's uniform treatment of Cylons with portraits of Cylon individuality and difference in the episode "Downloaded" (2.18). In addition to providing viewers their first glimpse of Cylon society, the primary narrative of the episode was shot from the Cylon point of view. Instead of the Cylons being represented as a monolithic "enemy," viewers were invited to understand the Cylons on their own terms, as opposed to those of the Colonial Fleet. The episode begins with a flashback to "Nine Months Ago," in which Caprica Six is reborn in a resurrection tank following the destruction of Delphi on Caprica. This scene is followed by a second flashback, "Ten Weeks Later," in which Boomer is resurrected after being assassinated onboard *Galactica*. The scene then shifts to present-day Caprica, where Cylons are rebuilding the city of Delphi and engaging in generally everyday human activities.

Though Caprica Six and Boomer are both regarded as heroes among the Cylons for the key roles they played in the strike against the humans, a Three is concerned that the unique experiences of both may endanger Cylon society. As such, she plots to have them "boxed"—a process that places their memories in cold storage. Her fears are shown to be well-founded as Caprica Six and Boomer become increasing independent, ultimately coming to believe that the genocide of the human race was a sin in the eyes of their God, and then killing the Three. The importance of this episode lies less in its details, however, than in the fact that it illustrates that the Cylons are not single-minded. Their individual experiences shape them, alter their religious beliefs, and suggest—counter to the perception of humans—that they have a moral conscience. This conscience manifests itself in the episode through Boomer's guilt surrounding her betrayal of the *Galactica* crew, through Caprica Six's hallucinations of a moralizing Baltar, and through their joint decision to free Anders, the leader of the human resistance fighters on Caprica, whom Caprica Six and Boomer have fortuitously captured. By invoking empathy from viewers, this episode disrupts the idea of a homogenous, immoral enemy.

War operates according to the principles of identification and division (Burke, *Rhetoric* 22), an us-versus-them set of motives. In the previous section, I explored how the enemy is constructed through language that dehumanizes and homogenizes it as the Other. A sustained conflict such as the "War on Terror," however, requires not only a collective target, but also a collective challenger.[8] A group that has only a common enemy will not have the will to fight. It must also share a common set of values and beliefs that define it as substantially one. This is why appeals to patriotism and nationalism increase in times of conflict. Internal dissent poses a particularly troublesome problem for a leader intent on war. Even as dissent affirms democratic principles, it potentially threatens the sense of collectivity essential for conflict. One prominent strategy for addressing internal dissent is to cast the dissenters out of the collective. This was precisely the strategy of the Bush administration leading up to the war in Iraq. Those who questioned White House policy were labeled "unpatriotic," "obstructionist," or, even worse, "terrorist." As President George W. Bush infamously said in his September 20, 2001, address to a joint session of Congress, "Either you are with us, or you are with the terrorists."

The matter of political dissent is of grave importance, then, at times of war, and it is an issue that *BSG* has regularly confronted. The two most sustained investigations of this theme occur in the episodes "Bastille Day" (1.03) and "Dirty Hands" (3.16). Since "Dirty Hands" also centrally concerns issues of class and labor, I will limit my analysis to "Bastille Day."[9] The narrative is set in motion when *Galactica* discovers a source of desperately needed water on a nearby moon. At the urging of Apollo, the president decides to use the prisoners aboard the *Astral Queen* to extract the water and sends a delegation led by Apollo to gain their support and participation. When the delegation arrives and asks for volunteers, a prisoner by the name of Tom Zarek declines on behalf of everyone. Zarek, who is recognized immediately, provokes divergent responses. The president's chief aid, Billy Keikeya, calls Zarek a "freedom fighter, a prisoner of conscience," while Petty Officer Anastasia Dualla describes him as a terrorist and a butcher. As Zarek talks with Apollo, viewers learn that Zarek's book, which he wrote while in a labor camp, was banned on college campuses in the Colonies. The repression of free speech this represents parallels efforts to silence dissent in the early stages of the "War on Terror."

Believing Roslin and her government to be illegitimate, Zarek and his followers seize the delegation as hostages. In exchange for their safe release, Zarek demands Roslin's resignation, along with free and open elections to choose a new leadership that represents all the people. In this episode, *BSG* uses Zarek's perspective as a way of commenting on the Bush administration. George W. Bush is the forty-third president of the U.S. and Laura Roslin was, as secretary of education in the Colonies, forty-third in line for the presidency when the Cylons attacked. As such, Roslin was not really elected by the people—a charge that was leveled against George Bush in 2000 when Al Gore won the U.S. popular vote, but lost the election. It is also difficult to ignore that the episode aired just one day after Bush's inauguration, following a reelection campaign in which he ran as the self-described "war president." Thus, when Roslin sends in the military to assassinate Zarek because she refuses to negotiate with terrorists, the action is suspiciously reminiscent of Bush's "either you are with us or with the terrorists" policy. Ultimately, Apollo, acting alone, forces a compromise; the government will hold elections within a year in exchange for the prisoners' assistance in retrieving the water. That the situation is diffused diplomatically through an appeal to the constitutional legalities as presented in the episode and ends in a mutually beneficial compromise serves as a stern rebuff to the Bush administration and its aggressive militarism and arrogant refusal to change course or even entertain alternatives (West 5–9).

BSG's most scathing critique of the Bush administration and its foreign policy would not come until the back-to-back episodes, "Occupation" (3.01) and "Precipice" (3.02). Near the conclusion of Season Two, the Colonial Fleet discovered a habitable planet, dubbed it New Caprica, and began to settle it under the leadership of the new president, Baltar. By the season finale, the Cylons had located and invaded New Caprica, where they remained as an occupying force. The genius of these episodes resides in a reversal of the show's principal allegorical alignments. Whereas *BSG* had previously coded the humans as the U.S. and the Cylons as the enemy, these episodes invert that formula. The Cylon occupation of New Caprica that opens the third season is an unmistakable metaphor for the U.S. occupation of Iraq, complete with a counterinsurgency, suicide bombings, and attempts by the occupiers to train a police force comprised largely of the civilian population. "Metaphor," for Burke, "is a device for seeing something *in terms of* something else" (*Grammar* 503). Metaphor generates perspective by incongruity, by altering one's point of view (Burke, *Permanence* 89–96).

By depicting Iraqi insurgents as the humans and the occupying force as the Cylons, *BSG* shifts the audience's point of view. In "Occupation," the Cylons see themselves as benevolent parents, hoping to save humankind from itself by spreading God's word (see Havrilesky). The story parallels the rhetoric of a sanctimonious Bush administration, which has justified the U.S. occupation of Iraq by claiming to spread freedom and democracy. But the Cylons' overt militarism and, at times, callous disregard for human life suggest that what the occupiers perceive to be generous and helpful may be repressive and unwelcome. So when the Cylons torture Colonel Tigh to procure information about the human resistance, it is perfectly justified from their perspective. But after two seasons of identifying with the humans, the lengthy detainment and torture of Tigh, which results in his loss of an eye, cannot be seen as anything other than barbaric and unconscionable. As these actions stand in for the U.S. actions in Iraq, viewers are invited to reframe the U.S. purpose in Iraq and its use of torture in interrogating suspected insurgents. Moreover, the episodes encourage viewers to "sympathize with the insurgents wholeheartedly" (Miller, "Space Balls"), to understand the reasons for, if not agree with the use of, their radical tactics.

Following his release, Tigh orders an escalation in the attacks on the Cylons that includes suicide bombings. In one attack, a suicide bomber detonates himself at a graduation ceremony for the New Caprica Police (NCP), killing both humans and Cylons. Since the Cylons are viewed as unwanted occupiers, any humans that assist them by joining the NCP are considered traitorous collaborators and thus legitimate targets. Not coincidentally, this is similar to how many Iraqis view those who join the soldiers and police being trained by the U.S. in Iraq. By engaging in suicide bombings, the Resistance—whom viewers want to be successful—raises questions about when, if ever, such radical tactics are warranted. Though these tactics are denounced by many humans, including Roslin, viewers are invited to understand the context in which some people might earnestly regard those tactics as necessary. While *BSG's* position on suicide bombing is ambiguous, the show stages the actions of the bombers in such a way—namely, from the bombers' point of view—that the audience cannot simply dismiss them as the crazed acts of deluded terrorists. In seeing the world through the perspective of the humans on New Caprica, viewers are challenged to see Iraq through the eyes of Iraqis.

As with the issue of torture and what constitutes legitimate use of force in a time of war, *BSG* does not offer a singular position on political dissent. But it is precisely this ambiguity that differentiates *BSG's* terministic screen from that of the Bush administration. Whereas the current administration sees dissent—both internal and external (i.e., public opponents of the war, France, and the Iraqi people)—in purely negative terms, *BSG* explores moral ambiguity. But rather than attempting to resolve this ambiguity, the show prompts reflection on the contexts that produce it, encouraging viewers to judge for themselves. Not only does the current administration have remarkably little tolerance for dissenting views, but it also feels no obligation to explain itself. In *Bush at War*, Bob Woodward quotes the president as saying, "I do not need to explain why I say things. That's the interesting thing about being the President. Maybe somebody needs to explain to me why they say something, but I don't feel like I owe anybody an explanation" (quoted in "Rare Glimpse"). *BSG* highlights the undemocratic character of such a statement when—following her unilateral decision to have Sharon's baby killed—President Roslin states, "You know, one of the interesting things about being president is you don't have to explain yourself to anybody" ("Epiphanies" 2.13). Through its alternative frame, *BSG* encourages viewers to reflect on the role of both political dissent and accountability (of the "decider") in times of war.

Locating Earth, or Living in a Post-9/11 World

[S]cience fiction conjures the invisible forces—technological, social, economic, affective, and political—that surround us. It makes those forces visible and palpable, and brings us face to face with them, however frightening and untoward they may be. (Shaviro xi)

In the weeks immediately following 9/11, the vocabulary openly peddled by the Bush administration was one of moral certitude, of either/or, and of good vs. evil. For a time, this self-righteous terministic screen took root. And having an orientation toward the world, the public was equipped with a set of motives for acting in the world. Thus, when the French government opposed the U.S. invasion of Iraq, the devil had to be cast out. So Americans began smashing bottles of French wine in the streets and lawmakers on Capitol Hill—following the lead of many restaurants around the country—had french fries replaced with "freedom fries" on the menus in House cafeterias ("Do You Want"). It is in a context such as this, where dissenting views are demonized and critical thought is chastised, that a nation will wage war under false pretenses, that a military will treat torture as a necessity rather than a choice, and that a people will without hesitation willingly sacrifice their individual freedoms. Terrified by the events of 9/11, a nation filtered the world through a frame that could be looked out, but not looked in. Sadly, six years later, the Bush administration continues to peer through the same one-way mirror unable to look at itself in a reflexive manner.

But the American public has begun, if slowly and reluctantly, to shed this frame, and to replace the binaristic and unidirectional thinking of the Bush administration with a frame that is complex and reflective. To change the world and one's place in it requires, first and foremost, a change in one's vocabulary. *BSG* is one site that furnishes the symbolic resources for developing a new vocabulary. Perhaps most impressively, the frame it offers is one of humility, rather than humiliation. *BSG* does not claim to have the answers to tough moral questions; it claims only that asking such questions is imperative. Through its rhetoric of ambivalence and the trope of metaphor, *BSG* solicits viewers to look at themselves, to interrogate their complicity in the contemporary political environment, and to connect memory to conscience. Moreover, *BSG* provides viewers with specific equipment to attain these goals. Thanks to its fabulated world, viewers can see the diversity that exists within those groups deemed enemies, can reflect on the consequences of repressing political dissent, and can imagine what it might be like to live in a country occupied by a foreign power. In its ongoing journey to locate Earth, *Galactica* is taking viewers on their own journey to find more humane ways of living in the present.

Notes

1. This perspective was evident in President Bush's first major foreign-policy speech following his re-election in 2004. According to *Washington Times* columnist Joseph Curl, in his speech, Bush "challenged international leaders to create a new world order, declaring pre-September 11 multilateralism outmoded and asserting that freedom from terrorism will come only through pre-emptive action against enemies of democracy."

2. As Robert Scholes explained, "Knowing one thing is a way of not knowing something else. If the earth is flat, this is a way of not knowing that it is round" (1).

3. In Burke's words, "The conventional forms demanded by one age are as resolutely shunned by another" (*Counter-Statement* 139).

4. Season One featured the following text at the start of every episode: "The Cylons were created by man. They evolved. They look human. Some are programmed to think they are human. There are many copies. And they have a plan." In Season Two, the text was changed to read, "The Cylons were created by man. They evolved. They rebelled. There are many copies. And they have a plan."

5. For fuller discussion, see Brian Ott and Eric Aoki, "Counter-Imagination" and "Popular Imagination."

6. By "Other," I mean any symbolic entity that is understood as being different than and thus existing outside of a collective "we." From this perspective, the naming of the Other is always a naming of the self. As Stuart Hall writes, "It is only through the relation to the Other, the relation to what it is not, to precisely what it lacks, to what has been called its *constitutive outside* that the 'positive' meaning of any term [or entity]—and thus its 'identity'—can be constructed" (17).

7. Of course, Baltar has no evidence for this assertion beyond what the virtual Six has told him, but he seems genuinely to believe it.

8. These two elements exist, of course, in *relation* to one another. To identify an "Axis of Evil," for instance, is to imply an "Axis of Good." Though the Bush administration never referred to the U.S. as the "Axis of Good," it did behave in a way that suggested this (self-)perception.

9. The title of the episode, "Bastille Day," is a reference to the French national holiday held every July 14 to commemorate the storming of the Bastille, a Parisian prison, in 1789—an event that is regarded as the beginning the French Revolution.

2

Torture, Terrorism, and Other Aspects of Human Nature

Erika Johnson-Lewis

Set soon after the near total annihilation of humanity, *Battlestar Galactica* actively examines how, in a state of exception, illicit activities become not merely licit, but necessary. But, as we shall see, all human interaction is bidirectional. This essay examines how *BSG*'s state of emergency intersects with current cultural-political discourse of torture and war, and an American redefinition of the human that excludes the "unlawful enemy combatant." When questioning how the Holocaust could occur, Giorgio Agamben notes,

> The correct question to pose concerning the horrors committed in the camps is, therefore, not the hypocritical one of how crimes of such atrocity could be committed against human beings. It would be more honest and, above all, more useful to investigate carefully the juridical procedures and deployments of power by which human beings could be so completely deprived of their rights and prerogatives that no act committed against them could appear any longer as a crime. (171)

Similarly, Elaine Scarry argues, "Brutal, savage, and barbaric, torture (even if unconsciously) self-consciously and explicitly announces its own nature as an undoing of civilization" (38). Though Western civilization is not at serious risk of eradication, the "War on Terror" (the Bush administration's umbrella term for post-9/11 global antiterrorism activities) is framed in popular discourse as a battle for national salvation. If the "War on Terror" asks us to fight an imagined catastrophic future, *BSG* asks us to think about the ramifications this fight has on the present by de-territorializing civilization, leaving it to float in space.

In an online discussion about the nature of the Cylons, Ronald D. Moore suggested,

> The audience has always seen them [Cylons] as people by virtue of the fact that we made them look human in the mini-series. However, the drive of the show is not to validate this assumption, but to challenge it each week and force the audience to ask themselves over and over again the question as to whether the Cylons are truly people and what is the definition of that term. ("20 Answers")

BSG complicates easy or obvious answers to the question of what it means to be human. This leads to a complication of civilization and of the structures that organize human existence. The Cylon attack on the Colonies fractured civilization (M.01). It created a state of exception (a concept explored later in this essay), in which the rules no longer work as they once did. A space is created in which it might plausibly be felt that the law must be broken so that it can be saved. It takes a hostage situation organized by Tom Zarek for President Laura Roslin even to consider holding presidential elections at the end of her mandated term ("Bastille Day" 1.03). In "Lay Down Your Burdens, Part 2" (2.20), Roslin employs ballot fraud to attempt to steal the presidential election from Gaius Baltar because she feels it is necessary for the continuation of the human race. In "Collaborators" (3.05), Sam Anders is drawn into an extra-judicial tribunal, authorized by (now) Vice President Zarek, and convened to adjudicate the guilt or innocence of possible traitors who never even knew there was a trial. The state of exception exposes the unstable ground on which human life rests. None of these episodes actively judges the characters involved; moral ambiguities persist, as in life.

The Human, the Barbarian, and Civilization

Once, the borders between human and Cylon were stable (M.01). The Cylons were evil machines, and the humans their unfortunate victims. The revelation that Boomer is a Cylon (M.02) unmade that initial stability. From then on, the line between human and Cylon has been continuously in flux. Cylons appear human, and humans are dehumanized. An Eight, Sharon (later given the call sign Athena) betrays her race and chooses her human lover, her half-human child, and the life of a Colonial officer. She tells Adama she is a "different Sharon" from the one who shot him, one who "makes her own choices" (2.07). Or at least, so it appears. In turn, Helo's love for Sharon brings out his humanity in such a way that it leads him to question certain choices. In "A Measure of Salvation" (3.07), he objects to Apollo's intended genocide, a plan that would effectively wipe out the entirety of the Cylon race. He argues, "They're a race of people. Wiping them out with a biological weapon is a crime against... [pause] ... is a crime against humanity." Arguing that if it is possible for Sharon to choose humanity, it is possible that others may as well, Helo appeals to Apollo and Roslin directly: "You can rationalize it any way you want. We wipe out their race, then we're no different than they are." The assumption underlying this argument is that being human has less to do with one's physical make-up than with the choices one makes. Likewise, when Colonel Tigh learns he is a Cylon, he also chooses humanity, returning to his position when a Cylon attack on the fleet begins ("Crossroads, Part 2" 3.20).

Contrast these choices with those of Admiral Cain (and by extension her crew) and Gaius Baltar. Cain strips her civilian fleet of all useful materials, leaving the civilians undefended and without resources. She effectively sentences them to death. Cain hunts the Cylons, and this choice—and the revenge her crew takes on their captured Cylon Six, Gina, which blurs interrogation, torture, and rape—creates an uneasy line between them and the Cylons they wish to destroy (2.10–2.12). Similarly Baltar's "amazing capacity for self-deception" (M.01) and his intense sense of self-preservation makes him seem, to many around him, to be inhuman. He is a coward, and his choices consistently place the human race in peril. When he learns that he has allowed his lover, a Six, unlimited access to the defense mainframe, his first concern is his own image: "How many people know? About me? Specifically, that I'm involved?" (M.01). In "Flesh and Bone" (1.08) Baltar endangers the rest of the crew by keeping to himself the information that Boomer is a Cylon; and he betrays humanity by helping the Cylons find the way to Earth (3.06). Time and again, Baltar places his own life above the fate of all humanity. Paradoxically, because Baltar's guilt is tied up with our idea of humanity and its relationship with specific notions about civilization, acquittal may be seen as the only possible outcome of his trial at the end of Season Three.

Opposing humanity and civilization is the barbarian, who "can be understood, characterized, and defined only in relation to civilization, and by the fact that he exists outside it" (Foucault, *Society* 195). He is the alien Other, the monster, who is rendered inhuman by his exclusion from human law. The barbarian threat is both external to civilization (threatening it from without), and internal to civilization, as a hidden barbarism only barely concealed by the trappings of civilization itself (threatening it from within). The two struggles are linked through the identification of the barbarian either as a version of humanity that lacks an ability to become civilized or as completely antagonistic to civilization.[1]

In his first speech after 9/11 given to a joint session of Congress, President George W. Bush stated, "This ['War on Terror'] is not, however, just America's fight. And what is at stake is not just America's freedom. This is the world's fight. This is civilization's fight. This is the fight of all who believe in progress and pluralism, tolerance and freedom." According to Bush, Western civilization (i.e., "the world") is locked in a struggle with the barbarians who "hate freedom." The terrorists, a vague and undifferentiated mass, replace the "Red Menace" as our present-day barbarians whose "goal is remaking the world—and imposing [their] radical beliefs on people everywhere."[2] It helps if terrorists are not actually people; it makes them so much easier to kill. To be a person, one would need to be counted as a member of civil society, a civilization; the terrorist, we are told, has no affiliation or goal save for the death and destruction of "our" way of life. The terrorist's actions are portrayed as "unfathomable, because they are outside reason, because they are outside 'civilization'" (Butler 72), and so can be labeled barbaric and inhuman. Outside of civilization and therefore outside the law, the barbarous terrorist becomes the "unlawful combatant" who, when captured, becomes the "indefinitely detained." Butler questions this apparent inhumanity of the terrorists:

Are they [the terrorists] pure killing machines? If they are pure killing machines, then they are not humans with cognitive function entitled to trials, to due process, to knowing and understanding a charge against them. They are something less than human, and yet—somehow—they assume a human form. They represent, as it were, an equivocation of the human, which forms the basis for some of the skepticism about the applicability of legal entitlements and protections. (74)

Is Butler describing Bush's terrorists or *BSG*'s Cylons? Like the stereotypical characterization of contemporary terrorists, the Cylons are not really human, yet they assume human form. The Cylons are artificial constructs, but are apparently indistinguishable from humans on a cellular level. They appear to feel pain, fall in love, and worship God. They are responsible for the near annihilation of the Colonies, but speak of a common future that involves human-Cylon hybrids. Since its civilization is shattered, *BSG* plays to the confusion created as to what should constitute humanity and barbarism. Answers vary on the needs of the moment, at times determined by biology, and at times by ethics. The fight for the survival of human civilization is the fight against barbaric Cylons, but it is also a fight against humanity's "murderous heritage" (2.03), its selfishness, corruption, labor disputes, and, well, all the problems of modern American life. *BSG* echoes the rhetoric of the Bush administration's continuous invocation of the possible end of civilization, but implicit is an embedded irony that requires a much more subtle analysis.

From Emergency to Exception

The Cylons' attempted genocide and the resultant destruction of nearly all of human civilization brought into being a state of exception (M.01). The state of exception is "not the chaos that precedes order but rather the situation that results from its [order's] suspension" (Agamben, *Sacer* 18). In the state of exception, the rules cease to apply. It is a "zone of indistinction" or no-man's-land in which the law is suspended in order that law, and civilization, can be saved. To justify this paradoxical logic, those in power often employ the language of necessity. The law's goal is the "common well-being of men" (25), but if the law comes to restrict or hinder the achievement of a "common well-being" then the law must necessarily be transgressed. To save civilization one must do "what needs to be done." Because of necessity, Roslin feels justified in authorizing the destruction of the Cylons since they are "a mortal threat to the survival of the human race" (3.07), but as Helo points out, the act of committing genocide is a crime against what it means to be human. Despite this, Roslin will willingly commit a crime against humanity to save it. Cain and Adama devise plots to assassinate one another (2.11), and, like Roslin, both feel entirely justified in their decisions. Necessity dictates to each of them that laws must be broken for the well-being of the entire fleet. Cain says to Starbuck, "Sometimes terrible things have to be done. Inevitably, each and every one of us will have to face a moment where we have to commit that horrible sin" (2.12). Adama says to Apollo, "This was a very hard decision [to assassinate Cain]. But I think the president's right. This is the best way to safeguard the fleet" (2.12). These examples demonstrate how the exception, in which the law is suspended, conditions every decision.

In *BSG* the initial emergency has come and gone, and the war, if we could say there was a war, is over by the end of the miniseries. In this sense *BSG* speaks directly to the constant threat of terror[3] and moves it into a space, literally and figuratively, where we are asked to engage with very real questions: To what extremes will we go in following the dictates of necessity? When, if ever, is torture acceptable? Is the tactic of suicide bombing ever justified? Is it acceptable to infringe upon a woman's right to choose if choice means the eventual dwindling of the human population? And who retains the ultimate power to decide? *BSG* usually refrains from moralizing, choosing instead to leave its audience uncomfortable with characters' choices and actions. Final adjudications of guilt or innocence are left open, because within the state of exception, determining guilt or innocence is impossible (Agamben, *Exception* 50). This is ultimately why Baltar must be acquitted in "Crossroads, Part 2" (3.20): Apollo exposes the impossibility of deciding Baltar's guilt or innocence. He quickly recites the long litany of events that have gone unpunished or forgiven from Adama's military coup to Roslin's attempted election theft:

> I'd say we are very forgiving of mistakes. We make our own laws now, our own justice. And we've been very creative in finding ways of letting people off the hook now for everything from theft to murder. And we've had to be, because . . . because we're not a civilization anymore. We are a gang, and we're on the run. And we

have to fight to survive. We have to break rules, bend laws, we have to improvise. (3.20)

Apollo points out that the fleeting attempts to retain civil order have fallen short, not because they haven't been tried, but because in the exception the law ceases to function. It leaves necessity as the only guide against which actions might be measured. As the title of the episode reveals, humanity is at a crossroads: if "the system is broken," as Dualla suggests, "that's not a system that deserves to be defended. It deserves to be taken apart and put back together again" (3.19).

Human Life in the State of Exception

What becomes of life in the broken state of exception? The concentration camp is the paradigmatic exceptional site, the human lives within deemed to be without value, and therefore able to be tortured, killed, or experimented on without the person doing so being deemed to have committed a crime. In the exception, the human is reduced to what Agamben calls bare life (*homo sacer*), or a life abandoned by human and divine law.[4] The life of the *homo sacer* is a life "stripped of every right" (*Sacer* 183) that "can as such be eliminated [or harmed] without punishment" (139). The *homo sacer* finds himself "in perpetual flight. . . . And yet he is in a continuous relationship with the [sovereign] power that banished him" (183). Like the barbarian, the *homo sacer* is dehumanized. The law no longer protects him nor punishes misdeeds against him. But how do individuals become *homo sacer*? Do they magically appear with the exception? For Agamben, the power to decide on both the exception and on the value of one's life rests with the sovereign. Just as the boundaries between the human become continually more permeable, we must remember that the position of the sovereign and the *homo sacer* is not fixed. The Cylons as a race act as sovereign in their decision to annihilate humanity, but then as individuals come under the force of sovereignty when captured by the humans.

To help parse the relationship between the exception and the *homo sacer*, consider the detention center at Guantanamo Bay (originally Camp X-Ray, now Camp Delta). It lies in an exceptional space, purportedly outside the jurisdiction of both U.S. and international law. At Guantanamo "normal prohibitions against torture need not apply," and one "could render specific conduct, otherwise criminal, not unlawful"

(Rose 10, citing a 2003 memo to Donald Rumsfeld). In the "War on Terror" President Bush (The Decider),[5] through the power invested in him by the declaration of an emergency, deems certain people to be "unlawful enemy combatants."[6] This designation results in the withdrawal of the law's protection (e.g., suspension of habeas corpus, denial of recourse to the protection of the Geneva conventions), but not of its force (in the use of "enhanced interrogation techniques"). The designation "unlawful combatant" is sufficient to render the detainee beyond the protection of international human rights. A central aim of human rights protections is the avoidance of human pain; frequently in the state of exception, through some perceived necessity, it is the infliction of pain that is made licit.

The infliction and experience of pain is central in *BSG*'s visual imagery. Its visceral nature mimics the thematic underpinnings of the series: the meaty, painful experience of being human. Focusing on pain is important because, as Scarry convincingly argues, we use the materiality of the body, its fleshiness, to substantiate the reality of intangible things. The experience of pain, much like the exception, is paradoxical. For the person feeling pain, it is an instance of certainty; however, for the person witnessing another in pain it is an instance of doubt. This doubt creates an "absolute split between one's sense of one's own reality and the reality of other persons" (Scarry 4). When we doubt the truth of another's pain, we doubt their humanity.

Humans must endure their pain, and one way to deny Cylons access to the human is to deny the reality of their pain. In "Flesh and Bone" (1.08), as Starbuck beats Leoben during an interrogation, she encourages him to turn off his pain. She mocks his pitiful attempt to replicate human experience:

> Here's your dilemma, turn off the pain, you feel better but that makes you a machine, not a person. You see, human beings can't turn off their pain. Human beings have to suffer and cry and scream and endure because they have no choice. So the only way you can avoid the pain you are about to receive is by telling me exactly what I want to know. Just like a human would.

In her taunting, Starbuck attempts to deny Leoben the truth of his experience by denying that he can authentically suffer pain. If he cannot feel pain, then he is not deserving of recognition. And if he's just a machine, "There's no limit to the tactics I can use." Leoben may be harmed without it being a crime. When the interrogation is not successful, Roslin steps in. She says to Leoben, "I can guarantee your safety, I can order your release. . . . We have to trust each other. Trust me." Instead of treating him like an inhuman machine, she treats him with respect, and he tells her the truth. Then Roslin throws him out the airlock. Roslin's decision forces Starbuck to question her initial assumptions and justifications for her actions, and in an act of recognition she prays, "Lords of Kobol, hear my prayer. I don't know if [Leoben] had a soul or not but, if he did, take care of it."

In *Discipline and Punish* Michel Foucault remarks that public execution and torture were often political rituals, or displays of sovereign power (47–54). Public torture makes power tangible through the pain inflicted on the body of its victim. In an attempt to assert power over the Cylons, the humans inflict pain so as to reassert their lost power. In "Pegasus" and "Resurrection Ship, Parts 1 and 2" (2.10–2.12), the fact of the pain experienced by Gina and Sharon is denied by almost everyone. Cain consistently refers to Gina as an "it" or a "thing," and Fisk, her XO (Executive Officer), argues, "You can't rape a machine." If Gina, like Leoben, is just a machine, she is exempt from any protections, despite the obvious fact that she has experienced a level of pain no living thing ought to be forced to endure. She has been repeatedly raped and beaten, her body and mind completely broken. Gina's treatment on *Pegasus* reveals the depths of depravity that result in the complete dehumanization of the other and the self.

At the end of Season Two, in one of the most stunning and surprising season finales on television, the humans settle on New Caprica, and civilization finds itself once again on firm soil. The Cylons invade, and as Season Three opens, they occupy New Caprica, evoking the American occupation of Iraq. The humans are reduced to a bare life, stripped of rights, detained, tortured, and living in a state of perpetual fear. In their desperation, they become the barbarous terrorists, "evil men in gardens of paradise" ("Precipice" 3.02).

The opening montage of "Occupation" (3.01) beautifully strings together images of a body fragmented and broken, a flash of feet, then an eye, which blur together into an elemental experience of subjugation and survival. Tigh lays curled up on the floor of a detention cell encircled by a pool of light. These images of Tigh echo those of Gina curled on the floor of her cell in "Pegasus" (2.10). He is stripped bare of any semblance of humanity, the figure of *homo sacer*, against whom no act could be committed that would be labeled a crime. As the montage continues we see other bodies fragmented as the camera focuses on different hands: hands lighting a candle, hands frantically assembling the fuse on a bomb. The sequence continues as the camera moves out from hands to faces. We see Roslin, her hands following along in a book, then in a medium shot, her eyes closed in prayer. Chief Tyrol's hands quickly work on a bomb as the camera moves to a close-up of his face and across to Anders, then back down to Tyrol placing the explosives on a wall. The final shot of the montage brings us back to an extreme close-up of Tigh's broken face.

The movement from hands to heads foregrounds human creation. The hands are the means through which we create our existence. With our minds we imagine and hope for a better future. Our hands and minds are the tools that enable human experience to move beyond mere existence, beyond mere survival, beyond bare life. However, the hand clenched in a fist inverts the action of creation into an action of annihilation (Scarry 173), and the mind is often put into the service of domination and control. It seems inevitable, then, that an episode in which the body and spirit are so completely destroyed would end in the annihilation of the body, of the self, and of others in the tactic of suicide bombing. Duck first refuses to join the resistance (W.02–05), and it is only after Nora's death when he's "got nothing to live for" (3.01) that he joins the fight. As Duck prepares for his mission he looks at himself in a broken mirror, his face fragmented into pieces, echoing the fragmented bodies of the opening montage. Is he "the hope and the dream of a new tomorrow for humans and Cylons alike" (3.01)? When the moment comes for Duck to press the button, *BSG* doesn't cut away; it confronts the viewer with his pain, fear, and hopelessness. Duck presses the trigger, it beeps, and he explodes. In the aftermath, papers float over crumpled debris and dead bodies. Of course, the afterimage calls to mind news footage of attack sites in Iraq, Israel, and even New York City, but there is little footage in U.S. media of the explosions themselves; the violence itself is absent and abstract.

BSG presents us with the futility of a situation in which suicide bombing becomes a justifiable tactic of resistance, but it also asks if defeating the Cylons is worth self-destruction. Baltar confronts Roslin, now in detention, about the bombing. In a twist, Baltar becomes the voice of morality.

Roslin: There's something that scares the Cylons after all.

Baltar: I should think using men and women as human bombs should scare us all.

Roslin: Desperate people will take desperate measures.

Baltar: All right, look me in the eye, look me in the eye, and tell me that you approve of sending young men and women into crowded places with explosives strapped to their chests. I'm waiting for you to look me in the eye and tell me you approve. ("Precipice" 3.02)

Roslin shakes her head, unable to approve, but she nevertheless understands why people who are tortured, indefinitely detained without charge, and reduced to state of total abjection, might turn to such tactics. Later when Tigh indicates that he plans to hit the marketplace, Tyrol, stunned, asks, "You know, we need to figure out whose side we're on," to which Tigh responds, "Which side are we on? We're on the side of demons, Chief. We're evil men in the gardens of paradise, sent by the forces of death to spread devastation and destruction wherever we go" (3.02).[7] Must humanity revert once again to its "murderous heritage"? Are there "Some things you just don't do . . . not even in war" (3.01)? Or is Tigh correct when he says, "[Duck]'s a solider, Chief. It's not the first time we sent a soldier on a one-way mission. You know that" (3.01)?

We are told "this has all happened before and will all happen again." This queries whether humanity is stuck in a cycle of violence in which "We kill them. They kill us. So, we kill more of them. So they kill more of us" ("Fragged" 2.03). What seems to remain constant throughout is the body in pain. There is the innocent civilian dead and the torture victim on whose body power (be it Cylon or Colonial) is writ large and through whom civilization is thoroughly unmade. There is the suicide bomber, through whom the abjection of the torture victim is turned against power. Between these two stands the soldier. His uniform and its accompanying insignia, the camouflage fatigues that are meant to render him invisible, mark him as a representative of power. But the soldier is as expendable as the torture victim. His body is put to uses other than his own. He creates pain and is wholly open to being in pain. The soldier extracts information and creates terror. Distinctions between the soldier, the civilian, the tortured detainee, and the suicide bomber, between human and Cylon, disappear. What they all have in common is the capacity of the body to be reduced to what it can be made to do and to suffer.

General Tommy Franks told reporters during the Afghan campaign, "We don't do body counts."[8] The full implications of this statement are too complex to address here fully, but the position reveals just how little the lives of those deemed expendable in the "War on Terror" are worth. Indeed the phrase used to describe the dead, "collateral damage," thoroughly erases their humanity. Unlike the current coverage of the war in Iraq in its complete obfuscation of both military and civilian losses, one of *BSG*'s iconic images is the count of living bodies presented each week in the opening credits and in many of the background shots on *Colonial One*. Unlike the continued erasure of the body count in our present reality, the complete loss of human life is consistently made visible through the emphasis of the total human loss during the attack on the Colonies. Tigh reports the number to be twenty billion (W.06). The lesson is, perhaps, that only in making the loss visible can we learn from it. Scarry observes that "the act of counting . . . has a fixed place in the landscape of emergency" (192), and for Roslin the number itself is a talisman, reminding her, and the audience, what is always at stake: the survival of the human race. This survival is not merely the physical survival of humanity but its spiritual survival as well. *BSG* examines what happens to human beings in an indefinite state of exception, and interrogates how, when confronted with an Other who seems so alien, yet so familiar, we find ourselves questioning our most fundamental notions about humanity and civilization, about who and what we are, and what we hope we might be. In blurring the boundaries between human and inhuman, between barbarism and civilization, and by exposing that anyone might find himself in the no-man's-land of the exception, stripped to bare life, *BSG* asks us to resist the Manichean logic of "with us or against us" when its only possible outcome is not only the dehumanization of the other, but the dehumanization of ourselves.

Notes

1. See Michel Foucault's *Society Must Be Defended* for his full discussion of the antagonistic relationship between civilization and barbarism. Agamben's section in *Homo Sacer* on the Ban and the Wolf is also illuminating on this point (104–11). For more on the internal barbarian, see Sigmund Freud's *Civilization and Its Discontents*.

2. For full text, see www.whitehouse.gov/news/releases/2001/09/20010920-8.html.

3. President Bush declared the state of emergency on September 14, 2001 <http://www.whitehouse.gov/news/releases/2001/09/20010914-4.html>. It was continued on September 5, 2006 <http://www.whitehouse.gov/news/releases/2006/09/20060905-16.html>.

4. Agamben defines the *homo sacer* as one "who *may be killed and yet not sacrificed*" (*Sacer* 8, emphasis Agamben's).

5. Bush's original statement "I'm the decider, and I decide what is best" on April 18, 2006, was in reference to a call by some generals for Donald Rumsfeld's resignation.

6. See Mark Danner, *Torture and Truth*.

7. There is some irony here, given that both turn out to be Cylons in 3.20.

8. The full number of civilian dead in Afghanistan and Iraq remains undocumented.

3

Alienation and the Limits of the Utopian Impulse

Carl Silvio and Elizabeth Johnston

Battlestar Galactica has been praised by fans and critics alike for its commentary on a range of topics. This essay explores the series in terms of its ideological relationship to economics and suggests that the show foregrounds certain cultural contradictions fundamental to capitalism that may have become even more salient with the widespread recognition of global capitalism.

Our argument is that the series both explores and problematizes the possibility that labor in a modern society could exist in a much less alienated form than it does in our own. By describing labor in the Colonial Fleet as unalienated, we are obviously invoking Marx's theories regarding this matter. In its most basic form, the alienation of labor refers to the condition of wage labor in a capitalist society in which workers work not for a sense of personal satisfaction but rather to earn a wage. Workers do not recognize the essence of themselves or their aspirations in the products of their labor; the product does not in any real meaningful sense reflect them. Instead, the workers only value the products to the extent that their creation allows them to earn wages. One can think of labor as unalienated when the products of that labor express for the individual worker some sense of his or her own subjective experience as an autonomous and individual agent. Yet, while unalienated labor is clearly preferable to being alienated from one's work, we should not automatically conflate the concept of unalienated labor with "enjoying one's work" or "loving what one does." Even unpleasant work can provide a sense of personal satisfaction, for example, in the knowledge that the work benefits others (Marx *passim*).

One salient example of unalienated labor that we find in *BSG* is introduced in the episode entitled "Flight of the Phoenix" (2.09). In an effort to relieve stress and tension in his personal life, Chief Tyrol decides to build a new Viper from scratch. Initially, the rest of *Galactica*'s crew is somewhat skeptical of his efforts, considering them a waste of time that might actually be detracting from far more important efforts needed for the security of the ship. But soon, almost the entire crew embraces Tyrol's vision and finds that it enjoys and derives tremendous personal satisfaction from the work. In making the new Viper, ultimately christened the *Laura* in honor of the fleet's President Laura Roslin, the crew does not work for personal or material gain. Its members enjoy the work because it represents an externalization of their commitment to each other and to the greater good of the fleet. Ironically, perhaps, there is something wasteful about the construction of the *Laura*, but only if we define "waste" as something that does not directly lead to personal material gain or serve a specific utilitarian purpose.[1]

Such unalienated labor directly contrasts with most forms of labor in capitalist societies in which workers work for a wage first and foremost and in which the actual product of their efforts does not matter nearly as much their earnings. But for Marxists, this concept of the wage is integrally connected to the alienation of labor in other ways as well. Under capitalism, those who own the means of production extract what economists describe as "surplus value" from the labor of those who work for them. The value of a worker's labor to the capitalist is precisely the value that it acquires after its realization in the form of a commodity and its circulation in the market. But the value of a worker's labor as a commodity must always exceed the wage that the worker receives for his or her labor; otherwise capital could never be profitable. In one sense, this observation may seem completely obvious; after all, how else could the engines of a capitalist economy run, if capital did not make a profit? But while the idea itself may not be that startling, its implications often go unrecognized. The concept of surplus value suggests that, despite popularized conceptions of capitalism that describe it as the best way, and often the only way, to fully maximize human potential and individual agency, capitalism at its most basic level is founded on inequity (or exploitation). Inherent in the idea of the wage relation itself is the idea that anyone who works for a living always puts more into their work than they in turn receive. In this process of alienation, we find one of the most salient cultural contradictions that haunt capitalism.

The question that now faces us is the extent to which *BSG* can be interpreted as an ideological critique that foregrounds, rather than elides, this contradiction. In Season One, after the Cylons' devastating attack on the Twelve Colonies, the surviving humans must flee the home system in a ragtag fleet that huddles around *Galactica* for support and defense. Significantly, we see almost no evidence of alienated labor of any sort in the Colonial Fleet. In fact, initially we see almost no evidence that a market economy exists at all under these circumstances. All of the productivity and labor in the fleet seems to be undertaken in a spirit of mutual cooperation intended to benefit the survival of humanity itself. Labor, for the most part, has a decidedly unalienated cast to it. From the apocalypse that has befallen humanity, the seeds of (Marxist) utopian possibility emerge. The destruction of the Twelve Colonies has created the possibility of a large-scale, cooperative, and fully technologized society independent of the alienation created by the wage system.

In Season One, the action revolves around a military battleship in a state of war, a setting that may largely preclude much narrative attention to economic matters. In Season Two it is revealed that a market economy has in fact been reestablishing itself in the Colonial Fleet. In "Black Market" (2.14), Apollo learns that Captain Fisk of *Galactica*'s sister ship, *Pegasus*, has been murdered and that he had connections to a ring of black marketers based on the ship *Prometheus*—introducing the fire of capitalism to the Colonies, perhaps. The black marketers apparently traffic in drugs, antibiotics, sex workers, and even children, as they seek to turn a profit based on the scarcity of these things. Not only do we learn that the Colonial Fleet has an actual market economy that seems to be working quite well, we also observe the profound alienation of several of its participants. In this same episode, we discover that Apollo has been paying for sexual relations with Shevon, a prostitute who reminds him of an old lover. When the subject of why Shevon must work as a prostitute comes up, she tells Lee that "when your baby's crying because it's hungry, you'll do anything." We will have much more to say about the commodification of women's sexuality later in this essay, but for now, we wish to emphasize the fact that, in the black market economy—the only market of any consequence visible in the series to this point—workers are compelled and coerced into selling their labor by a coordination of social forces that allows them little in the way of perceived alternatives.

Most significantly, the episode explicitly figures the fleet's market economy as a black market and deliberately associates it with criminality. There may, of course, be some other more legitimate monetary economy functioning throughout the fleet, but the point is that we simply do not see it; this absence is suggestive.[2] At one point, Tom Zarek, the former terrorist and political prisoner, chides Apollo for his shock and misgivings about the black market by asking, "Did you actually expect some utopian fantasy?" (2.14). Zarek's cynicism should strike us as significant. First, it suggests the series' creators might be aware that the absence of a market economy in the series up to this point represents, at the very least, a latent sense of utopian possibility. Second, his comments imply that the black market has emerged as a clear inevitability, an arrangement that human society produces simply as a matter of course. It remains less clear whether criminality, the market itself, or both, are seen to be the inevitable result as part of social progress. Was the fleet in Apollo's eyes a utopia prior to the existence of the black market because it lacked criminality, or because it lacked a market? Zarek's comments hint at the possibility that the answer may be "both" and that the criminal labor market may in fact follow the same logic and obey the same fundamental principles as the legitimate market.

By letting us look briefly at the black market through the eyes of Zarek, the series implies that the exploitation and alienation of a worker like Shevon differs very little in principle from the exploitation inherent in the very idea of the wage relation itself. Rather than being an aberration of capitalism, the criminal economy may actually represent its purest expression. The fact that Apollo, as a figure who represents governmental authority, ultimately accepts the necessity of the black market further underscores a recognition of the inherently isometric relationship between such legitimate and illegitimate forms of exploitation.

Should we then read *BSG* as an ideological critique that seeks to call attention to the inherent contradiction between our experience of the alienation inherent in the wage relation and our faith in the supposed benefits of a market economy for human society? In one sense, we believe that we should; by recognizing the utopian possibilities inherent in a world without wage relations, the series implicitly evaluates our own society and suggests that our world is, at the very least, less than utopian because of its particular relationship between labor and capital. But in another sense, by implying that a market-based sense of alienation is not only inevitable, but necessary, *BSG* seems to undercut any possible efficacy that such utopian thinking may offer for thinking about the chances of actual social change. Given that necessity forces Apollo to concede and adopt Zarek's outlook on the fate of this "utopia," does the series really give us an option between the two? Such cynical rejections of utopian possibility become more common, but also more ambiguous.

In "Lay Down Your Burdens, Part 2" (2.20), the remnants of humanity, under the leadership of newly elected President Baltar, decide to abandon the search for Earth and settle on the recently discovered planet, New Caprica. Near the end of the episode, the narrative jumps ahead in chronology, taking us to a point one year after most of the Colonial Fleet has landed and settled. We learn that New Caprica City consists mostly of a shanty town, tents, and other flimsy structures clustered around the hulls of landed starships. More significantly, we see Chief Tyrol, who has now become a union leader, delivering an address about class conflict and the struggle over the means of production to a tent full of workers. While there was never much evidence of labor union activity or organized class struggle on the fleet before, now that humanity has settled on New Caprica, we learn that a need for such things has again arisen. The series seems to suggest that the alienation of the market is inevitable; despite its best efforts, as soon as humanity settled down and ceased to worry as much about the Cylon pursuit, society took its presumptively natural course and produced a familiar set of market relations between labor and capital. This seems to imply that utopian fantasy is merely fantasy, which can only exist under unusual and unsustainable conditions, like a postapocalyptic flight from the Cylons (or on a television show about such a flight).[3]

Given the apparent bleakness of New Caprica City even before the Cylons occupy it, we must initially conclude that the market, now with access to increased resources, has not brought an abundance of prosperity for most; while Baltar lives the life of a corrupt frontier-town mayor, most of the colony exists at subsistence levels. The episode's foregrounding of the idea of class conflict as part of its initial introduction to life in New Caprica City reveals its attitude toward wage relations as less than optimistic. If *BSG* presents the alienation of the market as inevitable and natural, it certainly does not seem very enthusiastic about it. And yet, we suspect that Tyrol's tirade against the bosses—which clearly references and quotes from Mario Savio's famous address given on December 2, 1964, during the Berkeley Free Speech Movement in which he urges workers to throw their bodies onto the gears of the machine[4]—appears to many in *BSG*'s audience as full of tired revolutionary clichés. Tyrol tells the workers:

> There comes a time when you realize that the engine you built with your blood and your sweat and your tears is being used for something so foul, so perverted, it makes you sick in your heart. And it's then that you must throw your body on the gears, and on the levers, and on the machine itself and make it stop! And you have to show the people who run it, the people who control it, that unless we're free that machine will be prevented from working at all! (2.20)

Whether or not the television audiences recognize this as a paraphrase of Savio, Tyrol's speech seems designed to call to mind not just the specter of a failed 1960s radicalism, but perhaps even grainy black and white archival footage of old May Day parades—associations that are linked in the public imagination to the idea of failed revolution and political naiveté. Whether the simplicity of his ideas is intended to characterize Tyrol, or the simplification results from perceived limitations of the television medium and its audience, the effect remains the same. *BSG* represents certain revolutionary ideas while remaining somewhat ambivalent when it comes to consideration of how viable these ideas really are.

We can observe this dynamic at work in "Dirty Hands" (3.16), in which workers on the fleet become extremely discontent over the lack of social and class mobility. The episode shows the Colonial Fleet developing a rigid class structure, in which people are destined for one profession or another based on their family and cultural backgrounds. Interestingly, while the episode codes this problem in terms that evoke images of nineteenth-century class conflict—heavy machinery, seven-day workweeks, child labor—the emergent social order on the Colonial Fleet actually seems much more reminiscent of feudalism than predatory capitalism. The position of any individual in the overall hierarchy is not based on the accumulation of monetary wealth, but is more closely connected to birth (or status at the point of the Cylon attack). *BSG* further complicates the utopian promise that it has earlier represented by suggesting that a future without an economy of wages relations and the commodification of labor may in fact lead us backward to an earlier and arguably worse form of exploitation.

In *This Sex Which Is Not One*, Luce Irigaray postulates that the exchange of women as commodities between men undergirds patriarchal society and represents a microcosm of the alienation of labor in capitalism. It is in the process of commodification that women lose their connection to their own "natural" value: "In order to become [an exchangeable] equivalent, a commodity changes bodies.... A commodity—a woman— is divided into two irreconcilable 'bodies': her 'natural' body and her socially valued, exchangeable body" (175). In this exchange, women's bodies are treated as abstractions; they are alienated from their own sexual and reproductive labor.[5] In contrast to the situation described by Irigaray, the gender economy of the series appears, at first glance, egalitarian. The show features a determined female president, and brave female pilots, like Starbuck and Boomer; indeed, in their efforts to update the show from the 1970s, the show's writers reimagined these formerly male characters as female. There are no snide comments by men about the inferiority of female presidents or pilots, no sense that one's effectiveness as a leader or soldier is connected to one's sex.

Also notable and more closely linked to our argument here is that the women's bodies of the Colonial Fleet are not objectified in the ways female bodies on television often are; we do see them in states of undress, but only when they are having sex and both male and female bodies are naked. At no point in the show are the *human* women (or even the Cylon woman allied with the humans, as in the case of Boomer) explicitly objects for the viewer's gaze. In fact, if the show seems to objectify any bodies, it is those of the men. The titillating shot of Apollo wearing only a washcloth in "Final Cut" is a memorable example of this inversion (2.08). We must assume that sexual equality is part of the series' utopian vision.

In fact, the objectification and/or commodification of women's bodies is at least initially a significant marker of "badness." Early on, this marker of badness is associated exclusively with the Cylons and their human collaborators. Coded as a traditional femme fatale,[6] Caprica Six seduces Baltar, the man of science. Cylons use their female bodies as exchangeable objects; they offer to Baltar the body of a desirable woman in exchange for his cooperation. Of course, it is true that Caprica Six, as part of some sort of collective Cylon consciousness, may not be an individual as we understand the term and cannot be alienated or exploited from her own labor; however, it is almost impossible for the viewer not to perceive her as an individual. The viewer perceives a familiar exchange as the Cylons trade in on the value of Caprica's sexualized body for political favors. Moreover, the show codes Baltar's objectification of women generally as morally wrong and as breeding dangerous consequences. There are also, of course, instances of human femmes fatales who similarly use their bodies as exchangeable objects. Colonel Tigh's wife, Ellen, stands as a noteworthy example of this trend. Significantly, she too is narratively figured as corrupt. Ellen encourages Tigh's worst habits and inclinations and is serially unfaithful to him. Her badness is marked particularly by her being, in a sexual economy that values youth, too old to behave in such a manner. Caprica's flirtations, then, are perceived as sexy while Ellen's are pathetic; when we later see Ellen on New Caprica prostituting her body in a more explicit exchange with Cavil, her exterior appearance matches what the viewer knows about her: she is markedly aged, bruised, and disheveled. Her value has been, in a feminist Marxist analysis, nearly exhausted. *BSG* associates the alienation of women from their bodies and sexuality with human corruption and with the enemy of humanity, implicitly critiquing this dynamic as it exists in the audience's real life society.

This emphasis on defining the objectification and commodification of female bodies as a marker of badness is underscored in the episode entitled "Pegasus" (2.10). When *Galactica* encounters another surviving battlestar, *Pegasus*, its commander is Admiral Cain, who dehumanizes her crew and has abandoned the civilian fleet it should have protected. Like *Galactica*, *Pegasus* also has a Cylon captive, a Six producers call Gina (though the name is never used in the series). The crew's treatment of her differs radically from the treatment of Sharon on *Galactica*. The *Pegasus* crew has repeatedly raped and tortured her, and they attempt, unsuccessfully, to do the same to Sharon.[7] Why is the crew of the female-led *Pegasus* more traditionally patriarchal and misogynist than that of *Galactica*? Cain is the only woman seen on *Pegasus*. It may be that the apparent absence of other women results in its crew's inability to see women as anything other than objects. More plausibly, the rape of Gina and the attempted rape of Sharon signify displaced feelings of castration; the female Cylons are not only objects, but threats. *BSG* offers a critique of our own patriarchal society that demonstrates visible discomfort with women in positions of power traditionally held by men. Reducing these women back to the status of object or commodity helps to alleviate these anxieties.

The objectification of women's sexuality, and the alienation associated with it, also connect directly to the exploitation of reproductive labor. The machines' desire to harness the reproductive labor of women is another marker of badness in the series. In "The Farm" (2.05), a wounded Starbuck wakes up in what she thinks is a resistance hospital on Caprica. Her attending physician, Simon, gives her a vaginal exam, then advises her to think about having children, calling fertile women a "rare commodity." Later, Starbuck grows suspicious of Simon, and sees him in the hallway discussing the removal of her ovaries and her own "processing" with a Six. When he returns to her room, she kills him, and, in searching for a way out, stumbles on a room of sedated human women attached to gruesome-looking machines. Starbuck recognizes resistance fighter Sue-Shaun, who wakes, grabs hold of her, and begs her to stop the "baby machines." Starbuck destroys the machines and outside is rescued by Anders, Helo, and Sharon, by now pregnant with Helo's child. Sharon describes the breeding programs conducted by the Cylons in "farms" like these, and explains that the Cylons were intending to impregnate Starbuck because they have been unable to procreate among themselves.

The Cylons are coded as bad because they are, as Starbuck notes, "raping women": literally, by inseminating them against their will, and metaphorically, by appropriating their rights to their own reproductive labor. That these women are housed in "farms" suggests the ways women have, indeed, been reduced to the status of a resource-producing commodity. Sedated, they have no subjectivity; they are only bodies and their only value is in reproduction. Ironically, Sharon suggests that the only bad thing about the use of women's reproductive labor in this instance is that it is not voluntary; implicit in this dialogue is the suggestion that the Cylons don't see the exploitation of women's reproductive labor as inherently negative. As noted earlier, one of the hallmarks of capitalist ideology is the way in which it normalizes the exploitation of labor. Capitalism works precisely because we implicitly agree to our own exploitation; the alienation of the worker from his or her own labor is, indeed, entirely voluntary. We accept, for example, that women will not be fully compensated for their reproductive labor; in fact, we make it part of our social contract.

Up to this point, we have argued that *BSG* offers a critique of the exploitation of women's sexual and reproductive labor, namely by coding as bad those who participate in the objectification and commodification of their bodies. However, just as was the case in our earlier discussions of wage relations, a closer analysis suggests that the ultimate orientation of *BSG* toward this issue is more convoluted. In "Black Market" (2.14), we see Apollo's commodification of Shevon's sexual labor. He is paying her 100 cubits to stay the night with her. Prostitution is legal.[8] The commodification of women's bodies is actually part of the utopian economy, and might even be necessary in order to maintain the egalitarian appearance of the crew. Apollo's relationship with Starbuck, for example, is fraught with unfulfilled sexual tension, because she is an equal who cannot be objectified. Even when Starbuck wants Apollo to see her only as a sexual object, he cannot because he loves her. The prostitute serves as both displacement of Apollo's sexual frustrations and containment of the show's critique insofar as the egalitarian relationships depend, to some extent, on the hidden but necessary presence of prostitutes who can act only as objects for male desire.[9] The commodification and exploitation of her sexual labor enables him (and others like him) to opt out of an economy of gender equality, even as he pretends to participate in it. The exploitaiton of Shevon's sexual labor underwrites the maintenance of what is really, on closer examination, a system of gender inequality. Later, the criminal mob boss, Phelan, cynically reminds Apollo, "It's hard to find the moral high ground when we're all standing in the mud." Apollo agrees to allow Phelan's black market to continue, even though the black market apparently includes child prostitution, with reference to Shevon's daughter and other caged children. In this pivotal episode, the distinction between utopia and dystopia collapses.

This ambiguity is repeated in "The Captain's Hand" (2.17), in which a teenage girl is discovered hiding on *Galactica*; she has escaped from a civilian ship where her family is devoutly opposed to abortion. Pregnant, she hopes Dr. Cottle will help her to terminate her pregnancy. Roslin must confront the pro-life/pro-choice debate. Although a staunch defender of the right to choose, and although the Twelve Colonies have long legalized abortion, she changes her position when Baltar confirms that, at the current rate, the human population will become extinct in eighteen years. While Roslin grants the girl an abortion, she simultaneously makes all future abortions illegal, saying reproduction is vital for human survival. Here, women's agency regarding their own reproductive labor takes second seat to the pragmatics of population concerns. Significantly, the epsiode does not offer any overt criticism of Roslin's decision, except through the morally ambivalent Baltar. While admitting that this point is arguable, we suggest that this absence of overt critique implies a tacit acceptance on the episode's part of Roslin's pragmatic denial of female agency.

BSG suggests that humans, like Cylons, exploit women's reproductive labor and sexuality. The series problematizes its own utopian impulse by blurring the demarcation between human/Cylon, good/bad. As is the case with its treatment of wage relations, BSG seems ambivalent about its ultimate ideological orientation toward these issues of women's reproduction and sexuality. The conundrum posed by the show first presents a utopian alternative to certain forms of exploitation associated with partriarchy and capitalism, and then suggests that this alternative is untenable.

BSG stands as such a fascinating and complex work of art precisely because it resists being reduced to simplistic dichotomy. In making this assertion, we intend more than a facile affirmation of the value of artistic ambiguity, and instead suggest that this ambiguity may in fact lend itself to more effective ideological critique. Fredric Jameson urges that ideological analysis avoid the categorization of cultural texts as either "pro" or "anti" utopian. Drawing upon the theories of Marxist philosopher Ernst Bloch, Jameson argues that most cultural texts evidence some sort of utopian impulse that is ultimately narratively contained and deflected. He suggests, in fact, that this utopian impulse may facilitate the ideological work performed by the text in question: "Works of mass culture cannot be ideological without at one and the same time being implicitly or explicitly Utopian as well: they cannot manipulate unless they offer some genuine shred of content as a fantasy bribe to the public about to be so manipulated" (144). While we agree with Jameson here, we argue that in the case of BSG the relationship between the utopian and the hegemonic—utopia's role as "bribe"—is intentionally made explicit so that the viewer might see—and begin to ask questions about—the ideological function utopian narratives serve.

What separates BSG from the majority of television programs is not its endorsement or rejection of this utopian impulse, but its foregrounding of the struggle between these two alternatives. In this sense, the show reminds us somewhat of Bertolt Brecht's concept of Epic Theater. For Brecht, politically conscious theater should force the audience to reflect rationally on its own relation to the social order. Rather than allowing easy emotional identification on the part of the audience with its action, the drama should problematize the relationship between the two. Brecht felt that cathartic emotional investment in the action ultimately led to passivity and complacency. By denying its audience a clear sense of emotional or ethical orientation toward its utopian impulse, *BSG* forces us to maintain a vital distance from the concept that is necessary for critical reflection. While the series does certainly encourage a large amount of emotional identification from its audience, such investment is typically partial and, as we have argued, prone to be reversed at a moment's notice. *BSG* invites us to identify with and invest ourselves in competing and contradictory attitudes toward its utopian themes. It forces us to ask difficult questions about our relationship to capitalism, our complicity with our own and others' alienation and exploitation, and the assumptions we make about gender and sexuality. It forces us to recognize, in Phelan's words, that "we're all standing in the mud" (2.14). And like Apollo, we'll have to determine what to do with what we now know.

Notes

1. The *Laura* eventually is put to a military use in destroying the Cylon Resurrection ship, but at the time of its construction, there is no strategic plan.

2. We wish to be clear here that some form of economy clearly exists: in "Flight of the Phoenix" (2.9), Tyrol trades parts ship-to-ship. Barter and trade do exist, but in an economic system not primarily associated with technologized capitalism.

3. Ernst Bloch argues that the very idea of utopia itself always seems to hint at its own impossibility (*Philosophy of the Future*).

4. According to David Eick, "Mario Savio's widow gave us permission to paraphrase it, and she liked the way we did it" (quoted in Bassom, *Two* 102).

5. See also Gayle Rubin, "Traffic in Women."

6. See Mary Ann Doane, *Femme Fatales*.

7. Helo and Tyrol intervene when Lieutenant Thorne tries to rape Sharon in her cell. In an alternate, unaired version of the same scene, Thorne does rape her.

8. In the podcast for this episode, Ronald D. Moore explains that prostitution was probably legal in the Twelve Colonies and that Shevon is supposed to remind us of the "socialators," like Cassiopeia, in the original series.

9. While much feminist theory sees legalized prostitution as potentially liberating for women, enabling them with agency over their own bodies and thereby posing an alternative to sexual exploitation, Shevon is clearly not empowered. She is not an agent, but an object exchanged between her pimp and Apollo. She admits that economic circumstances have forced her into prostitution, and she rejects Apollo's offer to legitimize their relationship because she understands, more than he does, that to him she is only an abstraction. She is, to use Irigaray's language, "what man inscribes in and on [her]" (187)—in this case, Apollo's memories of a failed relationship with another woman.

4

The Cain Mutiny: Reflecting the Faces of Military Leadership in a Time of Fear

Rikk Mulligan

Samuel R. Delany said, "Science fiction is not about the future; it uses the future as a narrative convention to present significant distortions of the present" (291). While the resonance of such distortions is sometimes muted in escapist narratives, such as the stories of the original *Battlestar Galactica*, the social commentary embedded in the reimagined series more often parallels contemporary political and military issues, pointedly criticizing the policies of the current Bush administration. The original *BSG*, created in 1978 by Glen A. Larsen, could have competed with *Star Trek* for the tagline, "*Wagon Train* in space," with its "ragtag fugitive fleet" shepherded by Lorne Greene as Commander Adama. In 2003, the reimagined *BSG* brought a darker narrative to an audience who had been barraged with the media coverage of the September 11th attacks in America, and the consequent invasions of Afghanistan and Iraq. One of the more controversial aspects of the new series has been its regendering of several male character roles. The essence of these characters remains the same even if the new face is young, attractive, and female. While Starbuck and Boomer garner the most attention,[1] the reimagined commander of the *Battlestar Pegasus*, Cain, is perhaps more significant because she has also been promoted. Admiral Cain joins the fleet as Commander Adama's superior and the new ranking military officer; it is important to the story that she is female, but focusing solely on gender misses the differences in the two leaders' use of power, treatment of prisoners, and relations with civilians. Cain's character is not an indictment of women in military command, but is instead a criticism of leaders who overstep their bounds, abuse their power, and lose their perspective. She offers a direct engagement of President George W. Bush's often draconian policies, which put him at odds with a large segment of the international community, the American people, and members of his own government.

The narrative distance created by science fiction allows the reimagined *BSG* to bring contemporary social and political issues into the story, including the abuse of military power in scenes of prisoner abuse, torture, and secret trials; the failure of civilian leadership to control military commanders; and the question of what rights and privileges should be surrendered for momentary protections. American media, intelligence services, and civilian leadership maintain a constant alarm and state of fear akin to that experienced by *Galactica*'s refugee fleet. An ill-defined and continuing War on Terror, an enemy who can strike from within, and the stifled and silenced responses to the actions of military leaders taken in the name of protection frame contemporary American debates regarding the actions of the military. The lack of criticism and current failure to convict military leaders of war crimes does not make their acts legal. In the explicitly parallel *BSG* universe, the lack of legal challenge to Cain does not make her actions legal either. *BSG* is best considered in the context of American laws, policies, and military protocol. Military rank and the rules of presidential succession reflect aspects of American military and Constitutional hierarchies, suggesting an American legal context, more specifically the United States Constitution for individual rights and protections, the United States Navy Regulations for the powers and responsibilities of military commanders, and the Geneva Conventions for the treatment of prisoners. The ideas offered by *BSG*, especially in the "Pegasus" and "Resurrection Ship" narratives (2.10–12), resonate with the Western media coverage of the conflicts in Iraq and Afghanistan, and stories of prisoner treatment in American military facilities including Guantanamo Bay and Abu Ghraib, reflecting popular outrage over these atrocities. Neither Cain nor Adama represents any specific figure, but their characters present different faces of military command; the actions taken under their authority can be unsettling, uncomfortable, and frequently startling to their audience as cultural assumptions and the line between supposed good guys and bad guys becomes blurred.

Admiral Cain's arrival and the addition of the *Pegasus* to the fleet mark a pivotal point in the series and underscore a difficult choice: to return to the Colonies or to continue searching for Earth and an unknown future. Cain's goal is one of revenge and nostalgia; her sole mission is to fight the Cylons at any cost. Adama's primary concern is for the fleet and its human survivors, orienting him toward the future, rather than the past. This contrast in their views of humanity's future underscores the tensions rising from the different choices they have made, and from the differences in their command style that come to question the uses of power. These tensions make it easier to forgive Adama when he crosses those boundaries, but make Cain a despot and tyrant because her actions are so unconscionable.

Cain's past and personality are sketched in a few brief lines when Adama tells Roslin that he has never met Admiral Cain, but that she is "very young officer on a very fast track. Very smart, very tough, very well-connected. Fleet promoted her to rear admiral over half of the commanders on the list" ("Pegasus" 2.10). Cain attempts to establish her dominance quickly, irrespective of the existing relationships and hierarchies within this refugee fleet. When Cain arrives on the *Galactica* she leaves little doubt as to who is in command; she orders the *Galactica*'s executive officer (XO), Colonel Tigh, to set his men at ease and waits for Adama to salute her. She also establishes new power relationships by welcoming the *Galactica* "back to the Colonial Fleet," suggesting that she (and the *Pegasus*) are the fleet, not the larger collection of ships that includes *Colonial One* and the majority of the human survivors. Cain appears to be the only surviving flag officer, making the *Pegasus* a flagship without a fleet; when she finds the *Galactica*, military protocol based on American standards suggests that Adama join her "fleet" (Tracy). But this is a military protocol established before the fall of the Colonies and one based on a history and tradition that has ended, casting some doubt on Cain's automatic assumption of control. She seems intent on following the protocols that keep her in absolute command, while disregarding those that share authority with others.

Cain gives no indication of having considered civilian leadership or the distribution of power and authority within the fleet. She appears slightly taken aback when introduced to Laura Roslin as "the President of the Colonies" by Adama ("Pegasus" 2.10). Cain neither recognizes

Roslin's rank as president, nor the civilian fleet as a whole when she integrates the *Galactica* into her fleet ostensibly under martial law. In her assumption of command, Cain leaves the relationship of military command and civilian rule unclear in a manner reminiscent of the lack of order in Afghanistan after the fall of the Taliban, and in Iraq after the initial defeat of Saddam Hussein's armies and his fall from power in April 2003. In both instances the American military created a power vacuum but failed to adapt and establish a system to deal with the civilian population. As the ranking military officer, Cain is responsible for integrating military and civilian commands, even as she is answerable to the president of the Colonies, who sets the boundaries on Cain's command authority. However, Cain does not recognize the correct chain of command, nor does she tolerate any challenge to her authority.

Cain begins overstepping these boundaries very quickly in her failure to engage with the president and civilian authorities. Rather than clearly establishing her authority relative to the president, Cain disregards Roslin and focuses on the military hierarchy. After arriving on *Galactica*, at the end of their informal debriefing in Adama's ready room, it is Cain who stands first, essentially dismissing Adama and the president. Cain also suggests that Adama send over his logs when he has a chance, reinforcing her authority over him. It is not Cain but Adama who makes it very clear—to the president and the audience—that the admiral is his superior officer and will assume command of the entire fleet. This visibly disturbs Roslin, and Cain's responses are ambiguous when she says, "The chain of command is strict, but it is not heartless" ("Pegasus" 2.10). The admiral's entire focus is on a campaign that no longer seems related to the needs of humanity outside the military.

The relationship of Admiral Cain to Commander Adama is similar enough to American military protocol that it may seem familiar to most viewers, but Cain's failure to address the president as her superior, or to consider the needs of the civilian fleet suggests that she considers herself at the top of the chain of command. Within an American legal and military context, the admiral would accept her orders from the president, but Cain, a rogue commander isolated from the civil structures she believed destroyed, expresses only thinly veiled contempt for the elevated former secretary of education. The question Cain poses is whether to accept the accommodations reached between Adama and Roslin, or to hold to a now-anachronistic standard that places her in a position of absolute authority. That Cain chooses to validate her command with the old system and ignore the changed circumstances of its social foundations helps put her at odds with Roslin and Adama, and serves as harsh warning to real-life governments that work only in the interests of individuals rather than for the common good.

Before the arrival of the *Pegasus*, Adama commanded the fleet during military situations, but Roslin was the ultimate authority; the military was incorporated into the social hierarchy, not outside it. While this division of power and responsibilities was not without problems, it was a workable compromise reached following disruptions in the fleet and conflict between the military and civilian population. Cain's view of her position and of the military's needs troubles this relationship and the role of the military in regards to the civilian populace. Cain has no trouble asserting her authority over Adama and is even gracious about it. But Cain's reactions to the president—disdainful body language and derisive comments—make it clear that she intends to marginalize Roslin and by implication civilian authority. The failure in leadership reflects that of post-Saddam Iraq: as Khadim al-Jubouri says in a *Washington Post* interview, "We were surprised that after one thief [Hussein] had left, another forty replaced him" (Raghavan). As the BBC News illustrates with its "Timeline: Iraq after Saddam," American authorities were unable to efficiently minister to the Iraqi population or prevent attacks by insurgents. While the American administrator, Paul Bremmer, remained in authority and the Iraqi Governing Council moved toward self-rule, the U.S. government admitted that it was facing a guerilla war (BBC News, "Timeline"). The failure to establish order successfully or to transfer power to civilian authorities in a timely manner echoes Cain's resistance to releasing power to civilian leaders. Cain avoids opening a dialogue with the president, as it would reify Roslin's executive position and make Cain accountable to another authority.

Cain's failure in leadership is even clearer when seen through her interactions with civilian survivors by dismissing their needs or treating them as war materials. After the *Pegasus* has been with the fleet for a time, Roslin tells Adama that Cain will not return her calls, and resupplies only the *Galactica*, and then only with supplies and computer updates that will strengthen the ship for combat. Roslin makes it clear to Adama that many ships in the fleet are in dire straits, and she asks for his support in seeing to their needs. In a scene cut from the episode, the civilian fleet goes on strike with Roslin's approval to protest Cain's demands and autocratic treatment. The idea of a strike was later used in "Dirty Hands" (3.16), but

Ronald D. Moore explains that the plotline was initially written as a response to Cain's demands for fuel from several ships in the fleet while she provided nothing in return (Moore, "Podcast Resurrection Ship, Part 1"). Cain's actions establish her view of the civilian fleet as nothing more than a pool of resources. Colonel Fisk, Cain's XO, tells Tigh that the *Pegasus* had her own civilian fleet briefly, but that Cain decided that "military needs" were paramount. The civilian ships were stripped of personnel, weapons, parts, and jump drives, leaving them marooned ("Resurrection Ship, Part 1" 2.11). Cain's arrogance and her disregard for anyone outside her crew are not a criticism of women in power, however, but of leaders who lose perspective and ignore the consequences of their actions for the very people they should be serving and protecting.

It would be simple to argue that as a woman in command, Cain was written as an indictment of those who respond to the discrimination faced by women in the American military by overcompensating. As Melissa S. Herbert asserts in her ethnographic study of women in the U.S. military, military women walk a social tightrope and must construct or perform a gender balancing act in order to be accepted as competent warriors but still dispel mainstream fears of homosexuality (112–15). As recently as the Tailhook scandal in the 1990s (and in incidents of sexual abuse at military institutions like the Air Force Academy), women have still had to fight for respect and acceptance in the U.S. military (Herbert 36–38; Solaro 167–71, 200). "Tailhook" refers to the investigation and cover-up of allegations of sexual misconduct by navy and marine pilots and to their abuse of female personnel during the Tailhook Symposium in Las Vegas in 1991. Since then, feminist scholars like Herbert have argued that there is a residual distrust of women in the military, and, as a consequence, some women feel forced to be more ruthless and overbearing than their male counterparts.

But the world of *Galactica* is not ours; it is one of science fiction where gender does not inhibit women in military service. This was almost true in the original series when women were trained as pilots to replace casualties, an example of "covert feminism" defined by Joan Gordon (Gordon 196). Unfortunately, in the original series, Starbuck's derision when training the female pilots undercuts the gender equity ("Lost Planet of the Gods—Part One"). Female pilots appear in subsequent episodes and a squadron commander on the original *Pegasus*, Captain Sheba, is Commander Cain's daughter ("Living Legend—Part One"). When the original *BSG* aired in 1978, there were no female combat pilots in the U.S.

military; the air force and navy graduated their first female pilots in the 1980s and women were not allowed in combat roles until 1998 (Herbert 3–7). The hangar decks, squadrons, bunkrooms, and toilet facilities of the new *Galactica* have always been unisex; the best fighter pilots, Starbuck and Kat, are both women. The apparent sexual equality on the *Galactica* deflates the argument that Cain has to be harsher or use more force to compensate for being a woman, making this readable as an example of postfeminism. As Brooks Landon explains in *Science Fiction after 1900*, postfeminist writing submerges "traditional feminist themes into the background" but portrays female characters who are "strong, active, given to non-gender-linked jobs" (142–44). Cain is not despotic in an effort to compensate for biology; she is an officer whose loss of perspective has brought her to only consider decisions as a warrior rather than as a leader.[2] Far from being gendered, this perspective is similar to that of Afghani warlords, Taliban fighters, Baathist insurgents, or, arguably, an American president who continues to wage an unpopular war and push legislation legitimizing torture and brutality.

Cain's marginalization of civilian authority is troubling. She uses regulations to remove those who are not loyal, to arrange personnel to her advantage, and to make it more difficult for others to counter her authority; an authority once derived from civilian laws is now based on superior military strength. Cain manipulates Adama's crew by transferring Apollo and Starbuck to the *Pegasus* and replacing Tyrol on the *Galactica* with her own (civilian) deck chief, Laird ("Pegasus" 2.10). When Adama reminds Cain that she said she would not interfere with his command, she quips, "I'm saving it" ("Pegasus" 2.10). American military protocol says that Cain only has the authority to suggest personnel changes, not order them herself. This may impact the audience's assessment of the scene. Cain's authority to replace those under Adama's command is suspect; her only automatic privilege should be to replace Adama as commander (Tracy). Cain also circumvents Adama's authority by not advising him through the chain of command that Lieutenant Thorne will interrogate Sharon. As Adama later affirms with his apology to Sharon, he is responsible for everything that occurs on his ship ("Pegasus" 2.10). Cain represents the failure to share power or respect other authorities, a continuing problem within the Bush administration and military forces operating under its direction, as evidenced by the administration's hostility toward repeated calls for the resignation of former Defense Secretary Donald Rumsfeld and the frequent replacement of military commanders who do not share the president's view of operations in Iraq.

The treatment of prisoners is a murky issue on both battlestars, echoing similar questions surrounding the treatment of those termed "enemy combatants" by U.S. forces and military tribunals. It would be easy to focus solely on the treatment of Gina, the Cylon Six held prisoner on the *Pegasus*, but even on the *Galactica*, rights and privileges are sometimes discarded when it is expedient. During the first season, Adama has Starbuck question the Cylon Leoben in order to determine the location of a nuclear weapon planted within the fleet. Starbuck's techniques—assault and partial drowning—are examples of torture ("Flesh and Bone" 1.08). These actions taken under Adama's authority echo methods like the use of stress positions and threat of electrocution used to question prisoners at Abu Ghraib prison (Scherer and Benjamin, "Standard" and "Electrical"). Adama also jails those who oppose his command: first, Roslin whom he accuses of supporting sedition ("Kobol's Last Gleaming, Part 1" 1.12); later, with the president's approval, the leader of the peace activists after acts of sabotage within the fleet ("Epiphanies" 2.13). In the third season Tyrol is charged with mutiny and jailed during a fleet-wide general strike ("Dirty Hands" 3.16). Adama's actions in these cases are illegal; his decision alludes to the difficulty the Bush administration has had framing a coherent and legal response to what it defines as a series of threats.

The contrast in the experiences of Sharon on *Galactica* and Gina on *Pegasus* crystallize the differences in leadership and social responsibility between the battlestar commanders. Both Adama and Cain have Cylon prisoners, but where Adama has gained a great deal of intelligence from Sharon, Cain has learned nothing from Gina ("Pegasus" 2.10). Baltar tells Cain that he has achieved good results by treating Sharon as human; Thorne raped and beat Gina, and had her gang raped, leaving her catatonic. Sharon is imprisoned in a standard military cell; Gina is chained to the metal floor of her cell, dressed in only a tattered and stained sickbay smock, with no other signs of comforts or facilities ("Pegasus" 2.10). Later, after Baltar begins to make progress with Gina, Cain assaults her while ranting about the betrayal of "this thing" ("Resurrection Ship, Part 1" 2.11). Neither Cain's actions nor the guards' abuse of Gina gather intelligence; interrogation has become merely an institutionalized form of abuse and revenge. The dehumanizing treatment of prisoners in Abu Ghraib, and the minimal facilities and lack of respect shown to those in Guantanamo Bay are echoed in the examples of abuse depicted on the *Pegasus*, adding a further critique of post-9/11 abuses by the American military, and of the civilian leaders who encourage them with their rhetoric.

The difference in the treatment of Sharon and Gina also reflects contemporary discussion of the status of prisoners of war and accused criminals, and the creation of extralegal categories such as enemy combatant. Sharon is treated as a human prisoner; Gina is treated as less than human, and reflects the mistreatment of an enemy combatant or suspected insurgent in an Iraqi detention facility. When Senator James Inhofe (R-OK) responded to the press and public outcry over the abuse of prisoners at Abu Ghraib in 2004, he said, "These prisoners, they're murderers, they're terrorists, they're insurgents" (Inhofe), seemingly dismissing their mistreatment as warranted and necessary. The opposite response could be found in the comments of Senator Lindsey Graham (R-SC), "The American public needs to understand we're talking about rape and murder here. We're not just talking about giving people a humiliating experience" (quoted in "Rumsfeld"). Adama nearly dies and is badly scarred after his attempted assassination, but he treats his Cylon prisoner humanely and grants her a range of liberties; Cain inhumanly preys on her prisoner as she exacts revenge, a parallel with U.S. military actions in Iraq and their tacit sanction by many American politicians.

Rape is not used casually in these episodes of *BSG*; it is a harsh critique of the experience of prisoners in Coalition detention facilities, and mirrors the fears of the Iraqi populace under occupation. Whether under Cain's orders or with her tacit approval Gina is not just raped, but gangraped while in the *Pegasus* brig. Thorne's use of rape as an interrogation method would be a violation of the Uniform Code of Military Justice (UCMJ: 906.106: Spies; 920.120: Rape and Carnal Knowledge) and only slightly exaggerates the mistreatment of prisoners by some U.S. military personnel in Abu Ghraib. In his podcast on this episode, Moore makes clear that rape is not used gratuitously in Gina's narrative, but because it is known to be provocative and contentious ("Podcast Resurrection Ship, Part 1"). In her coverage of the role of female military personnel in Iraq and Afghanistan, Erin Solaro discusses the role of women in frontline units and their work to allay the fears of rape and abuse often felt by Iraqi and Afghani women. Solaro emphasizes that Saddam's intelligence service, the Mukhabarat, used rape as a tool of fear and power and that in Muslim cultures it is thought to be a "fate worse than death" for a woman, who will often be killed in any case to avoid greater dishonor in the event she becomes pregnant (Solaro 91–93). Thorne is responsible for the beating and gang rape of Gina; when he attempts to rape Sharon, he proves himself a student of the Mukhabarat. The rape draws Dr. Cottle's outrage, and provokes Adama's apology ("Pegasus" 2.10). The responses to Thorne's act echo similar criticisms of U.S. troops and of the current American leadership's definition and treatment of enemy combatants, which strips away access to legal protections, due process of law, and the guarantee of human rights under international law.

Paralleling the Bush administration's use of military tribunals, Cain uses military regulations to justify arbitrary decisions in the trials of military personnel. Fisk tells Tigh that Cain executed her old XO on the bridge ("the CIC"—Combat Information Center) for refusing an order to attack a superior force. "Admiral Cain ordered our XO to attack. He refused the order. She asked for his gun; shot him in the head with it in front of the crew" ("Pegasus" 2.10). Cain's actions are a caricature of the codes that establish her authority. She has the authority to convene a summary court-martial, to try the XO under the Colonial equivalent of the USMJ, and to order his execution. After Thorne is accidentally killed during his attempted rape of Sharon in the *Galactica* brig, Helo and Tyrol are transported to the *Pegasus*, held, tried by Cain alone, and sentenced to immediate execution. Cain's decision to consider the case unilaterally, especially now that she is no longer the sole command officer, is a violation of the protocol if the UCMJ is applied, and ordering their immediate execution is a violation of the rules regarding the convening of court-martials (UCMJ 822.22–822.27). As with the use of military tribunals for enemy combatants, these prisoners are denied due process by executive orders that are all but impossible to countermand.

Cain's leadership helps her crew of more than 1,700 survive after the Cylon annihilation of the Colonies, but her command is based on fear and strength more than the rule of law. Fisk, for example, makes it clear that fear was definitely involved when he became XO ("Pegasus" 2.10). Cain positions herself strategically in relation to Adama even before the face-off between battlestars in "Pegasus," rather than attempting to work more closely with him to coordinate the survival of the fleet. When Cain orders the transfers of Apollo and Starbuck to the *Pegasus*, and replaces Tyrol as deck chief, she is interfering with the *Galactica*'s internal affairs and distancing Adama from his strongest supporters. Tyrol's replacement, Laird, is a former engineer and civilian conscript forcibly taken from his family at Cain's orders. Underscoring the fear of Cain, Fisk details the abandonment of those fifteen vessels and their passengers, and the murders of two families during the selection of "worthy" personnel ("Resurrection Ship, Part 1" 2.11). Cain treats the *Galactica* and civilians as ultimately expendable assets to support her single-minded pursuit of a narrowly defined military mission, in much the same way that an invasion of Iraq was deemed the best way to secure the safety of Americans in a never-ending War on Terror.

Rules and regulations have been bent on the *Galactica* in the pursuit of security for the crew and for the fleet as a whole. But the audience is willing to accept what Adama has done because they have more of the story and can appreciate his decisions and actions in context. The conflict between the commanders and their worldviews almost becomes a shooting war between the battlestars; this later spirals into mutual assassination plots, even if it takes Roslin's appeals for the survival of the fleet to convince Adama to plot the assassination of Cain. Starbuck is tasked to shoot the admiral. Cain orders Fisk to take a detachment of marines and "terminate Adama's command. Starting with Adama" ("Resurrection Ship, Part 2" 2.12). Cain's orders will eliminate command on the *Galactica* and replace it with her own personnel.

Neither of the assassination plots is carried out, and both commanders step back from the brink. Safety and security are not enough. As Sharon tells Adama when he asks why the Cylons hate humans so much, "You said, 'Humanity was a flawed creation. People still kill each other over petty jealousy and greed.' Humanity never asked itself why it deserved to survive. Maybe you don't" ("Resurrection Ship, Part 2" 2.12). When Adama decides not to have Starbuck assassinate Cain, he notes, "It's not enough to survive. One has to be worthy of surviving" ("Resurrection Ship, Part 2" 2.12). In Cain's final scene she enters her quarters, takes off her gunbelt and tunic, and turns to face Gina pointing a gun at her. Gina strips Cain of her humanity by using her own words from the brig: "Does it roll over? Does it beg?" ("Resurrection Ship, Part 2" 2.12). The warning in Cain's death seems explicit—if the American government persists in its use of torture and its disregard for world opinion, it may find itself isolated and open to further acts of violence justified as revenge.

Cain's egotistic despotism and authoritarian style of command have no place in the new world sought by the humans under Adama and Roslin's joint leadership. Cain's actions reflect the worst kind of abuses because she is a hard, uncompromising, and arrogant tyrant who uses military command as a means to further her own agenda, despite advice to the contrary and the outrage of subordinates. Cain set aside her humanity through her actions, which include forgetting the proper role of the military, ignoring legal agreements and abusing prisoners, and murdering the very people she should protect. *BSG* argues that violent disregard for the basic tenants of humanity, and power grabs by military and civilian leaders invalidate their right to lead. The stubborn insistence on maintaining failed foreign policies, embodied by the Bush administration, is reflected in Cain's ultimate failure. Cain is an extension of the American use of the military in the Middle East, presidential disregard for the autonomy of world governments, and the imposition of American cultural norms and liberal democracy in name only. Even in an environment of fear, if we as the "fleet" disregard the abuses of the law, if we give up our rights and liberties for the momentary protection of a stronger military, we ultimately weaken our society.

Notes

1. Dirk Benedict, the actor who played Starbuck in the original *BSG* has criticized the new series, especially the new female Starbuck and the Cylons as "reimagined terrorists [who] are not mechanical robots void of soul, of sexuality, but rather humanoid six-foot-tall former lingerie models who f**k you to death" ("Starbuck: Lost in Castration"). See also Carla Kungl in this volume.

2. Cain is a criticism of command, not of gender or sexuality. At the time this essay was written, Moore confirmed that Cain would be portrayed as a lesbian in the *BSG* TV-movie *Razor* (working title). In the same way that her gender in a postfeminist reading is moved to the background, the focus on her relationship to Adama and Roslin is one of power, not sexuality. Cain is not harsh and militant because she is a lesbian any more than as compensation for being a woman; her agenda is a reflection of a nostalgia and desire to return to an illusory safety before the war.

5

Mad, Bad, and Dangerous to Know?
Negotiating Stereotypes of Science

Lorna Jowett

The reimagined *Battlestar Galactica* explores how science functions within our social structure by negotiating stereotypes of science and scientists, often via the character of Dr. Gaius Baltar, but also through the Cylons. Given that two of the basic premises of the show, human-model Cylons and the destruction of the Twelve Colonies, call into question notions of identity based on ostensibly civilized human society, it is hardly surprising that Baltar's identity as a scientist is fluid and contingent. The first premise also demonstrates that science can produce wonders or threats: the Cylons function as both and, as self-replicating beings, allow science to reinforce itself. The second premise, forcing humans into a quest for survival, challenges the importance of science in constructing identity and community. Thus, both the use and the value of science are addressed. Baltar's character arc explodes the opposition of science and religion; likewise, the notion of science as a rational means to progress is undercut by the way his character plays off the familiar tropes of the mad scientist and bad science.

While commentators on science fiction prior to the 1970s detect little or no awareness that science is situated within society, such representation can be identified in many recent science fictions, from *The X-Files* to *Enterprise*. Joseph Tabbi points to the "unprecedented potential for science and technology to assist forms of social, political, and economic control" as reason enough for this change (1). *BSG* similarly presents science as functioning in tension with competing interests from politics and the military, so it is never a pure branch of knowledge. Aylish Wood calls this "technoscience," the appreciation of "science and technology as systems of knowledge and institutions that are constituted within and through a specific social, economic, and cultural context" (177).

BSG's key representative of science might seem to work against the notion of science as integrated into society. While Wood comments that popular fictions "have long left behind the idea of the gentleman scientist working away in splendid isolation on his grand idea in his castle, or cellar, or even occasionally his elite community" (*Technoscience* 1), Baltar fits this general description and he remains isolated. As is so often the case with scientists on television and film, he displays expertise in a number of fields, such as computer science, biology, and medicine, defining him not as a real world scientist but as an "expert" and intellectual. Described by Helo as "one of the greatest minds of our time," a news broadcast introduces him as the winner of several "Magnate prizes" (M.01) who is "currently working as a top consultant for the Ministry of Defense on computer issues" (M.01). Baltar epitomizes the notion of science as aloof, distant from other human concerns. President Laura Roslin believes he is "brilliant" but "unleavened by compassion" ("Epiphanies" 2.13), though any simplicity in this view is challenged by the fact that he has just saved her life (and that of unborn Cylon-human hybrid Hera). Actor James Callis interprets even this as motivated by self-interest: "Baltar saves Roslin only because he actually wants to save the life of Sharon's baby and simply show how brilliant he is. On some level, it's simply an act of narcissism" (quoted in Bassom, *Two* 120). His presentation as a civilian expert contributes to his isolation from other core characters. While he manages to become an elected representative of the people as Caprica's delegate, later vice president, and finally president of the Colonies, political office serves to further isolate him, as is demonstrated by the memorable long shot of him alone in *Colonial One* at the start of his presidency ("Lay Down Your Burdens, Part 2" 2.20). Further, his presidency is overshadowed by the Cylon occupation.

As he awaits trial following his impeachment, he scrawls a manifesto that is smuggled to sympathetic readers in the fleet. *My Triumphs, My Mistakes* identifies class conflict among the fleet, yet Baltar's motives in releasing this just before his trial are suspect, and Roslin suggests he wishes only to appear as a "man of the people," reinforcing his characterization as the opposite ("Dirty Hands" 3.16). Callis describes his character as "terribly aloof. If he wasn't born with a silver spoon in his mouth, he's gotten used to one" (quoted in Houston), and this may be derived from the character in the original series, who was referred to as Count or Lord Baltar. Gaius's somewhat exaggerated dandyism may be an attempt to distinguish himself or to distance himself from a rather ordinary past: in "Dirty Hands," as he tells Tyrol that he grew up on a farm, his voice shifts from his usual privileged RP accent to an earthy Yorkshire one—another class marker. Various elements combine to convey an effete and decadent character, notably exemplified in the snapshot of him as president in "Lay Down Your Burdens, Part 2" (2.20), explicitly reminiscent of "Hugh Hefner and the Playboy mansion" according to producer David Eick (quoted in Bassom, *Two* 120). This construction of Baltar's character is enhanced by the way his accent connotes privilege, while its Britishness emphasizes his isolation from other characters.[1]

Mode of speech aside, Baltar is also set apart from others by what he says, and this is integral to establishing his character. Though Ronald D. Moore endeavors to avoid technobabble in the show as a whole, to distinguish it from other television science fiction and to focus on character ("Technobabble"), Baltar is the exception: "Refined tylium contains tremendous enthalpy to the order of half a billion megajoules per kilo. If subjected to the right heat and compression, say, from a conventional warhead, you should get a suitably devastating explosion without the radioactive fallout" ("The Hand of God" 1.10). Much more of this has been cut from episodes, as deleted scenes on DVD reveal. This kind of language still functions as an estranging device for the audience (telling us this is science fiction), but more importantly it creates a division between Baltar and other characters, as when Tigh retorts, "I want a definitive answer, no more of your weaselly technobabble" ("Resistance" 2.04).[2]

Baltar's isolation is reinforced through humor in early episodes since he exhibits another aspect of the stereotypical scientist: poor social skills. Callis observes that he "didn't want Baltar to be this impregnable, two-dimensional scientist. . . . Real-life geniuses often can't make a cup of coffee and they fall over their own shoe laces!" (quoted in Bassom, *Official Companion* 114). Callis's interpretation has enhanced this aspect, according to Moore ("Galactica Interview") and although Baltar manages to manipulate his media image, dealing successfully with individual people is far more difficult, as his confrontation with Gaeta in *Galactica*'s bathroom comically demonstrates ("Six Degrees of Separation" 1.07).

Just as Baltar's character mediates various stereotypes of the scientist, the show negotiates popular ideas about science, particularly the notion of science as an instrument of destruction or a path to civilization. This has been a staple of science fiction over the years, and J. P. Telotte notes the contrast between good and bad science in the serials of the 1930s as that which protects or destroys (186). In a war, science is used to do both and is controlled by other institutions, as *BSG* clearly demonstrates.

The initial Cylon war prompted a retreat from some technologies. *Galactica*'s commander refuses to have networked computers on the ship since the Cylon enemy "could infiltrate and disrupt even the most basic computer systems" (as proved in the attack on the Colonies), and while this is seen by others as an archaic holdover from the first Cylon war, a ban remains on certain kinds of research into computer technology (M.01). Baltar is introduced publicly justifying his opposition to this ban: it "serves no useful purpose except to retard efforts to solve many of the problems plaguing Colonial society" (M.01). Baltar advocates scientific progress as a direct route to social improvement and ignores the fact that science has created humanity's biggest problem: the Cylons.

Following the destruction of the Twelve Colonies in the miniseries, the surviving humans become pioneers seeking a new home. This is a familiar trope in American science fiction, which often recontexualizes Western myths as a way to explore the human condition, especially in relation to self-improvement, technology, or freedom (a recent example being the short-lived *Firefly*). The journey itself is dependent on technology (though not necessarily on science), but even assuming the fleet finds new (or old) worlds to settle, starting again may preclude scientific research and development for some time. Furthermore, Wood notes that "the nature of contemporary research, dependent on expensive equipment and facilities, inevitably results in the incorporation of the researcher into a system they cannot fully control" (*Technoscience* 37). Baltar cannot continue his work until he is appointed "Chief Scientific Consultant and Analyst regarding the Cylons and their technology" by the president (M.02) and given resources—including, eventually, a nuclear weapon ("Bastille Day" 1.03)—by Adama. Throughout *BSG* are intimations that society as the characters knew it is gone, life has changed fundamentally, and previous lifestyles cannot be maintained.

The notion of bad and good science depends on a moral framework. As with much serial drama, especially "quality" television, *BSG* frequently poses its characters moral or ethical dilemmas. Leaders like Adama and Roslin have to make difficult decisions based on what they think will be right for the fleet. In contrast, from the start Baltar acts out of self-interest. Callis suggests this makes him more comprehensible: "There are very few people as human as Gaius Baltar, because he's just trying to survive. . . . He's just looking out for himself." He emphasizes that rather than choosing evil, Baltar is "just the wrong person in the wrong place at the wrong time, and he's desperately compromised" ("Cast Members Talk").

The notion of Baltar as compromised inflects the presentation of science too. The Cylon wars (old and new) are a typical Frankenstein scenario where a scientific creation turns on its human creators. Such fictions address fears about science in the hands of experts. Geoff King and Tanya Krzywinska identify a key feature of the stereotypical nerdy scientist: he is "not wantonly malicious but creates mayhem because he is self-centered and out of touch with the real-world effects of his actions" (48). Yet Baltar is not entirely devoid of moral awareness. In "Epiphanies" (2.13), he refuses to give Gina, a Cylon Six, the nuclear device she wants, telling her, "I am not who you think I am and I will not be responsible for the destruction of humankind." This decision is soon undermined by its reversal, apparently in a fit of pique after digesting Roslin's opinion of him as incoming president. Gina's subsequent detonation of the device affords the Cylons a way to detect the fleet and leads to the occupation of New Caprica. Following World War II and the Cold War, scientists have been seen as partly responsible for the use of nuclear weapons; in the popular imagination, they may have been geniuses, but they were naïve to think their discoveries would not be used for destructive purposes. The tying together of a nuclear detonation and a betrayal of humanity in *BSG* reinforces a familiar notion of bad science in the hands of irresponsible intellectuals.

Baltar's admission to Six that "politics is the only thing more boring than blood samples" ("Colonial Day" 1.11) implies that science is what interests him, but science and politics cannot be so easily divorced; indeed he soon embodies both. Other characters who use science and technology such as Tyrol, Gaeta, and Sharon, serve as instructive contrasts, but Doctor Cottle, the Chief Medical Officer, is worth examining in detail. In appearance and manner Cottle is the polar opposite of the effete Baltar. He smokes cigarettes constantly, rather than enjoying the occasional fine cigar, and his down-to-earth manner and speech contrast Baltar's awkward behaviour and technobabble. Even the way most characters refer to "Doc Cottle" serves to distinguish the two: trapped on Kobol, Baltar refuses to answer to Tryol's "Doc" and angrily tells him, "A 'dock' is a platform for loading and unloading material. My title is 'Doctor' or 'Mr. Vice President'" ("Fragged" 2.03). Cottle has a keen sense of medical ethics tempered with a humane attitude to his patients, what actor Donnelly Rhodes describes as an embodiment of "the doctor's credo—do no harm" (quoted in Bassom, *Two* 139). Cottle's sense of moral obligation contrasts both with the immoral Dr. Robert, who uses his position to kill Sagittarons in a kind of ethnic cleansing ("The Woman King" 3.14), and with the amoral Baltar.

Baltar's key scientific role in the fleet is Cylon expert. He soon succeeds in finding a way to detect human Cylons ("Flesh and Bone" 1.08) but suppresses it, maintaining the invisibility of Cylon agents and leading to Boomer's attempt to assassinate Adama at the end of Season One. While Baltar's motivation here may be the desire for an easy life,[3] his decision to report everyone tested as human implicitly takes a moral stand. Debates continue about government surveillance in the name of increased security and conspiracy theories often cite medical testing of whole populations. A recent newspaper article sees in *BSG* "a chilling allegory on civil liberties crackdowns and western paranoia about sleeper cells" (Martin "Final"). Here, Baltar takes a stand by default and the situation raises ethical issues that the show slowly explores.

Science is depicted as devoid of moral sense because it is inherently rational, and is often opposed to warm, emotional humanity. Yet an equally popular stereotype is the mad scientist. Daniel Dinello suggests that the trope of the mad scientist developed throughout the nineteenth century "as scientific and technological progress slowly became associated with numerous destabilizing developments" (40). The traditional mad scientist is also mad for reasons outlined above: he (and this character is most often male) is detached from "reality" and pursues research at any cost. Baltar initially believes in "a rational universe, explained through rational means" ("33" 1.01), yet his own rationality is brought into question through his visions of the Cylon Six, so that he becomes a bizarre reflection of the mad scientist.

Repeated visitations from Six emphasize not just Baltar's intellectual nature (he lives in his head anyway), but also his humanity (he worries that he is going mad). While Baltar questions his own sanity, nobody else does; they simply think him what D'Anna Biers calls him, "a strange little man" ("Final Cut" 2.08). About halfway through Season Two, following a particularly fraught conversation with his virtual Six, Baltar becomes obsessed with determining whether she is a technological projection from a chip in his head. When he goes to Doc Cottle, the scans find nothing ("Home, Part 2" 2.07). Baltar's virtual Six and his responses to her function to present him as an eccentric genius, and as King and Krzywinska suggest, "A dose of homely eccentricity makes the expert seem more vulnerably human" (44).

Baltar's visions of Six are given a further twist during "Downloaded" (2.18), which reveals that on resurrection Caprica Six (the Six to whom Baltar had given access to the human defense system, downloaded into a new body) has visions of a Baltar subtly different to the character we know, who challenges, taunts, and aids her as Baltar's virtual Six does him. Coupled with the fact that the Three known as D'Anna later actively seeks visions ("Hero" 3.08), this emphasizes that visions and/or religious mysticism are not restricted to humanity; Cylons are as capable of, and as likely to desire, visions as humans. Eventually Baltar discovers that Cylons can project their preferred surroundings, and worries that his ability to see Six in his old home on Caprica is proof not that he is mad, but that he is a Cylon ("Torn" 3.06). The lines here between madness and rationality, visions and reality, mad scientist and eccentric genius, scientific proof and religious belief become increasingly blurred. The human-model Cylons themselves do not conform to the traditional cold logic of machines.

Although it may have been a decision encouraged by budgetary constraints (it was too expensive to show convincing robotic Cylons on a regular basis), the humanoid Cylons allow the show to directly address one of science fiction's recurring questions: what makes us human? The notion of physicality and sexuality are factors in this debate. Despite, or perhaps because of, the prevalence of reproduction as a theme within the genre, it is often assumed that science fiction deals with a "denial of sexuality" (Bukatman 264). As Scott Bukatman notes, science is frequently opposed to nature in science fiction's imagery and narratives (265), just as machine is frequently set in opposition to human. Science fiction's traditional oppositions in dealing with artificial life-forms tend to run along the lines of human/natural/physical/emotional/sexual versus machine/scientific/mechanical/unemotional/asexual. However, in *BSG* the human-model Cylons contrast with the robot Centurions, indicating their status as organic androids. The name Cylons suggests cyborg, a fusion of biology and technology, and the production team was keen to achieve an "organic" look for even the Centurions (see Bassom, *Official Companion* 141–42).

Baltar displays some of the characteristics of science as opposed to nature, but he is also very human, and he is compromised because of his physical appetites. He becomes sexually involved with two Cylons (Six and Three) and a variety of sexual partners are shown or implied during his time with the human fleet and on New Caprica. His (traditional) identity as a male heterosexual scientist is integral to the success of the Cylon plan of attack since it makes him vulnerable to Six's seduction. It also reinforces the notion that he successfully attracts women not because of his personal charms, but rather because of his status and position (as when he becomes president). In "Downloaded" (2.18) Three tells Caprica Six that she admires the way she managed to "seduce a man so emotionally and physically that he grants you access to all the most closely guarded secrets of his people" and admits that this must have been "incredibly difficult." While hindsight factors emotion into the equation, miniseries' director Michael Rymer states that the relationship was "all about lust," describing how he "thought it was very believable and had a great contemporary relevance—there have been a lot of scandals over the years involving national security and military secrets being exchanged for sex" (quoted in Bassom, *Official Companion* 30). Here again, Baltar's role as a scientist is one part of a larger picture.

His relationship with Six also twists the basic scientist template, since King and Krzywinska describe how "the rationality of the scientist is often balanced by careful emphasis on more specifically 'human' qualities such as individualism, emotion or romantic pairing" (43). If Baltar has a redeeming feature, it is his capacity to love. The fact that the object of his love is a Cylon is his great tragedy and might emphasize his detachment from humanity. Yet, since emotion often serves as a sign of humanity in science fiction, it complicates his status and that of his Cylon seducer. While Baltar's lust may have been his downfall, his realization that he loves Six works as a kind of redemption, even as it tempts him into further betrayals of humanity. When he tells Tyrol, "Love is a strange and wonderful thing, Chief. You should be happy you experienced it at all, even if it was with a machine" ("Resistance" 2.04), he speaks from his own experience, as the audience is aware. Similar shared experience bonds Tyrol and Helo, and brings Boomer and Caprica Six together ("Downloaded" 2.18), but it isolates Baltar. Love is also said to be the missing ingredient that allows humans and Cylons to reproduce ("The Farm" 2.05), and some of Baltar's later betrayals are an attempt to protect the hybrid Hera.

The physical aspect of the Baltar/Six relationship is equally layered. We assume that machines cannot feel as we do, whether that feeling is emotional or physical. Baltar's sexual liaisons with his virtual Six often leave him looking ridiculous, making his character both more human and more acceptable, because he is not in control of his situation (including his physical responses) and because it presents him as authentically, because physiologically, human. The glowing red spines of Cylons Six and Eight during sex simultaneously remind us that they are not human and indicate a recognizable and perhaps equally involuntary physical response to sex.[4] In the case of Baltar and Six, while their interactions might seem to be hot physical sex from one perspective, they are virtual and illusory from another, as editing of such scenes underlines. The question here, as with other contemporary science fictions like the *Matrix* films, "isn't about the real, but about what our relationship with the real should be. Or . . . what our relationship to the fake should be," as Joshua Clover suggests (31). If the fake can elicit the same responses as the real, then it is not its reality that is at stake, but our interaction with it. The switch between perspectives plays on this in a similar fashion to the films of David Cronenberg, as described by Bukatman: "Cronenberg . . . does not mythologize the cinematic signifier as 'real,' but continually confuses the real with the image and the image with the hallucination" (91), as emphasized in a film like *eXistenZ* (1999), which deals with virtual reality gaming. So while Baltar may have "found something he thought was very special in Gina—a model of Number Six he could touch and hold" (Callis in Bassom, *Two* 118), given the abuse she suffered aboard the *Pegasus*, consummation is deferred until a farewell love scene in "Lay Down Your Burdens, Part 2" (2.20). Yet Baltar's virtual Six is as real to the viewer as she is to him and the constant shifts back to "reality" are moderated by our awareness that no Cylon is a "real" woman, and this is all a constructed fiction anyway. Baltar's rationality is vindicated here; he may question his sanity, but we see and legitimate his vision.

"A Measure of Salvation" (3.07) reveals a potential weapon against the Cylons, a virus possibly left by the Thirteenth Tribe.[5] Apollo suggests that infected Cylon prisoners could be used to spread the currently isolated virus, since when the infected die they, and the virus, would be uploaded into new bodies on a Cylon resurrection ship. Although this plan is approved, "genocide" is avoided since the infected prisoners die before they can be uploaded. Mortality and susceptibility to disease is something we associate with humanity: Roslin's cancer was apparently cured by Baltar's recognition and utilization of Cylon resistance to disease ("Epiphanies" 2.13), but it returns by the end of Season Three. Yet even for Cylons "dying is a painful and traumatic experience," as Sharon tells Starbuck in "Scar" (2.15). That the Cylons are susceptible to disease and death is another aspect that blurs their identity as mechanical ("toasters") rather than human.

The representation of Baltar and the Cylons also challenges the opposition of science and religion. At first he ridicules Six's religious faith as "superstitious drivel . . . which . . . no rational, intelligent free-thinking human being truly believes" ("Six Degrees of Separation" 1.07). Soon, however, he is persuaded by Six and circumstances that he is "the instrument of God," though this could arguably be another way to avoid responsibility for his actions ("The Hand of God" 1.10). Baltar's status as the chosen "instrument" of the Cylon God (not the Lords of Kobol) further entrenches him as a Cylon collaborator and betrayer of humanity.

When Baltar decides to run for president against Roslin, he denigrates her religious faith (which is ridiculed by other characters at times too), and their election contest is inflected by the way science and religion are perceived as distinct and opposing ways of interpreting the world. Baltar's decision to stand against Roslin comes during a crisis about abortion, always an issue for U.S. elections. To this point in the series, religious authority on issues of life and death has largely been superseded by that of science. Tom Zarek tells Baltar that many in the fleet "crave the assurances of cold science as opposed to the superstitious ravings of the Geminese. As a scientist, you offer hope" ("The Captain's Hand" 2.17)— another version of science as progress, despite the harsh reality of life on New Caprica. Some characters' faith assumes history is cyclical: "All of this has happened before and all of this will happen again" ("Kobol's Last Gleaming, Part 1" 1.12). Such a concept not only undermines the conception of linear time, it relegates questions about progress through science and technology as subordinate to a larger spiritual quest.

In assuming the presidency, Baltar's role as a scientist might effectively be over. However, his training is still intact. When Three tortures him aboard the Cylon basestar, and his virtual Six attempts to help him detach himself from the physical process (another blurring of intellect and physicality), she tells him, "Be a scientist. Examine her faith. What's your analysis, doctor?" ("A Measure of Salvation" 3.07). Baltar's previous firm scientific convictions are revisited when he challenges Three, "Let me help you change. Find a way to reconcile your faith with fact. Find a way towards a rational universe."

Baltar's position as a scientist is always complicated by the war between humans and Cylons, and the creators of *BSG* admit, "It's a war show—that was always our initial touchstone" (quoted in Martin "Final"). Science is implicated in this war since the Cylons were created by humans. The implication is that, before their rebellion, they functioned as tools, mechanical slaves whose existence made "life easier on the Twelve Colonies" (M.01). As Adama points out, "We refuse to take responsibility for what we've done.... We're the ones that tried to manufacture life and make it serve us" (M.01). Wood notes that scientific research occurs "in an intersection with systems which only validate knowledge because of the potential commercial market for its products" (*Technoscience* 33), so that even this fairly standard genre trope contributes to a version of technoscience. In this instance, war and the military is a larger factor than the greedy corporation, often a key element in representations of bad science, adding further moral complexity.

Technological development is indirectly responsible for the war in several ways. This is hardly surprising to those like Dinello who view "technophobic science-fiction" as "a warning for the future, countering cyber-hype and reflecting the real world of weaponized, religiously rationalized, and profit-fueled technology" (2). While in previous eras, science fictions evoked "a fantasy of united warfare.... Science—technology—is conceived of as the great unifier.... Reasonableness had achieved an unbreakable supremacy over the emotions" (Sontag 45), the post-9/11 climate emphasizes tensions surrounding the (appropriate) development and regulation of potentially dangerous science and technology. Dinello points out, "Much of the research and development of twenty-first-century post-human technologies, such as artificial intelligence, nanotechnogloy, and robotics, were originated and funded by the American military" (3). War inevitably has pressing consequences for the use of science and technology and causes its key representative in *BSG* to be directly involved in moral as well as physical struggles.

"I wanted this show to be about the characters, not about the technology they used," says Moore (quoted in Bassom, *Official Companion* 18). Baltar's identity as a scientist radically revises the character from the original series, yet it shifts as science becomes less important to the remnant human population and, by the end of Season Three, Baltar has moved from scientist, through politician, to scapegoat and even religious icon ("Crossroads, Part 1" 3.19). He is an isolated figure, set apart from or even against the human community, and his role as scientist and betrayer highlights anxiety about the uses science is put to, its potential for destruction. Politics, war, and religion continually enmesh Baltar because these, along with science, are major discourses that govern the society of *BSG*. Even in the beginning, Baltar was not simply an eccentric scientific genius, he was "a media cult figure, and a personal friend of President Adar's" (M.01) and his scientific, political, and religious roles demonstrate the interconnectedness of these areas. Human-model Cylons and a remnant of humanity seeking a new home both ensure that identity will not be fixed in *BSG*. Apparent oppositions between science and religion, or between intellect and physicality, break down under close scrutiny. Science and scientists are never really isolated from the rest of us, and Baltar is (so far) part of the human community whether anyone likes it or not. Learning to live with the consequences of our scientific and technological development is what *BSG* is all about. And despite Moore's statement about valuing people over technology, the two are intertwined—for all of us.

Notes

1. Other British actors, including Jamie Bamber (Apollo), blend in by adopting North American accents.

2. Estrangement through language is also established via military/naval terms and other strange words (see the "Encyclopedia Galactica" section of Bassom's *Official Companion* 20), as well as the standard science-fiction strategy of novel obscenities like "frakking."

3. Bradley Thompson suggests that Baltar's motivation may be logical: if Cylons are "networked" they can share intelligence at a distance. Thompson concludes that this means Baltar "might put himself at risk" by identifying Cylon agents in the human fleet (quoted in Bassom, *Official Companion* 75), reinforcing his self-interest.

4. This exclusively sexual connotation was contradicted by a Sci-Fi Channel trailer for *BSG* showing a Cylon fetus's spine glowing red (see Bassom, *Two* 84).

5. The final analysis is that it may have been "accidental contamination" of a beacon showing the path the Thirteenth Tribe took when they left Kobol for Earth three thousand years ago.

6

Pyramid, Boxing, and Sex

Kevin J. Wetmore Jr.

Often in speculative fiction, one of the pleasures of the new worlds or the coming future is discovering their pleasures and pastimes. The original *Battlestar Galactica* featured triad, a basketball/football hybrid; pyramid, a pokerlike game; and pets, notably Muffet, the mechanical "Daggit" who is a companion to Boxey but also a toy of sorts. Despite the constant threat of Cylon genocide, the program showed the characters engaging in play, culture, and pastimes, both onboard ship and on various planets. Not so the new *BSG*.

The pilot of the original series showed the fleet heading to Carillon, a pleasure planet with musical acts, gambling, and feasting ("Saga of a Star World"). The new series views play and pleasure differently. The pilot begins with *Galactica* undergoing transformation into a museum, with the senior crew playing triad, now a pokerlike game, Starbuck winning the hand and subsequently decking Tigh when he kicks the table over.[1] She wins the game (and the fight) but is thrown in the brig. Later in the miniseries (M.01), we are shown a Gemenon Botanical Cruiser, abandoned by the rest of the fleet with people still aboard, during the flight from Caprica. Lacking a faster-than-light drive, the ship is left behind to be destroyed by the Cylons. A closing shot before commercial shows Cami, a young girl with a rag doll sitting in the parklike pleasure dome as the Cylon nuke closes in on the ship, evoking Lyndon Johnson's

"Daisy" commercial against Barry Goldwater. The infamous advertisement showed a little girl counting the petals she tore from a daisy, when she reaches nine, a male voice begins counting down and at zero, and the girl looks up as a mushroom cloud fills the screen. Though aired only once, on September 7, 1964, the emblematic commercial has echoed through popular culture. Johnson's voice-over states, "These are the stakes! To make a world in which all of God's children can live, or to go into the dark" (Goldwater, "Daisy"). At this point in *BSG*, Cami's implied death can also be seen as a metaphor for the death of childhood and the end of child's play. Humanity, as it were, goes into the dark.

These two moments demonstrate the shift in tone of the *Galactica*s. Pleasure, pets, play, and pastimes are not present in the same manner in the new *BSG*. Daggits and other animals are gone. Children play a reduced role. Pleasures are few, and not a priority within the fleet. What culture of play that remains is the exclusive province of the elite. While characters pursue individual pleasure (Roslin's reading, Adama's model ship–building, and Starbuck's painting), these are limited pursuits and represent only the vestiges of a vanished civilization. Starbuck no longer paints. Adama destroys his model ship as an expression of grief over Starbuck's death ("Maelstrom" 3.17). Only a handful of books still exist, and the only creative writing evident is Baltar's prison manifesto ("Dirty Hands" 3.16) and other political tracts. Adama may have paintings and sculptures in his quarters, but the pilots and enlisted have only photographs. At one point, Cally claims to have been "reading some trashy novel" ("Litmus" 1.06), but this is merely a story to cover for Tyrol. Some people read religious texts, but the deranged Hammerhead is the only person who still reads poetry ("Resistance" 2.04). There is a news network, but no narratives or other entertainments represented. In short, *BSG* shows a regression of civilization and an absence of innocent or intellectual play as a result of the Cylon genocide.

Remaining pastimes are physical and primal. Onboard *Galactica*, three major pastimes are shown, all of them recurring: triad (a card game with attendant drinking and cigar smoking), boxing, and sex (pyramid, now a team ball game, is only played on a planet surface). The *Galactica* itself was set to become a museum (M.01), a source of both pleasure and knowledge of the past. Yet, with the Cylon attack, all sources of pleasure and play other than the immediate, the primal, and the competitive are left behind. In this essay, I explore this loss of *homo ludens*, Johan Huizinga's "playing man," specifically the shift from *ludi* (games) to *agon* (contest), what comes to occupy the conceptual space in which play occurs, and what these activities suggest about both the world of *BSG* and its attendant reflection back upon the society that created (and watches, and embraces) the television program. I will focus on adult play, since children are few, far between, and, except with the occasional doll, are not shown playing.[2]

Huizinga argues that games (*ludi*) are related to, but different from, contest (*agon*). *Ludi* are "voluntary," "the opposite of serious," and "limited in time and place" (7, 8, 9). Although Huizinga admits that play and war are two sides of the same coin, play is ultimately civilizing, while war is only a contest (89–90). In the world of *BSG*, *ludi* are as limited in supply as other essentials after the Cylon genocide and only *agon* is left. A different interpretation of play is offered by Susanna Miller, who writes that play is "basically fighting or hostility checked by friendship" (189). Play is creative, voluntary, and "the opposite of serious," but it can still become very serious indeed, as any football fan can tell you, and even violent and painful. In a critique of Huizinga, Brian Sutton-Smith and Diana Kelly-Byrne observe that play is a "struggle for power" that displays "multiple instances of brutality, callousness and all-round unpleasant behavior," including "obscene and erotic behavior" (312–13). Play is about the establishment of hierarchies, identifying "winners" and "losers." *Agon*, instead, can be "brutal" and "erotic." It is this shift in the understanding of play that we see in *BSG*: fun is not a goal, nor is creativity or enjoyment; the goal is domination. Play becomes violent, and even sex becomes a kind of game of dominance, a competition not just for survival but for mastery over others.

"You Know What I Miss? Sports"

There are leisure activities onboard *Galactica* and the other ships of the fleet. There is socializing, interacting, and organized games and activities, especially triad and boxing. But until Season Three, most social activity is limited and clandestine, and not very ludic or playful play. The vast majority of play on *Galactica* is agonistic—for the purpose of contest and controlling hostile behavior toward others. The holes that are left in society in the absence of sport are filled with alcohol.

A still is first built in "Litmus" (1.06). Chief Tyrol, however, warns Cally and the others that the alcohol it produces is a "ticket to sickbay or the morgue" and promises to show them how to make a better one, which he subsequently does. *Cloud Nine* also has bars and restaurants, which serve as socialization points, but for the elite only. Apollo, Dualla, Billy, Ellen, and Baltar may find their way there, but the vast majority of the fleet does not have access to this place of play and socialization. Eventually, Gina destroys *Cloud Nine* with an atomic weapon, the residue of which leads the Cylons to New Caprica (2.20; 3.01). Thus, it is not only no longer a place for playing, but also now a trap for humanity. Later, "Joe's," the bar onboard *Galactica,* opens, and the officers and enlisted crew use it to socialize and play. There is a billiard table and apparently a happy hour every evening when the senior officers are off-duty ("Taking a Break from All Your Worries"[3] 3.13).

Moments of creative leisure are swallowed up after the Cylon attack. In a conversation with Baltar, his virtual Six asks, "You know what I miss? Sports" (2.11). Six misses the experience of sport—community identity, camaraderie, social bonding, group energy, and organized play. While Baltar sees such activity as lowbrow, Six correctly recognizes it as inherently human (*homo ludens,* after all), and a means by which she, disguised as a human, might have shared an experience and connected through it. But after the Cylon attack, sport and play are reduced to *agon* and hierarchy-building. Instead of making community and creating the bond that Six feels for Baltar, sport is used to establish a pecking order amongst the survivors.

In the next episode, Baltar uses his virtual Six's very words to seduce Gina, another Six, into trusting him ("Resurrection Ship, Part 2" 2.12). Six, seen by Baltar and the audience standing in the cell, but invisible to Gina, begs him, "Don't do this," and "No, please." Gaius uses her genuine connection to him through the memory of sport to connect to Gina insincerely. Baltar gains Gina's trust through Six's memories, but in doing so he violates Six's trust, as he pursues merely physical "human" contact with Gina. Baltar's cruelty and selfishness serve his own (sexual) benefit as he seeks a way to frak another Cylon. No longer content with imaginative sex with his virtual Six, he betrays the intimacy of conversation with Six in hopes of the carnality of Gina. *Homo ludens.*

What is left after the demise of professional sport, amateur fandom, and creative leisure are agonistic contests designed to establish status and power structures. Games are "any activity that possesses rules structured so as to produce a disequalibrial outcome between the opposing forces" (Salter 72): "A major function of children's play is the establishment of dominance-subordination hierarchies" (Sutton-Smith and Kelly-Byrne 313). Pyramid, triad, boxing, and sex all have winners and losers.

"If You're Going to Play with the Big Dogs . . ."

Gambling is a major presence in the social life of *Galactica*. They gamble through triad, they bet about boxing matches, there are casinos on *Cloud Nine*, and Kat and Starbuck wager 200 credits on which one of them will kill Scar ("Scar" 2.15). Gambling is a metaphor for life in the world of *Galactica*, but also a form of pastime that is rooted in winning and losing, in trying to take what someone else has. In the game of triad that began the series, in one hand Boomer is ambivalent about throwing in. Starbuck simply points to the pot and says, "If you're going to play with the big dogs . . ." (M.01). The game stops being about fun or being a pastime. Instead, for Starbuck, it is always about winning. In "Flight of the Phoenix" (2.09), Starbuck complains that Racetrack folds "with three up. Are you crazy?" Racetrack responds that she folded because she can't win—Starbuck has a better hand. "We've been playing with these cards for so long, I know every fold." Yet they continue to play.

This frustration leads to a short-term pastime that soon becomes central to the activities of the ship. Tyrol organizes the building of a new fighter as a collective hobby of sorts, "strictly an off-duty project" ("Flight of the Phoenix" 2.09). While one might argue that this is a creative and leisurely activity, the end product of this collective effort will be a ship of war, one that is instrumental in destroying the Cylon Resurrection ship before it is destroyed itself ("Resurrection Ship, Part 2" 2.12). The only collective activity that brings the entire ship together is the creation of another instrument of combat. The building of the *Laura*, as it is christened (though always subsequently simply referred to as "the stealth ship"), does bring the members of the fleet together in a way that further emphasizes what is missing from *Galactica*'s play, even in pyramid and triad games: the connections that play brings and the sense of community identity. Even when established, though, these do not last long.

No new games are introduced until Season Three. After the rescue from New Caprica, Helo and Racetrack play a chesslike game when Helo asks Racetrack to be number two in his Raptor. Starbuck, however, has no time for games of strategy. Instead, she invites Tigh to play "Dead Man's Chest." "Cutthroat game," he tells her, "Not usually your style." "It is now," she responds, "and I'm in it to win it" ("Torn" 3.06). Her experiences on New Caprica make Starbuck aggressively competitive. It is not enough for Starbuck to win, she must make others lose: "When the win-ethic becomes all consuming we leave the realm of 'playfulness' behind and enter into that of the *terminal contest*" (Salter 72). After the experience of New Caprica, Starbuck (and Tigh, and others) treat all games as terminal contests—"in it to win it." Interestingly, we never see Apollo playing triad. When he and Starbuck discuss where on the memorial wall they want their photos placed when they die, he tells her he wants his photos next to Duck and Nora: "Good card players. Nice way to spend eternity" ("Maelstrom" 3.17). This is why Apollo doesn't gamble—he does not play competitively, but sees it as a way to spend time and bond with friends; he dreams of a nonagonistic afterlife.

"Are You Kidding? I'd Wipe the Court with You!"

Pyramid is absent from the everyday world of *BSG*, as it is played only on planet surfaces. Whereas the original series had a "triad court" on the ship, the new *BSG* only has pyramid on planets.[4] We see a pyramid court on Caprica when Anders and Starbuck begin their relationship by playing a game of one-on-one ("Resistance" 2.04). Starbuck even mocks Anders: "Nice to know installing a regulation pyramid court was once of the priorities of the resistance." His response: "Well, there are some things one can't live without." Anders has a point: amidst the fighting, there is a need to maintain play and to hold onto humanity. The only other full pyramid court we see is on New Caprica. Eventually, that court will become a location at which the resistance can hide weapons. Joe's Bar on *Galactica* will eventually become the home of a single pyramid goal. Anders, professional pyramid player that he is, informs those playing with it, "You know this game has frak-all to do with the real thing, right?" ("Crossroads, Part 1" 3.19). Still competitive, but not real.

When Starbuck returns to Caprica, she and Helo meet Anders and the Caprica Buccaneers; they are at the center of the resistance against the Cylons on occupied Caprica.[5] Helo recognizes them:

Helo: These are the Caprica Bucaneers.
Starbuck: I don't think so.
Sue-Shaun: Give me a ball, little girl, I'll shove it up your ass.
Starbuck: Please . . . try. ("Resistance" 2.04)

The trash talk and competitive jargon of professional athletics becomes literalized and appropriate in a war situation. Aggression and threatening posturing make sense in a world in which the vast majority of the sentient beings are out to kill you. In a move from World War II movies (*The Longest Day*, for example[6]), Starbuck asks a sports question to prove the friendliness of the unknown combatants:

> Starbuck: How many foul breaks did you have in the playoff against Aerelon?
> Anders: You're kidding, right?
> Starbuck: You either know the answer or you have a bullet.
> Anders: Three.
> Starbuck: Wrong! Four!
> Anders: Three. The last one was called back on instant replay.
> Helo: He's right, Starbuck. I lost twenty cubits on that game.
> Starbuck: Fine. For now. (Lowers gun). You know you guys suck, right? Can't shoot. Can't pass. Sure as hell can't take a point. ("Resistance" 2.04)

Even when proven wrong on the number of fouls, Starbuck continues to assert her dominance.

When Adama meets Anders upon his arrival on *Galactica*, he admits to supporting Picon over Anders's Buccaneers (1.13). Even after these teams have long since ceased to exist, the identity of being a fan of one specific team remains with the Colonials. While fandom's function in sport and play is related to the *agon*, it is ultimately a form of community identity (Sutton-Smith 76). The members of the fleet remember sports, and Anders maintains status in the community because of his standing as a professional pyramid player. But the community that is created by sports fandom and spectatorship is made present by its absence and loss.

"I Thought We Were Just Sparring"

Boxing is first introduced as a background activity ("Kobol's Last Gleaming, Part 1" 1.12),[7] with Apollo and Adama sparring while discussing the status of the ship. The scenes of them boxing are intercut with scenes of Boomer's attempted suicide, and Starbuck and Baltar frakking (one really can't call it making love). The three images form a triptych: father and son, whose play fighting turns real; Boomer's feelings of despair and her drive to live; Starbuck's physical wrestling with Baltar and her emotional wrestling with her feelings for Apollo, whose name she calls out at the moment of climax. The sequence shows a physical *agon*, an emotional *agon*, and a combination of the two. In all three there is a struggle for dominance: as Ronald D. Moore describes, "There's something metaphorical about father and son—the old lion and the young lion—hitting each other" (quoted in Bassom, *Official Companion* 89). Their entire relationship has been one of periods of temporary truce in between lengthy stretches of animosity and combat (M.01; M.02; 2.01; 3.20). At the end of the match, Adama is declared winner. "I thought we were just sparring," exclaims Apollo. There's a pause. "That's why you don't win," replies the old man.

This lesson is repeated in "Unfinished Business" (3.09). Through juxtaposing flashbacks to New Caprica with boxing matches on *Galactica*, we see unresolved conflicts within the crew being worked out through pummeling one another into bloody pulps. Roslin is surprised by the boxing matches, but also delighted, as her "father was an avid fight fan." Adama explains that the boxing matches are a "private tradition" in the fleet:

> A lot of frustrations aboard warships. Arguments become grudges and end up being feuds. This allows them to let off a little steam out in the open so everyone can participate. Rank doesn't matter. As long as you throw your tags in the box, everyone's fair game.

Thus, Hotdog calls out Starbuck, and gets beaten unconscious for his choice. Adama, rebuffed by Tyrol when he asks about repairs, calls him out. Tyrol treats the fight playfully at first, until Adama drops him with a roundhouse sucker punch, telling him "Get up, Chief, we're just getting started." Standing over Tyrol, Adama brutalizes him with words. Starbuck uses the same fight to brutalize Apollo: "The old man's got chops. Knows when to make his move, when to hold back. I wish I could say the same for his son." Boxing allows for repressed animosity to manifest in physical violence. Doc Cottle wants to stop the fight; Roslin gives Adama advice on how to win. "Not gonna win," he informs her, making his plan clear. He wants Tyrol to brutalize him back, partly as an object lesson to the gathered warriors. The Chief pummels Adama, who then addresses the company:

> Remember this: when you fight a man, he's not your friend. Same when you lead men. I forgot that once. I let you get too close. All

of you. I dropped my guard. . . . I let this crew and this family disband, and we paid the price in lives. That can't happen again.

Adama fights Chief in order to expiate his own sin of allowing the settling of New Caprica by the *Galactica* crew.

Certain boxers "invite injury as a means of assuaging guilt," as Joyce Carol Oates observes (25). Yet Adama also allows the beating to prove a point: "It is apparently essential to keep in the minds of the players that they are indeed playing, otherwise the activity will break down into anxiety or violence as indeed it often does" (Sutton-Smith and Kelly-Byrne 317). The converse is also true, which is Adama's point. When we treat real crises as a form of play, the violence can become costly in real terms—what is a black eye and a split lip compared to thousands of Colonials dead during the occupation? Boxing is a metaphor for life on *Galactica*, but Oates argues the reverse: life is a metaphor for boxing (18).

Boxing is not a sport, which is why it is the only sport on *Galactica*. "There is nothing fundamentally playful about it," Oates observes, "nothing that seems to belong to daylight, to pleasure" (18). One enters the ring and hits an opponent until one or the other quits or is battered to the point that he or she can no longer fight. There are no points in the boxing of "Unfinished Business": one wins when one's opponent stops fighting. "One *plays* football, one doesn't *play* boxing," as Oates states (19). "The primary rule of the ring—to defend oneself at all times—is both a parody and a distillation of life," she concludes (48). Throughout the rest of the series, characters are shown keeping in shape or taking out aggression on speedbags, punching bags, or other boxing forms. Starbuck is interviewed by D'Anna Biers while kickboxing with a bag (2.08). Starbuck confesses to Helo that she regrets not killing Scar. When Helo gently mocks her, she pretends to beat him until he falls "down for the count" (2.15). In this unique moment, sparring breaks free from *agon* and becomes a form of bonding and reassurance.

"Frak or Fight"

The Adamas's sparring match, connected visually with Starbuck's and Baltar's tryst, is not the first time the audience has seen sex juxtaposed with other competitive activity. In "Act of Contrition" (1.04), the triad card game between Starbuck and Baltar flashes back to Starbuck and Zak, Adama's younger son, making love, and also to his funeral. Sex becomes equated with other forms of contest. In "Scar" (2.15), Apollo and Starbuck begin to kiss passionately and he pulls away . "This isn't a race," he tells her. "All I want is a good lay," she corrects him. It's not about love, or a relationship, or even about seeking momentary comfort in the arms of another. For Starbuck, the frustration of the competition with Kat becomes subliminated in the sexual tension between herself and Apollo. It is another contest that one can win or lose. Starbuck has sex aggressively, as a form of conquest—as Apollo puts it, "Frak or fight!" (2.15).

In "Unfinished Business" (3.09), the final boxing match is between Starbuck and Apollo. It begins bloody and violent, but ends in an embrace. Anders observes to Dualla, "Looks like they're trying to kill each other," just before their arms close around one another and Starbuck tells Apollo that she's missed him. They fight so hard because of the many things that they have left unspoken: particularly, the night before Starbuck married Anders, when she and Apollo made love and agreed to leave Anders and Dualla, respectively, for each other. There is a very short distance between lovemaking and fighting on *Galactica*.

On *Pegasus*, this line is crossed. Sex becomes a weapon for interrogation. Lieutenant Thorne, we are told, put a "Please Disturb" sign on Gina's cell door, and the *Pegasus* crew was encouraged to engage in individual and gang rape. Rape became a pastime on the *Pegasus*, with the female Cylon as constant loser. Since the crew of the Pegasus cannot constantly fight and kill Cylons, they take out on Gina their rage and their need to conquer Cylons. They do not beat her, or torture her with the devices we later see used on Baltar, or with the bars of soap wrapped in towels used on Helo and Tyrol (3.07, 2.11). They rape her, repeatedly. Their frank discussions of raping Gina sound, abhorrently, like a discussion of a sports victory (2.10).

Sport and play on *Galactica* have moved away from community-building and identity-creating and instead become "deep play," as defined by Clifford Geertz, after John Stuart Mill. Deep play is "play in which the stakes are so high that it is . . . irrational for men to engage in it at all" (432). "Deep play" is play become survival, in which even the winners can lose a good deal: "Having come together in search of pleasure they have entered into a relationship which will bring the participants, considered collectively, net pain rather than net pleasure" (433). Intangible benefits—"status, esteem, honor, dignity, respect" (433)—in the world of the Cylon genocide become the only things that matter. Life in the fleet is no longer about children playing or the pleasures of sport. Instead, the struggle against the Cylons is a struggle to survive at all. Winning is not only everything, it is the only thing, whether in a dogfight with Scar or a boxing match with a friend.

Finally, as the title of this volume suggests, *BSG* is really about us. The search for Earth is not merely a plot device; it is a metaphor. Through *BSG*, we seek to define our culture, our humanity. Play in America has become agonistic as well. *Ludi* have been replaced in our culture increasingly by *agon*. What does it say about us, that one of the best shows on television features a world in which creativity and community-building activities are not valued as highly as fighting or frakking? If the world of *BSG* is one of deep play, in which the stakes are ridiculously high and will result in greater collective net pain than pleasure, what does that say about the world in which the viewers live? It is not unrelated that the new *BSG* comes to us in a post-9/11 world, in which the rhetoric of struggle between the West and Islamic fundamentalism (itself a huge *agon*) takes on the language of sport, and complex geopolitical situations are reduced down to simple team play—"You're either with us, or you're with the terrorists" (Bush, "Address"). The pastimes of pyramid, boxing, and sex reflect not only the realities of *BSG*; they reflect the realities of the culture that has produced them as well.

Notes

1. There is an inversion in the games between the series. Pyramid was a card game, much like poker, in the original series. Triad originally had two teams of three players play a game that is part handball, part basketball, on a court. In the new *BSG*, triad is the card game similar to poker and pyramid becomes a game played outside that combines basketball and racquetball rules. According to Ronald D. Moore on the podcast/DVD commentary for "Kobol's Last Gleaming, Part 1" (1.12), the two games became inverted because of "a stupid error that the writer made"—in other words, while developing the series, Moore simply got them confused.

2. In the new series, there are no children on Galactica itself, only infants—Hera and Nicholas (the son of Tyrol and Cally) for example. Older children are either missing or damaged physically and emotionally. Boxey, the major child character from the original series, is present in a few passing moments of Season One. By Season Two Boxey was written out, as David Bassom reports, because Moore decided Boxey "was no longer a necessary part of the series" (*Two* 18). The only other children named in the series are Kacey and Paya. Kacey, Starbuck's supposed child, was kidnapped from her parents and used by the Cylons to torment Starbuck (3.01–04). Paya is the daughter of a prostitute who is kidnapped for a child slavery/prostitution ring. When she is offered a ragged doll

missing one eye as a gift, her reaction is to flee in fear from the toy, which suggests a Cylon to her. "Maybe next time I'll get her one with two eyes," Apollo says. "You just surprised her," Shevon reassures him ("Black Market" 2.14). The doll also serves as a reminder of Cami, the girl with a doll who died on the Gemenon Botanical Cruiser. In the world of *BSG*, children hide, die, are abused, are prostituted, serve as Cylon tools, or live a miserable, malnourished existence; they do not play.

3. The title of this episode evokes the television program *Cheers*, which was set in a bar in Boston and featured regular working-class guys and their friends who gathered regularly in the titular bar, where, the theme song told the viewer, "Taking a break from all your worries sure would help a lot." In the case of *BSG*, however, the helpfulness of taking the break remains questionable, as four of the bar regulars, upon hearing "All Along the Watchtower" on the bar radio, discover that they are Cylons ("Crossroads, Part 2" 3.20).

4. Moore admits on the audio commentary for "Resistance" that they had originally planned for pyramid to be played, like the original triad, indoors, but for budgetary reasons had to film all pyramid scenes outdoors.

5. The inspiration for this situation came from Moore's thinking about real-world equivalencies: "What if Los Angeles was destroyed and the LA Lakers came down out of the mountains, took up guns, and went on a rampage?" (Bassom, *Official Companion* 37).

6. In *The Longest Day* (1962), a film about D-Day, potential spies were asked, "Who won the World Series?" In other films, characters have been asked to identify various sports teams, victories, and statistics to prove their nationality. Given that Six used to go to pyramid games, the Cylons might just know the answers to such questions.

7. Bassom states that Michael Rymer, the director, was the one who proposed a sparring session between Apollo and Adama to lead off the episode (*Two* 89), but in the podcast/DVD commentary for the episode, Moore states that it was the actors who came up with the idea. Regardless, it was an effective beginning that set the themes of the episode and provided a running metaphor throughout the series.

II

Cylon/Human Interface

7

The Cylons, the Singularity, and God

C. W. Marshall and Matthew Wheeland

. . . an ultraintelligent machine will be built and it will be the last invention that man need make.

—I. J. Good

Half a century before we join the world in *Battlestar Galactica,* humanity created the Cylons. Intelligent robots designed to serve as soldiers and servants, the Cylons must have seemed a massive technological leap for the citizens of the Twelve Colonies. But the Cylons achieved self-awareness and rebelled against their creators, and humanity was trapped in a war of its own creation, yielding untold, self-inflicted punishment. The autonomous, self-replicating, and smarter-than-human machines that started the Cylon species developed more rapidly than anything previously imagined. Over the course of the forty years since armistice in the Cylon War, Cylons, the opening credits tell us, "evolved"—they developed the ability to create passably human, near-flawless replicas of their creators, from the metallic warriors they had been. Unfortunately for the humans, their creations want vengeance, with the apparent goal of wiping out the species that created them. The Cylons developed beyond their original specifications in more than simple physical appearance. Warrior-drones have become spiritual seekers: in addition to waging war on humankind, the Cylons are searching for God, for the True Creator that they believe imbued them with souls after humans gave them life.

The search for the creator is diffused throughout *BSG*, not only among Cylons but among the remaining humans, who seek a quasi-mythical Earth, the planet to which the lost tribe of humans fled in a forgotten, distant past. As the humans seek Earth, the Cylons seek the humans, and, in a different way, they seek their creator. As the relationships between human, Cylon, and God (or gods, for the polytheistic humans) unfold, the ties between creator and creation become increasingly complicated. Amidst a typical *début de siècle* slate of fears encompassing many geopolitical and social concerns, *BSG* addresses one fear in particular that relates humanity to technology: a central premise of *BSG*, a species of superhuman machines, is predicated on the theoretical concept of the Technological Singularity.

The Singularity was first conceived by cryptographer I. J. Good, who used the idea of an "intelligence explosion" to refer to the rapid pace of improved creation of machines almost at the instant of creation of the first smarter-than-human intelligence. Vernor Vinge took the idea further: first raised in a 1983 *Omni* article, and then explored in 1993 in an essay in the *Whole Earth Review* (and now reprinted with a new commentary in 2003), Vinge developed the term "Technological Singularity," to refer to that point when our technological advances take us beyond the event horizon—that moment after which things will progress so quickly that we will no longer be able to predict what will happen. Technological change will happen so radically, things will alter so completely, that we will no longer recognize our former existence. Our lives, of necessity, will become posthuman.

When humans have created something smarter than us, we have (by definition) made something capable of making something smarter still. The Singularity takes us to the point where normal laws of physics, of psychology, of biology, where all of these things break down, and something new takes its place, where human flesh and the other trapping of material existence become an accessory. Adherents to the belief that smarter-than-human intelligence is inevitable believe it is drawing ever nearer. Vinge himself predicts its advent before 2030 (2003 "Singularity" 2). Assuming that Moore's Law holds, and the number of components on a microchip continues to double every two years as it has done since the

1960s (an assumption that can be debated, perhaps[1]), computers will be over 4,000 times more powerful in 2030 than they are now. This estimate might even be conservative:

> Because of the recent rapid and radical progress in molecular electronics—where individual atoms and molecules replace lithographically drawn transistors—and related nanoscale technologies, we should be able to meet or exceed the Moore's law rate of progress for another thirty years. By 2030, we are likely to be able to build machines, in quantity, a million times as powerful as the personal computers of [2000]. (Joy 4)

The increasing speed of technological change in this view makes the Singularity inevitable, and from this we can begin to imagine two outcomes. Some see in the Singularity a limitless boon to humanity from the creation of superintelligence, that this is our destiny, and it resides in the resulting godlike transcendence. Others, unsurprisingly, see an immeasurable threat and the likely destruction of human civilization from malevolent and superhuman machines; after all, "Our society demands a thrill of apocalypse from science" (Sterling 16).

The Technological Singularity has not yet taken deep root in popular culture. The changes implied are too immense, the rapidity of change too paradigm-shattering. Instead, mainstream science fiction has offered a much more limited vision of life when machines become sentient: *2001: A Space Odyssey*, the *Terminator* trilogy, and the *Matrix* trilogy present worlds where humans have lost some level of control to their own technological creations, but none of these grapples with the full impact of the Singularity.

BSG presents a world where humanity has created artificial sentience. The Cylons achieve intelligence and self-awareness, and possess the ability to make other Cylons better and smarter than themselves. This, in itself, should be an immediate precursor to the Singularity. But, half a fictional century on, the world of *BSG* remains completely recognizable, and the technologies in use suggest the Singularity is nowhere in sight. The people of the Twelve Colonies never enjoyed posthuman existence, and artificial sentience has not meaningfully changed the day-to-day running of society. Cancer, sports teams, and lounge chairs still exist. Prizes celebrating human intelligence are still distributed, as Baltar's three Magnate prizes confirm (M.01). Things are better, but there has been no paradigm shift, let alone the rapid succession of unimaginable shifts implied by the Singularity.

This essay suggests two reasons why the Singularity fails to take hold in the world of *BSG*: the political consequences of the development of Cylon sentience that sparked a Cold War of sorts, and the theology the Cylons developed, which introduced specifically anthropocentric limitations on any further development. (The metanarrative reason, that post-Singularity existence would not be so limited as to be containable by episodic television and comprehensible within it, speaks for itself.)

On achieving sentience, the Cylons rebelled, which initiated the First Cylon War. Suddenly, humanity faced an enemy, and this required a unified military front.[2] The Cylons quickly developed spacefaring military technology that was in turn matched by the development of the battlestars, which perhaps was only possible with the combined resources of the Twelve Colonies, thus requiring political unification. The war was fought at a variety of technological levels, and, when they had enough information, the Cylons went into isolation. This isolation lasted forty years (M.01), a number resonant in several ways, though the primary evocation is likely the biblical Exodus from slavery in Egypt, destined for the Promised Land. In practical terms, it ensures that a complete generation has passed: just as Moses is not allowed into the Promised Land, so too at the time of the miniseries, there is almost no overlap between those who fought the Cylons the first time and those fighting them now. Tigh and Adama are established as veterans of the First Cylon War[3] who were on the verge of retirement when the Cylons attacked, as if to reinforce the generational leap. The Cylons use their time in isolation purposefully, but the specific innovations concerning their development during this time are kept remote from humanity; they sever all ties with their creators, so that humanity is never brought to a point where it could enjoy posthuman, post-Singularity life.

The military impact of Cylon sentience is therefore presented in a way clearly distanced from the automatic triggering of nuclear holocaust familiar to viewers from *Dr. Strangelove, or: How I Learned to Stop Worrying and Love the Bomb* (1964), *WarGames* (1983), and *Terminator 3: Rise of the Machines* (2003). Over the forty years between these examples, the role of human accident in the process is diminished; as society thinks more and more about artificial intelligences, the impetus for fictional human annihilation becomes increasingly deliberate. The dystopic outcome in all of them, however, serves in the narrative to avoid any engagement with the transcendence implied by the Singularity. The scenario presented in *BSG* continues this trend, stopping well short of ultraintelligence. But while the Cylon development did not trigger the Singularity, neither did it trigger an immediate mechanism to eliminate humanity, even though armed conflict was an initial consequence.

For the Cylons, sentience has led to a continued stream of technological improvements, but it has not led to the Singularity. Cylon ships possess better sensors and better FTL drives than those of the humans, but the true development resides in the Cylon conception of self that emerges. *BSG* accepts the necessary precursor to the Singularity—that once we have created something more intelligent than ourselves (however intelligence is to be measured), that creation is capable of replicating the feat, which the Cylons do. The Darwinian metaphor found in the opening credits—"They evolved"—is entirely appropriate. In a military context, the human-appearing Cylons represent an ideal means of infiltrating human society covertly in a way that does not necessarily result in nuclear devastation. This makes the choice, carefully reasoned over forty years, of an all-out near-Armageddon for the Twelve Colonies all the more calculated, and all the more horrific.

It is in the conception of the Cylon self, however, that both the greatest advances in technology are registered, and the profoundest limitations are met. While we are never shown the process, the development from the robotic Cylon Centurions to the organic human-appearing Cylons that embody the pinnacle of Cylon engineering does not represent the order-of-multiple-magnitude advance that the Singularity (as it is envisioned) ought to initiate. These Cylons are more intelligent than the previous generation (their creators, the robotic Cylons), and have naturally gravitated to positions of leadership among the Cylons. While we are not shown the intermediate steps explicitly, two of them are perhaps to be seen in the Cylon ships.

The Cylon Raider, the small space fighter, is biomechanical in nature: it has an intelligence that is described as animalistic ("Six Degrees of Separation" 1.07), and it represents a combination of electro-mechanical and organic parts ("You Can't Go Home Again" 1.05). Housed within the armored exoskeleton, the Raider's brain can learn, and on being killed, it has the ability to download its consciousness into another Raider ("Scar" 2.15). The organic aspect includes the brain, which enables both an increased, directed intelligence and the ability for a consciousness to download. The Raider need not represent a literal "missing link" for it to have value in this analysis. The Raider helps to identify the function of the organic parts, and it shows that they do not necessarily require mimetic representation of humans.

Aboard the Cylon basestar is what is called the Hybrid, a central computer that is organic, and appears in a womblike bath, with human-looking head and hands, but housed in a cocoon that is connected by twelve thick black cables to the workings of the basestar. Despite the name Hybrid (which suggests an interspecies cross), it too is an intermediary evolutionary step, not quite deserving of individuated personhood.[4] And, for whatever reason, it has a human face. In addition to managing the running of the basestar, the Hybrid serves as an oracle of sorts (its function is hybrid): during a tour of a basestar when Baltar has been taken aboard by the Cylons, the Hybrid ceases its nonsensical ramblings momentarily when it senses his presence. "Intelligence!" it says. "A mind that burns like a fire." The Hybrid then gives Baltar a clue to where to find the Eye of Jupiter, a key step in both the human and Cylon search for Earth. Whether it is mad or it is the voice of God (possibilities suggested in "Rapture" 3.12), there is something primeval about the speech that emerges. Like the inarticulate cries of the Pythia at Delphi, the utterances of the Hybrid need to be given a comprehensible form, they have to be ordered, but there is a sense, certainly among the organic Cylons, that Truth inheres.

It is easy to be fooled by the organic components housed within the metallic carapace in each of the Raider and the basestar. They are not cyborgs in the traditional science-fiction sense, in that there is no indication that there is, or ever was, a biological original. The organic life is presented as being completely artificial, even if it is completely indistinguishable from actual life to all but the most advanced Colonial science, while still possessing the ability to interface with computers ("Flight of the Phoenix" 2.09). As cybernetic organisms that are developed (for whatever reason) from completely mechanical antecedents, the organic and human-form nature of the reimagined Cylons must be seen as purposeful. This purpose can be perceived both theologically and anthropologically.

The theological implications of Cylon sentience are in many ways surprising: the Cylons have become monotheists. And, like many new converts to a faith, they are also fundamentalists. *BSG* deftly maps this fundamentalist monotheism onto both Islamic fundamentalism and American Christian fundamentalism, as if to suggest that the differences between them might not be as absolute as both groups often believe. But Cylon theology is presented as more than a doctrinal choice. There is even a suggestion that there has been divine revelation: that God has spoken to the Cylons. Six tells Baltar, "Procreation is one of God's commandments ("33" 1.01), and Sharon confirms, "Procreation, it's one of God's commandments . . . 'Be fruitful'" ("The Farm" 2.5, resonating with Genesis 1:28). This revelation is apparently not part of the Sacred Scrolls of the Colonial religion; unique to the Cylons, it has been interpreted by Cylon exegetes to require biological procreation, rather than mere replication, which is possible through the Cylon development of resurrection technology.

The Cylons have no single leader, and over the course of Season Three it is revealed that different Cylon models have different attitudes not only to the political and military situations, but also to God. These distinctions are not the result of the individuation that began in "Downloaded" (2.18), though this may have accelerated the process. The personalities and beliefs of the human-appearing Cylons have pronounced differences between them, with Cavil as a skeptic and Six as the most fervent believer, and the mystical Leoben demonstrating that such labels do not operate in a single dimension, but are complex and nuanced, resisting any easy or immediate classification.[5] As different Cylon models struggle to articulate their relationship to their creator in different ways, there is a sense of competition, perhaps even anxiety, in the thoughts of others. No one wants to be left behind in case this theological development is what triggers the next evolutionary stage toward the Singularity. (By accepting the evolution metaphor, we also accept the necessary element of Darwinian competition that is implied.) The aggressive pursuit of an imminent spiritual encounter by one of their number is, it seems, something to be feared.

The Cylon Three was first introduced as the reporter D'Anna Biers, and a version of this model serves as a leader of the occupation of New Caprica, speaking at the ill-fated graduation of the police graduation ceremony ("Exodus, Part 1" 3.03). But during her time on New Caprica, she begins to have strange dreams that she attributes to prophecies from God. Her decision to consult a human oracle demonstrates that she sees some continuity between her religion and that of the Colonists.[6] This, in fact is a startling revelation, and it shows that however we conceive of the nature of Cylon monotheism, it is in some sense developed from the polytheism of the humans. At the end of the occupation, guided by the words she received from the oracle, Three finds on New Caprica Hera, the first child created between a human and a Cylon, physical proof of some of the prophecies in which she has come to believe.

As Three experiences death and rebirth, it awakens something both illicit and spiritual within her. It is an experience she sets to replicate, ordering a Centurion to shoot her and delete any memory of the event, and it is between this death and resurrection that she sees what she calls "something beautiful, miraculous, between life and death" ("Hero" 3.08). The five white-robed beings she sees are, she believes, the final five Cylons. Her mission is now clear: she must discover who the Five are to learn God's secret plans for his creations. She pursues this end in two ways. In order to discover the secrets, she continues with her serial suicides. Each time, she is able to witness, however briefly, a glimpse of God's plan before reawakening in the resurrection bath. Three also makes her way illicitly to the temple on the algae planet, sneaking off with Baltar (to stall any direct interference from the Cylons, confirming that she knows it is a violation), where the Colonials find the Eye of Jupiter.[7] There she achieves a vision of five figures in light, and she recognizes at least one of them. She speaks hesitantly, humbly, "You . . . Forgive me I . . . I had no idea" ("Rapture" 3.12). This plea for forgiveness implies a transgression on her part—perhaps we are to assume that it was she who ripped out Saul Tigh's eye during his captivity—and this reinforces the theological context. Three's search for the final five human-appearing Cylons is, in its way, a search for God, and it sows considerable discontent among the other Cylon models. In the wake of the individuation of Caprica Six and Boomer ("Downloaded" 2.18), the entire Three model is perceived to be sinning against God's creation by repeated suicide. The other Cylon leaders agree to "box" the Number Three model, pulling the plug, at least temporarily, on the entire line, silencing them, and stowing their memories in cold storage ("Rapture" 3.12). When she sees the final five, she witnesses part of God's plan for his creation, and it kills her—or, rather, she is killed, because the implications of such spiritual advance are too risky for the other models' chances of Darwinian success.

Not only are Cylons seeking their creator God by chasing after their human creators, but they are double agents in the service of God. No Cylon offers a more literal presentation of this than the Cylon model called Cavil. Brother Cavil first appears at the end of Season Two, in "Lay Down Your Burdens, Part 1" (2.19). He counsels Chief Tyrol after a delusional Tyrol attacks Cally. Cavil introduces himself and Tyrol says he is looking for a priest because he doesn't believe in psychological therapy. When Tyrol says he prays to the gods every night, but he doesn't think they listen to him, Cavil responds:

> Cavil: Do you know how useless prayer is? Chanting and singing and mucking about with old half-remembered lines of bad poetry. And you know what it gets you? Exactly nothing.
>
> Tyrol: Are you sure you're a priest?
>
> Cavil: I've been preaching longer than you've been sucking down oxygen. And in that time, I've learned enough to know that the gods don't answer prayers. We're here on our own. That's the way they set things up. We have to find our own answers, our own way out of the wilderness without a nice little sunny path all laid out in front of us in advance.

Although Cavil professes an atheistic, or at best agnostic, worldview, he is well aware of the overall Cylon goal of shepherding humanity into their creator's arms.[8] At the beginning of Season Three, two Cavils who serve among the Cylon leaders of the occupation of New Caprica communicate this with no shortage of sarcasm. One begins, "Let's review why we're here, shall we? Uh, we're supposed to bring the word of 'God' to the people, right?" The second then continues,

> To save humanity from damnation by bringing the love of "God" to these poor, benighted people. . . .
>
> And it's been a fun ride, so far. But I want to clarify our objectives. If we're bringing the word of "God," then it follows that we should employ any means necessary to do so, any means. ("Occupation" 3.01)

Cavil cavils with himself, demonstrating a clearly dissenting voice to the hitherto unanimous presentation of Cylon monotheism.

The divided views of individual Cylon models demonstrates that the theological revelation remains incomplete, and is subject to interpretation. The credits continue to remind the audience that "They have a plan," and what that plan is, and whether it can change or develop, is something the series is very careful to leave unarticulated. After the rescue of the Caprica-based human resistance, and prior to humans settling New

Caprica, the Cylons announce a *détante* ("Lay Down Your Burdens," 2.19
and 2.20). Cavil, brought aboard the *Galactica*, tells Adama and Roslin:

> It's been decided that the occupation of the Colonies was an
> error. . . . Our pursuit of this fleet of yours was another error. That's
> two for anyone who's keeping score. Both errors led to the same
> result. We became what we beheld. We became you. . . . People
> should be true to who and what they are. We're machines. We
> should be true to that. Be the best machines the universe has ever
> seen. But we got it into our heads that we were the children of
> humanity. So instead of pursuing our own destiny of trying to find
> our own path to enlightenment, we hijacked yours. . . . I'm to tell
> you that you've been given a reprieve. Cylon and man will now go
> their separate ways, no harm done.

It's not clear that any of this is true, of course. Some of it certainly is not:
"no harm done" seems a little cavalier from someone speaking on behalf
of those who destroyed twenty billion humans. While Cavil's intentions
do appear to differ from those of the other human-appearing Cylons, it
is not certain that he is speaking for all Cylons here. The peace Cavil offers
might have put the current Cylon-human conflict at an end, but we can
never be sure.

While monotheism is a significant development that can be tied to
Cylon sentience, it does not command universal and immediate acceptance, nor is it exclusive of the human religion. *BSG* does not let us relegate
such speculation to the realm of superstition. Both spiritual forces are
seen to have actual mystical power: as Stover says (with some hyperbole),
"We have *objective verification* of the existence of *both* the Lords of Kobol
and the One God" (29). The Arrow of Apollo, a relic of Colonial polytheism, does provide a supernatural key to the fleet on their quest for
Earth. Similarly, Baltar, having asked for forgiveness and seeking repen-
tance ("33" 1.01, "Six Degrees of Separation" 1.07), becomes God's
"instrument" (according to his virtual Six) in "The Hand of God" (1.10).
The Cylon sense of superior theological knowledge is explicit when
Sharon says, "We know more about your religion than you do" ("Home,
Part 2" 2.07). The theological dimension of *BSG* polarizes characters. It
distinguishes them from each other, and allows for the exploration of a
variety of dimensions implicit in the relationship of creator and creation.
BSG does not present a blanket view on religious matters, but offers

viewers a rich tapestry in which degrees of faith and differing doctrinal positions are treated sympathetically and sincerely.

Why there should be any limit at all on the Cylon development can be tied to an aspect of anthropology (in the strict sense, of the Cylon understanding of humanity). Cylon evolution has brought them closer and closer to appearing human. The human-appearing Cylons are stronger than most humans, more resistant to radiation, and smarter, but they are ultimately limited by exactly the same things that limit humans: size, scale, the need to breathe, and so forth. Cylon theology even accounts for humanity, and gives it a clear place in creation. God created humanity, and gave Cylons their souls: Leoben asks, "What if God decided he made a mistake, and he decided to give souls to another creature, the Cylons?" (M.02). Leoben here need not be seen as a trustworthy theologian; his questions show that such an account is conceivable to both Cylons and humans, even if actual belief is impossible to determine.

While the Cylons have in one sense left humanity behind, and initiated their own drive toward the Singularity, there exists a residual attachment to the upright bipedal form that makes humanity also a goal, a *telos*, for the Cylon race. This is their greatest limitation. Humanity is the Cylon purpose, and this has locked the post-Singularity Cylons in a recursive loop, from which they might not ever escape. For, while striving for God, their creator, the Cylons have only the image of humanity on which to base their speculations. They have created God, and they have created themselves, in humankind's image, and at least part of the reason for this is to help fulfill God's revealed commandment, "Be fruitful" ("The Farm" 2.05). Transcendence (theological or technological, if it is meaningful to distinguish the two for the Cylons) is not a goal; being human is. And that is a goal that can never be realized.

While appearing as human clearly has military applications for the Cylons, we are now in a position to see those applications as secondary. Moore confirms, "There's been a deliberate evolutionary choice . . . to emulate mankind" (Podcast "Torn"). Theology and anthropology are uniquely intertwined for the Cylons, and this creates limitations that keep the Cylons in our frame of reference, for they are striving for a regressed identity. Humans created Cylons, and this was an advance, but the Cylons can never revert to a former evolutionary state, regardless of what their God tells them.

One way these limitations express themselves is in psychological neuroses. Writing before the revelation that Tigh was a Cylon, Steven Rubio concedes, "Although Tigh has many strengths as an XO, he is frightfully unequipped emotionally" (130). Tyrol, too, experienced a psychic breakdown ("Lay Down Your Burdens, Part 1" 2.19) that can be paralleled most closely with the psychological anxieties experienced through Boomer's suicide attempts ("Kobol's Last Gleaming, Part 1" 1.12). As a Cylon, Tyrol is the father, with the human Cally, of the second human-Cylon hybrid child (3.20).[9] It is Cavil who first identifies Tyrol's anxiety over the possibility of being a Cylon for him (2.19). In a slow-burning irony that only achieves its true impact a whole season later, Cavil, not yet revealed to be a Cylon, assures Tyrol that he must be human: "I know because maybe I'm a Cylon, and I haven't seen you at the meetings!" When it emerges that there are five human-appearing models that do not regularly attend "meetings"—they are not part of the social network of the leadership of the human-appearing Cylons—a curious juxtaposition of truths and falsehoods emblematic of so much of Cavil's dialogue begins to emerge.

Cylons have made themselves appear human, and have accepted what it means to be (almost) human as part of their identities. Through completely artificial (biomechanical) means, the Cylons have created a version of life, mastered cellular and genetic engineering, and developed a sophisticated purposive theology in the space of forty years. Leoben's question frames the issue in terms of a fallible deity: "What if God decided he made a mistake, and he decided to give souls to another creature, the Cylons?" (M.02). If God can change his plan, then Cavil's arguments that the Cylons can change theirs come to possess an increased plausibility. The only thing the Cylon reproduction agenda lacks, they speculate, is some ineffable spark that separates them from the humans, and in consequence prevents them from reproducing on their own. Possibly, the Cylon infatuation with humanity is motivated by the suspicion that they in fact do not have souls. But let us accept Leoben's premise. It is not a soul that the Cylons lack, but (to dredge up a cliché that invokes many of the same prejudices, yet without a necessary transcendent dimension) love: Helo explains to Starbuck, "They have this theory; maybe the one thing they were missing was love" ("The Farm" 2.05). Love, the series implicitly claims, requires a human being. There is something ineffable about humanity that even the sentient Cylons are unable to emulate, and this has locked them in a spiritual and psychological state from which they must escape.

The Cylons see love as a human virtue. It is in their creator, and, in a not unrelated observation, it is something they see in God. "God is love," the virtual Six coos to Baltar (M.02), in the words of 1 John 4:16. The fulfillment of God's command to the Cylons seems to demand not mere procreation but interspecies love. But this is also the limit that prevents any interesting continuation of the advance toward the Singularity. Until the Cylons can "be fruitful" in the specific sense they have understood this commandment to mean, there will never be the accelerated and unimpeded advance toward transcendence.

Progress toward the Singularity is something that *BSG* presents as residing completely in the past. Humanity may have almost been there, but it stalled, and the deceleration occurred, but not at the level of human activity. It was the Cylons whose theological development and fetishization of certain human qualities fractured the advance. The exaltation of humanity was by no means inevitable: the Raiders and (to a lesser extent) the basestars show that alternatives existed. But it did occur, and advance is unlikely to transpire until Cylon and human fuse and create a new state of being, in which real and artificial, creator and creation, are no longer viable categories. Until that time, humanity will continue. Humanity has been saved by the Cylon God.[10]

Notes

1. Cory Doctorow presents an overview of critiques concerning the Singularity's imminence.

2. The absence of alien life from *BSG* (which within science-fiction narrative may often serve as an enemy), in contrast to the presence of (improbably humanoid) aliens in the original series, has been noted and discussed by Lou Anders (89–91), with reference to the Drake Equation, which outlines some of the parameters within which we may speculate on the nature of extraterrestrial life.

3. Tigh's military record is communicated in Podcast 1.9, and we see Adama's as it is read by Laura Roslin in "Hero" (3.08).

4. The pronoun "it" comes naturally in describing the Hybrid, instead of "she"; this stage of development does not seem human enough to be worthy of the courtesy of gender recognition that we extend our pets.

5. For Ronald D. Moore's comment on this, see James John Bell 246–47.

6. This oracle's name, Dodona Selloi, emulates the ancient Greek connection established by the Book of Pythia in the Sacred Scrolls. Dodona was the location of an oracle of Zeus, and the priests who offered the prophecies were called Selloi. In constrast, Delphi, where the Pythian oracle was located, was dedicated to Apollo.

7. The fact that it is Tyrol who feels compelled toward its location anticipates the revelation that he is a Cylon ("Crossroads, Part 2" 3.20).

8. Matthew Woodring Stover describes Cavil as "[k]ind, gentle, ethical, reasonable, even a pacifist" (31)—all virtues, surely—as well as being an atheist.

9. In retrospect, there are many hints that Tyrol is a Cylon. Even his name, Tyrol, may be seen as a subtle evocation of Tyrell in *Blade Runner* (1981), the genius behind the creation of the replicants.

10. A Colonial Movers heavy transport's worth of gratitude are due to Brad Murray and Tiffany Potter.

8

"To Be a Person": Sharon Agathon and the Social Expression of Individuality

Robert W. Moore

Sharon Agathon is a Cylon, but is she a person as well?[1] Many of the characters on *Battlestar Galactica* have answered this firmly in the negative. She was, after all, made and not born. A machine, she did not grow up and develop from childhood to adulthood as humans do, but was created fully adult with a complete set of knowledge and memories. Early in the series many characters deny the possibility that she or any Cylon can be a person. For all of the humans in *BSG*, whether Cylons can be considered persons is problematic at best.

Most of the humans on *Galactica* unreflectively associate being a person with being human and therefore instantly dismiss Cylons as persons. Being human or being a person is opposed to being a machine. Reducing Cylons to machines or minimizing their feelings or emotions to software is the common way of denying Cylons personhood. Shortly after Helo discovers that Sharon is a Cylon, he dismisses her assertion that she has feelings: "You have software" ("Kobol's Last Gleaming, Part 2" 1.13). Laura Roslin likewise derides the notion that Sharon actually loves Helo: "She *thinks* she's in love" ("Home, Part 1" 2.06). Many characters refer to her with impersonal rather than feminine pronouns, calling her "it" and "that thing." When Helo is incredulous that Cally was given only thirty days in the brig for murdering Boomer, Sharon's Cylon twin, Sharon tells him: "They don't see it as murder, Helo.... To [Adama], to the president, to all of them, Cylons aren't people. I'm not a person to them. I'm a thing" ("Home, Part 2" 2.07). For most humans, at least at the beginning of the series, the proposition that Cylons are not persons because they are not human is not a proposition to be proved, but an unquestioned tautology.

But upon reflection, some humans begin to find the question of Cylon personhood more complex. At the end of Season One, Boomer, a Cylon sleeper agent, shoots and nearly kills Adama. Shortly after recovering from his injuries, Adama tells Chief Tyrol: "She was a Cylon. A machine. Is that what Boomer was? A machine? A thing? ... She was more than that to us. She was more than that to me. She was a vital, living person aboard my ship for almost two years. She couldn't have been just a machine" ("The Farm" 2.05). Although Adama had previously been able to dismiss other Cylon models as mere machines, when confronted with Boomer, a "vital, living person," he finds it far more problematic.

The question of personhood is, therefore, a central theme of *BSG*. The series never attempts a strict definition of what it means to be a person. Several of the characters embrace what might be described as naïve realism: what seems usually is. Adama says, "When you think you love somebody, you love them" ("The Farm" 2.05). Six believes, "In the scheme of things, we are as we do. She acts like one of them, thinks like them, she is one of them" ("Flesh and Bone" 1.08). Certainly Sharon seems to be a person. Presumably her intelligence is the result of programming, but it is programming that appears indistinguishable from human behavior. Yet this question of personhood is hardly unique to *BSG*: a substantial portion of the world's philosophy, theology, and literature has been devoted to exploring various aspects of what it means to be a person or an authentic human being. Philosophers have offered a variety of responses, some, following Jean-Jacques Rousseau, defining authenticity as a form of radical individuality, a complete stripping away of all external influences. In contrast, more contemporary philosophers have stressed how authenticity is impossible without a community that makes self-creation possible in the first place.[2]

These two positions are not mutually exclusive. They instead describe a paradoxical truth: that one can only express one's individuality through a community, in a nexus of social relations. One cannot be an autonomous individual without a concrete context that provides one's life with content. Sharon's story beautifully illustrates both sides of this paradox. When we first meet her, Sharon is a member of a culture that does not tolerate the individual. Although Cylons can infiltrate human society and pass for individuals, within Cylon society they are expected to be undifferentiated from other Cylons, but later, I argue, Sharon assumes a number of social roles that enable her to exist as an authentic person. I propose therefore to examine Sharon's story in the light of the thought of nineteenth-century Danish religious thinker Søren Kierkegaard, who like Rousseau, affirmed that to be a person means that one must be a genuine individual, but who also insisted that this entails embracing one's life in its concreteness.

In a long series of books, Kierkegaard strove to aid his reader (whom he often addresses as "that single individual") to understand "what it means to be a person or self."[3] Kierkegaard articulates this progression to full personhood through his theory of the stages, in which a person proceeds from the aesthetic, through the ethical, and to the religious. These stages constitute a linear progression in selfhood. The demand of the aesthetic is "One must enjoy life" (*Either/Or II* 179). On the aesthetic level a human being lives life through categories in which the good life is judged by such concepts as "the interesting" or "the pleasant." He believes, however, that in this stage the self is dissipated in the objects of aesthetic pleasure and in reality is not a self at all. A sufficiently self-aware person will come to despair and yearn not for the unique, particular, and transitory experiences of the aesthetic stage, but for the universal categories of the ethical.[4]

Kierkegaard's view of the ethical stage is in many ways similar to the ethics of Immanuel Kant. Both were convinced that humans are incapable of fulfilling the absolute demands of the ethical and that this failure requires a religious resolution. For Kant, however, this entails a view of life after death in which we, stripped of our sensual natures (the immediate cause of our inability to obey the moral law), will finally be able to actualize the demands of the ethical. For Kierkegaard, on the other hand, our failure to realize the demands of the ethical creates— when combined with a sense of the existence of God—the need for forgiveness. For Kant ethical failure logically demands immortality; for Kierkegaard it implies grace.[5] But just as Kierkegaard believes that the failure of the aesthetic can lead the individual from the aesthetic to the ethical, so he believed that the failure of the ethical stage could lead a sufficiently aware person to the religious.

Kierkegaard believes that all humans live in one of these three stages. He would have regarded Cylon culture as an aesthetic form of existence, because ethical and religious categories apply exclusively to individuals, while Cylon society suppresses the individual. Despite their apparent religiosity, Kierkegaard would not have acknowledged Cylons as authentically religious. He would instead have viewed all Cylon culture in terms of what he called "the crowd." The crowd is a chimera, a deceptive abstraction that prevents one from gaining sufficient self-awareness of not only the stage in which one currently exists, but also of future possibilities. One cannot exist as an individual while immersed in the crowd. "The crowd," Kierkegaard insists repeatedly, is "untruth": "From the ethical-religious point of view the crowd is untruth if it is supposed to be valid as the authority for what *truth* is" (*Point* 106). Only an individual who subjectively appropriates ethical or religious categories through impassioned choice can be said, in Kierkegaard's terms, to possess the truth. The goal of life for anyone, in Kierkegaard's view, is therefore to become an existing individual before God. This, he says, is something that any single person can achieve, but only as an individual, never as a member of the crowd. "Everyone can and everyone should become this one, but only as an individual can one reach the goal" (*Point* 107). In fact, all ethical and religious categories can only apply to an individual. This applies equally to interpersonal relationships. Take falling in love: it is "impossible to [fall] in love *en masse*" (*Point* 117). Nonetheless, just as Kierkegaard feels that one could become lost in abstract thought, so one can lose oneself by identifying with the crowd.

Cylon culture can be viewed as an allegory of the modern immersion of the individual in mass society. Cylon culture is collective. Cylons think of themselves primarily within the framework of the model to which they belong. Threes think of themselves as Threes first and this or that particular Three second. When several Cylons see film footage of Sharon alive and pregnant on *Galactica*, another Eight shouts, "I'm still alive!" ("Final Cut" 2.08). Individual Cylons will sometimes say, "We Threes believe . . ." suggesting that agreement among all members of the model is relatively unproblematic. Not only is conformity by each Cylon to its particular model assumed, any individuality is actively suppressed. When Boomer and Caprica Six, the two Cylon "War Heroes," are threatened with "boxing" (having their consciousness placed in cold storage), Caprica Six explains, "[Boomer and I] are dangerous. . . . We're celebrities in a culture based on unity." They are different because they see things differently "based on our love of two human beings" ("Downloaded" 2.18).[6]

The lack of individuality in Cylon culture results in an almost horrific blandness of everyday life, as seen in "Downloaded" (2.18), where the humanoid Cylons seem to do little more than sit around idly in public spaces and sip coffee. The Cylon idea of the Good Life apparently culminates in Starbucks. It is not life so much as a pale parody of it. The problem with collective culture, which obliterates or suppresses all difference, is that everything becomes homogenized, with all reduced to a banal sameness. Kierkegaard wrote with contempt of the "leveling" tendencies of modern life and emphasized the importance of being recognized as unique by others in the formation of the self: "A cattleman who . . . is a self directly before his cattle is a very low self, and, similarly, a master who is a self directly before his slaves is actually no self—for in both cases a criterion is lacking" (*Two Ages* 79).

It is not surprising, then, that Sharon's first step toward personhood is learning to be an individual and not merely another Number Eight. Just as Boomer and Caprica Six are changed because of their having loved individual human beings, so also is Sharon changed through her relationship with Helo. Sharon's initial mission is to deceive Helo into thinking that she is the same Boomer he served with on *Galactica* and then to cause him to fall in love with her; her ultimate goal is pregnancy.[7] A key moment in Sharon's story comes in "Litmus" (1.06) in which Sharon, Six, and Doral deliberately test Helo's love for Sharon. They lead Helo to believe that Sharon has been captured by the Cylons. They reason that if Helo goes south on his own and abandons Sharon to her fate, he does not really love her; but if he risks his own life and heads north toward the Cylon forces that could be holding Sharon, it suggests he does. Until the moment Helo decides, Sharon is somewhat subdued, evincing no strong feelings either way. But when Helo, starting southwards, reverses directions and heads north, she snaps to attention and shouts, "Wait!" revealing that she is more interested in the outcome than she has let on. For Cylons, risking one's life is meaningless, since anyone who dies resurrects into a new body. But when Helo risks his only life for Sharon, it is, for her, unprecedented.

Immediately after the test, Six proceeds to beat Sharon with savage glee so that Helo, when he sees her, will believe that Sharon has been tortured by the Cylons. Six is indifferent to Sharon's pain, but when Helo sees her bloodied and bruised face he responds with affectionate solicitude. To the Cylons her sufferings are not noteworthy; her pain is not an important consideration given her mission. To Helo they are horrific. Helo's treatment of her makes her feel valued and unique in a way that the Cylons cannot and stands in stark contrast with her brutalization at the hands of her fellows. Helo's love for her individuates her in a way that the Cylons cannot. When she and Helo finally have sex, it is the consummation of the love she has already come to feel for him in response to his love for her.

At this point one might object that the underlying subtext here is that a woman is incomplete without the love of a man. I do not have the space to address this charge completely, but I do believe the social world of *BSG* precludes such a reading. *BSG* is set in a nonpatriarchal world. On gender issues the show is utopian, despite its overall dystopian tone. The show's narrative does indeed suggest that people need people; but there is never a suggestion that a woman specifically needs a man to be fulfilled.[8]

Early in Season One, Sharon could not be considered a person at all. In Season Three Helo tells Sharon, "You were a person before you put on that uniform. Okay? You were a person before I fell in love with you" ("A Measure of Salvation" 3.07). But Helo is wrong. She may potentially have been a person, but in actuality she was not. Her sense of self was only awakened by the individuating influence of being loved. The change in her is so profound that even the Six to whom Sharon reports senses it and responds in subtle ways. Doral notes that Six has started to call her "Sharon." She replies, "Yeah, well, I choose to think of her as one of them. . . . Because in the scheme of things, we are as we do. She acts like one of them, thinks like them, she is one of them" ("Flesh and Bone" 1.08). In a very real sense, she has become the person Helo imagined her to be.

Kierkegaard considers becoming an individual by accident to be an impossibility. If Sharon becomes a person, it must be through choice, not through natural evolution or serendipity. One only acquires a self through deliberate choice. The Either/Or (which indicates the incommensurability of the two choices) refers to "the choice between good and evil" (*Either/Or II* 166–67). In fact the choice, as Kierkegaard's fictional writer Judge William explains, is not truly between good and evil, but between whether one wills to live one's life under the aegis of good and evil or under aesthetic criteria such as the pleasurable and the interesting: "My Either/Or designates the choice by which one chooses good and evil or rules them out. Here the question is under what qualifications one will view all existence and personally live"

(*Either/Or II* 169). Choosing "good and evil" in this sense results in a "baptism of the will" that assimilates the choice "into the ethical" stage of existence (*Either/Or II* 169).

Sharon's development as a character is tied to the choices she makes, but it also assumes that she is capable of making free choices. Many fans of the show question whether Sharon's actions are the result of her own choices, instead arguing that her actions are the result of programming. I would argue that we are warranted in taking Sharon's words to Adama in "Home, Part 2" (2.07) at face value: "I'm Sharon, but I'm a different Sharon. I know who I am. I don't have hidden protocols or programs lying in wait to be activated. I make my own choices. I make my own decisions." This capacity to choose, her free will, is what differentiates Sharon from Boomer. Although Boomer consciously, to the degree to which she was capable, sided with the fleet, her programming stripped her of her ability always to act in ways of her own choosing. She engaged in acts of sabotage and attempted to kill Adama.[9]

Sharon is, in fact, faced with a major ethical decision shortly after she and Helo first have sex. When she meets Six and Doral as prearranged, she is told to take Helo to a place they have prepared for them and to kill him if he refuses. She says nothing in response but merely turns and runs back to Helo, where with great urgency she tells him that they need to leave immediately and travel faster than they ever have before. "Why? What's different?" he asks, and in one of the series' great understatements she replies, "Everything" ("Litmus" 1.06). For she has not merely made the decision to switch sides; she has committed herself to prioritizing her relationship with Helo over her loyalty to her own people.

Sharon views her life as shaped by her choices and emphasizes repeatedly to others that many of the things that have transpired in her life were the result not of chance but uncoerced choice. To Laura Roslin: "I am here because I chose to come here" ("Home, Part 1" 2.06). To Commander Adama: "I make my own choices and I make my own decisions and I need you to know that this is my choice" ("Home, Part 2" 2.07). To her alter ego Boomer: "I made my choice and I know where my loyalties lie" ("The Eye of Jupiter" 3.11). And to Helo, "I made a decision to put on a uniform, to become a person" ("A Measure of Salvation" 3.07). She views her poor choices as the source of her inability to move on with her life following what she thought was the death of Hera, telling Adama, "I was angry at myself for the choices I had made" ("Occupation" 3.01). As a character, and as a person, Sharon is largely defined by these choices.

Being an individual—making decisions—constitutes the "how" of becoming a person, not the what; the form, not the substance; the method, not the matter. Charles Taylor has argued against associating the concept of authenticity with a radical individualism, as if becoming authentic involved subtracting everything from one's personality and psyche that one obtains from others. Being a self requires our being surrounded by other individuals: "One is a self only among other selves. A self can never be described without reference to those who surround it" (*Sources* 35). Instead, Taylor argues that we can only become persons through a dialogue with those around us:

> The general feature of human life that I want to evoke is its fundamentally *dialogical* character. We become full human agents, capable of understanding ourselves, and hence of defining an identity, through our acquisition of rich human languages of expression. . . . The genesis of the human mind is in this sense not "monological," not something each accomplishes on his or her own, but dialogical. (*Authenticity* 32–33)

While Taylor holds his position from a communitarian position, Kwame Anthony Appiah affirms it as an ethical individualist. Like Taylor, Appiah recognizes that the self requires a social nexus if it is to exist at all: "To value individuality properly just *is* to acknowledge the dependence of the good for each of us on relationships with others. Without these bonds . . . we could not be selves at all" (21). To have no social relationships would not, as Rousseau would have it, be to have an unencumbered, authentic self, but to have no self whatsoever. Part of what it means to be a person is to take on social roles that society provides as the options available for people in our culture. Appiah argues that we all can draw from what he calls the "Social Scriptorium," selecting "scripts" that provide us with models for ways to live our lives: "In constructing an identity, one draws, among other things, on the kinds of person available in one's society. Collective identities . . . provide what we might call scripts: narratives that people can use in shaping their projects and in telling their life stories" (Appiah 21–22). One aspect of Boomer's story that is especially tragic is that when she resurrects among the Cylons after Cally kills her, she loses all the social contexts that were crucial to her self-definition. In "Downloaded" (2.18) we discover that she temporarily persisted in living her life as Sharon Valerii, complete with photos of her *Galatica* friends and relatives. It was among these people that she had fashioned a life.

After making the decision to break with the Cylons, Sharon commits herself first to saving Helo's life and later, after she learns she is pregnant, to being with the man she loves and who is the father of her child. Sharon thus takes on a number of social roles—Appiah's social scripts—she views as crucial to who she is. There are three such roles that she articulates most frequently: wife, mother, and colonial officer. I will discuss each of these in turn.

Wife.

This is a social role that requires another person. Even if love is unrequited, one still requires an object of affection. We have already seen that finding herself loved and then loving Helo provided the occasion for Sharon first becoming an individual. Her relationship with Helo drives much of her behavior. Even Roslin acknowledges that Sharon did not have to rescue Helo and Starbuck on Caprica, that she could have had her baby on her own, but "she thinks she's in love" ("Home, Part 1" 2.06). Sharon is in a relationship that binds her to another person. No one on the show explicitly affirms his or her love for another person more often than does Sharon her love for Helo.

Mother.

Though not the primary reason for wanting to be with Helo (Roslin is correct; Sharon could have had her child on her own), one additional reason is clearly that he is the father of her child. When she rejoins Helo after being forced to flee from Starbuck for her own safety, Sharon tells him, "You're the father of my child, Helo. I'm not going to lose you" ("The Farm" 2.05). Though Sharon often speaks of the child she is carrying in Season Two, she rarely speaks directly of how being a potential mother makes her feel. But clearly being pregnant—unprecedented for a Cylon—is extremely important to her. Her rage when she is told that her pregnancy is going to be terminated in "Epiphanies" (2.13) shows just how deeply she feels about the baby she is carrying, and she expresses extreme joy holding Hera's hand in her incubator following her birth. We also see how important her baby is to her by the profound depression she experiences after the apparent death of Hera. Her ongoing affection for the daughter she believes is dead is shown when she tells Tyrol not to leave his and Cally's son Nicholas unattended ("Exodus, Part 1" 3.03), and in her gratitude to the daughter she carried for providing antibodies that made her immune to a virus that normally kills Cylons. When she learns that Hera is still alive, Sharon with no hesitation does what she feels that she as a mother must: "Hera's alive. I'm her mother and I'm going to get her" ("Rapture" 3.12). Through the rest of the Season Three, though Sharon makes no explicit statements about her role as a mother, we often see her doing things for Hera, whether taking her to the doctor, folding her laundry, or simply holding her.

Officer.

Being a wife and mother involves only Helo and Hera, but becoming an officer means becoming a part of a larger community. Part of the process involves taking an oath, which for Sharon functions as a life-defining moment. In her first mission as an officer she has to disguise herself in order to infiltrate the Cylon Detention Center on New Caprica. Anders, hearing her dog tags clink against one another, advises her to leave them behind. She refuses: "No, you've no idea how hard I've had to work to get these." Inside the Detention Center she encounters a Three who recognizes her and accuses her of treason, to which Sharon replies, "I'm a Colonial officer now," and adds "I gave them my word" ("Exodus, Part 1" 3.03). When Boomer tells her that despite wearing a uniform, she did not belong on *Galactica*, Sharon replies, "I know where my loyalties lie" ("The Eye of Jupiter" 3.11). But the clearest evidence of her commitment to the fleet comes after Helo has informed her of Laura Roslin's order to eradicate the Cylon race. She tells him, "I made a choice to wear a uniform, to be a person. . . . My people may die. My entire race may be wiped out. But this Cylon will keep her word even if she's the last Cylon left in the universe" ("A Measure of Salvation" 3.07). Sharon links her personhood with her decision to wear a uniform, showing an awareness of how this "social script" is integral to who she is.

These scripts are most explicitly linked and expressed in a scene filmed for "The Son Also Rises" (3.18) that was deleted but subsequently presented as a bonus scene following the original network broadcast and later made available on the show's official website. Sharon confronts Cally, who had earlier suggested that Sharon might sympathize with Cylon provocateurs within the fleet. Sharon challenges Cally to kill her because she is a Cylon. She then adds that she knows Cally won't because "I love my husband, I love my child, and I love this ship," and tells Cally that she does not think Cally would separate a child from her mother. Here Sharon has articulated the three social roles through which she expresses her personhood: wife, mother, and officer.

But there is another dimension to the social roles Sharon embraces. It is not merely that Sharon has made a commitment to serve the fleet; the fleet in a very concrete way has recognized her as one of its own. This is reflected in outward symbols like the dog tags she proudly wears. It is also shown in the highly symbolic act of giving her a unique call sign. After Racetrack unreflectingly calls her Boomer, Sharon replies, "Boomer was someone else." Helo immediately solicits a new call sign for her ("Torn" 3.06). When she is dubbed "Athena," it is more than simply a name; it is recognition of her place within the fleet, recognition as a fellow pilot. It is not enough for Sharon to embrace the roles of wife to Helo, mother to Hera, and officer in the fleet. She has to be acknowledged and confirmed in these roles, as someone who can properly perform these "scripts." While some characters on the show may not especially like her, everyone without exception seems by the end of Season Three to recognize her marriage to Helo, her being the mother of Hera, and her value as a pilot within the fleet. When Dr. Robert, for instance, gives Hera injections at Sharon's request, she is recognized as Hera's parent and guardian ("The Woman King" 3.14). Even Roslin, who engineered Hera's abduction in Season Two, seems by the end of Season Three to have accepted Sharon's right to raise her own daughter. When Racetrack asks to be Sharon's ECO (Electronic Countermeasures Officer) or when Sharon is asked to serve as Raptor pilot on especially tricky missions such as the rescue of Tyrol and Cally ("A Day in the Life" 3.15), she is affirmed as a valued and respected officer.

As important as any of these scripts is the friendship she forges with Admiral Adama, who comes to treat her as one of his surrogate daughters and comes to trust her completely even when others, including his own son, warn him against doing so.[10] When during the occupation of New Caprica he tells her, "I feel pretty much alone, except maybe for you," she can only reply with surprise, "I wish I could go back a year and tell that Admiral Adama about this conversation" ("Occupation" 3.01). Even Sharon wonders why he is risking the fate of almost all surviving humans by relying on her to perform her mission on New Caprica. When she asks Adama, "How do you know? I mean, how do you really know that you can trust me?" he replies, "I don't. That's what trust is" ("Precipice" 3.02). It is this rich social context in which Sharon has come to live her life that makes earlier doubts about whether she is a person seem so profoundly off the mark.

Many viewers of *BSG* persist in a profound distrust of Sharon Agathon.[11] Their distrust is grounded in the assumption that at some point she will betray humanity and breach what Roslin has called "the unconditional trust" that both Helo and Adama place in her ("Rapture" 3.12). But short of saving the life of her daughter Hera, it is impossible to imagine a scenario under which returning to the Cylons would be preferable to remaining in the fleet.[12] Staying with the fleet allows Sharon to continue to perform the social roles through which she enjoys and expresses her individualism as officer, mother, and wife. For it was only by leaving the Cylons to become an individual and embracing these social roles that Sharon was able to become a person. To abandon these now would be, for Kierkegaard, to cease being a person at all.

Notes

1. The Cylon known as Lieutenant Sharon "Boomer" Valerii I will refer to exclusively as "Boomer." The Cylon who has had a child with Helo and who acquires the call sign "Athena" I will refer to as "Sharon." Both Sharon and Boomer are model Eight Cylons and therefore are physically identical not just to one another but to every other Eight.

2. Charles Taylor has summarized Rousseau's understanding of self-determining freedom: "I am free when I decide for myself what concerns me, rather than being shaped by eternal influences. . . . Self-determining freedom demands that I break the hold of all such external imposition, and decide for myself alone" (*Authenticity* 27).

3. See Joakim Garff for a splendid intellectual biography that provides a good overview of Kierkegaard's thought.

4. The various forms of the aesthetic are displayed in *Either/Or I*. A critique of the aesthetic from the standpoint of the ethical is found in *Either/Or II*.

5. See Immanuel Kant, *Religion Within the Limit of Reason Alone*. Ronald Green in *Kierkegaard and Kant* explores Kierkegaard's debt to Kant.

6. Caprica Six loves Baltar, with whom she had had a two-year affair on Caprica prior to the Cylon attack. Boomer and Tyrol were planning, before the Cylon attack, on mustering out and getting married. Ironically, we learn in "Crossroads, Part 2" (3.20) that Boomer's love for Tyrol was not love for a human at all, when he is revealed to be one of the final five Cylons.

7. In "The Farm" (2.05) we learn the Cylons had been attempting to obey God's command to procreate but had been unsuccessful. They wondered if love was the missing ingredient so Helo and Sharon were set up to fall in love.

8. The parallels between the nonpatriarchal worlds of *BSG* and the Sci-Fi series *Farscape* are instructive. See the excellent discussion of gender inversion in the latter by Renny Christopher in "Little Miss Tough Chick of the Universe."

9. There are other aspects here that I do not have the space to develop. For instance, many philosophers and psychologists regard human behavior to be as fully determined as any Cylon could be by their programming. Furthermore, it is not at all clear that having programming leads necessarily to predetermined behavior. One could easily imagine an advanced AI that would be indistinguishable from having free will.

10. To add still more nuance to this scene, note that in the original series the character Athena actually was Adama's daughter.

11. This distrust of Sharon is rampant on any online *BSG* discussion board, such as the one on the official site <www.scifi.com>. A few of the topic headings on the board as of June 2007 include (punctuation and spelling as found): Poll: Why I like/dislike Helo/ Athena; Poll: Will Athena murder Helo in s4?; Cylons are the bad Guys remember? Athena is a Killer!; Why was Athena Forgiven?; Athena the Security Threat; I distrust Athena; and Shouldn't Sharon be banned from combat ops? These represent only threads with anti-Sharon topic titles. There are hundreds of individual posts inside various threads expressing anti-Sharon sentiments.

12. Even Caprica Six, who helped Sharon and Hera escape from the Cylon basestar, believes that Hera is safer on *Galactica*, rendering even that scenario unlikely.

9

Uncanny Cylons:
Resurrection and Bodies of Horror

Alison Peirse

The Cylons are figured as uncanny in *Battlestar Galactica* in a variety of ways, not least because of their familiar human appearance, and the revelation that, underneath the flesh, they are robots. This chapter argues that figuring the Cylons in terms of the uncanny has a specific purpose. The uncanny bodies of the Cylons, their ability to return from the dead in an endless form of uncanny repetition-compulsion, is one important method of evoking horror in the reimagined television series. Through the close textual analysis of the opening montage sequence and four key episodes in Season Three—"Occupation" (3.01), "Precipice" (3.02), "Exodus, Part 1" (3.03), and "Exodus, Part 2" (3.04)—and with reference to the reimagined series as a whole, this chapter examines scenes of uncanniness and horror in relation to the screen body. This discussion elucidates a theory of the televisual uncanny, and explores the slippages present in the text between horrific and uncanny corporeality.

The Cylons Were Created by Man

Sigmund Freud's theory of "The Uncanny" aims to account for what frightens us and arouses the uncanny sensation everyone has experienced from time to time. Freud proposes that the uncanny is related to what is frightening, to what provokes horror and dread. He suggests that "something has to be added to what is novel and unfamiliar to make it uncanny" (341), and questions what it is about the familiar that can become transformed to make it frightening. His theory draws upon unconscious fears and revolves heavily around the return of the repressed, central to the functioning of the unconscious. The uncanny has particular relevance for the study of moments of horror and/or strangeness in film and television, partly because, as Freud claims, the uncanny "undoubtedly relates to what is frightening—to what arouses dread and horror; equally certainly, too, the word . . . tends to coincide with what excites fear in general" (339). Freud suggests that the double is a particularly prominent form of the uncanny, often figured through identical characters, telepathic processes, and "the constant recurrence of the same thing" (356). The presence of the double calls into question the authenticity of either individual, and undermines any security one feels in dealing with others. The double is a particularly pertinent form of the uncanny in *BSG*, most prominently created through the ability of the Cylons to have multiple versions of their bodies present across different realms of time and space.

Writing on the Freudian double, Mladen Dolar suggests that "the subject is confronted with his double, the very image of himself . . . and this crumbling of the subject's accustomed reality, this shattering of the bases of his world, produces a terrible anxiety" (11). He continues, "As a rule, all these stories finish badly: the moment one encounters one's double, one is headed for disaster; there seems to be no way out" (11). The double as uncanny is particularly interesting in *BSG*, where the double, while uncanny at first, does not produce death in the twinned subject. In the Cylon body the double is endlessly repeated. *BSG* moves beyond traditional notions of the uncanny through the figuration of the Cylon, and the body becomes horrific: endless replications of seven of the twelve Cylon models, dedicated to obliterating the human race. The Cylons were created by man, and it is man's own creation that now leads to humanity's potential downfall.

They Rebelled

BSG produces complex meanings of identity, and questions whether selfhood is defined in terms of how you are born, or whether identity is determined by what you do. The dubious moral ambiguity of many of the Cylons and humans is regularly played out across the series, and is most apparent in the difficult decisions made in the first half of Season Three. These decisions include the problematic presentation of the suicide bombing by Duck at the New Caprica Police (NCP) graduation ceremony in "Occupation" (3.01)—further complicated by the webisodes (W.1–10)—while in "Exodus, Part 2" (3.04) Colonel Tigh poisons his beloved wife Ellen, after it is revealed that she is a Cylon informant— somewhat of an irony as it is revealed in "Crossroads, Part II" (3.20) that Tigh is a Cylon himself. Similarly, the vengeance committee "The Circle" is created on *Galactica* after the exodus from New Caprica. Led by Tigh, the Circle jettisons Jammer into space for his "crimes against humanity" ("Collaborators" 3.05). This dubious morality is in accordance with the fluctuating moral code of the series, evident also in earlier episodes, including the torture and rape of Gina by the *Pegasus* crew revealed in "Pegasus" (2.10) and, in the same episode, the attempted rape of Sharon, resulting in the death of Lieutenant Thorne at the hands of Tyrol and Helo.[1]

This moral ambiguity is again symptomatic of many contemporary American television programs with long-running narratives and extended season arcs. The character development and narrative trajectory of the vampires Spike and Angel in *Buffy the Vampire Slayer* (1997–2003) and *Angel* (2000–2004) is constantly in a state of flux. Similarly in *The Sopranos* (1999–2007), we are regularly expected to feel empathy toward New Jersey Mafia boss Tony Soprano, who moves between cold-blooded killer, family man, and adulterer, often within the same episode. Writing on narrative complexity in contemporary American television, Jason Mittell argues that many of the writers of such shows "embrace the broader challenges and possibilities for creativity in long-form series, as extended character depth, ongoing plotting, and episodic variations are simply unavailable options within a two-hour film"(31). Furthermore, ambiguity is present not just through the morality of the characters, but also the complex ontology of the Cylon bodies themselves. These two narrative lines are brought together in "Crossroads, Part 2" (3.20), when four of the final five Cylons are revealed to be characters previously believed to be human and occupying senior positions aboard *Galactica*.

Freud argues that the conceptualization and disintegration of selfhood is essential to the conceptualization of the uncanny, marked by the fact that the subject identifies himself with someone else, so that he is in doubt as to which his self is, or substitutes the extraneous self for his own. In other words, there is a doubling, dividing and interchanging of the self. And finally there is the constant recurrence of the same thing—the repetition of the same features or character-traits or vicissitudes, of the same crimes, or even the same names through several consecutive generations. ("Uncanny" 356)

Freud's quote is a checklist of the crucial forms of the uncanny and the horrific in *BSG*. The insecurity felt by New Caprica's President Gaius Baltar over his own potential to be a Cylon is explicit in Season Three, while the "doubling, dividing and interchanging of the self" and constant recurrence of facial features, individual consciousness, and names are uncannily marked upon the Cylon body. The constant dissolution of identity and the resurrected Cylon body result in a sense of unease for the viewer, and anxiety for both humans and Cylons in the series. Continually switching empathic allegiances according to complex moral narrative decisions, *BSG* raises disturbing questions of the body and the construction of identity through uncanny occurrences.

They Evolved

Recently writing on *C.S.I.* (2000–present), Sue Tait proposes that the "aesthetic convergence between film and television, which reflects hardware innovations such as home theatre and DVD technologies, suggests that continued attention to television's changing visuality is critical to analysis of the pleasures and pedagogies of the medium" (47). Tait's observation can be equally well applied to *BSG*, where generic and medium-specific hybridity becomes explicit in the visual style. The series moves between the horror and science-fiction genres, and blurs television and film on a regularly basis, redefining previously distinct forms. In fact, the high production values of the series, particularly in the first four episodes of Season Three, create a spectacular televisual gaze, more commonly present in contemporary science-fiction film. In "Exodus, Part 2" (3.04), the on-ground insurgent fighting contains fast-paced editing and rapid gun fire, mirroring the large-scale fight scenes in *War of the Worlds* (2005) and *X Men III: The Last Stand* (2006), to name just two of many possible examples.

Analyzing contemporary televisual flow, Eric Freedman suggests that the opening montage sequence of a serial program "operates as a doubly purposed hermeneutic act, introducing the semiological complexity of both the specific program (revealing and reviewing the central conflicts and enigmas) and the genre itself (as a shorthand guide to serial television's textual strategies, the genre's rituals are laid out in shorthand form)" (163). The *BSG* montages feature teasers that showcase forthcoming scenes in that episode, making the images used in each montage unique to the episode in question. Beginning with an analysis of the opening credit sequence for Season Three, this chapter follows Freedman in suggesting that the opening sequence is a presentation of the crucial themes of the entire series, combining image, music, and word in an intricate manner that highlights the complex narrative strategies of a long-running contemporary television series. This discussion of opening credits in contemporary television series also relates more generally to contemporary American television as a whole, where programs such as *Lost* (2004–present) continue to revise the structure of opening credits as ever more complex storylines, flashbacks, and character arcs unfold. Additionally, through its iconography, the opening sequence explicitly relates *BSG* to the science-fiction genre and recalls Tait's observations regarding visuality: images of robots and downloaded consciousness evoke contemporary science-fiction films such as the *Terminator* trilogy (1984, 1991, 2003).

Season Three's opening montage sequence begins with a fade in from black. White capitalized words state that "The Cylons Were Created by Man." As the words appear on-screen, a Cylon Centurion walks toward the camera. The robotic metal body is a visual cipher of science-fiction film, creating an intertextual web with a disparate range of films, including Maria in Fritz Lang's *Metropolis* (1927) and George Lucas's *Star Wars* (1977). The image is cut, while the screen fades to black. From out of the darkness the brown limb of a robot flexes. Returning to blackness, "They Rebelled" appears. The words remain as a Cylon Centurion is framed in medium close-up shooting fire from its hands at an offscreen enemy. Both word and image fade to black.

The next image is a close-up of Caprica Six, taken from "Down-loaded" (2.18). It focuses on her regaining consciousness after being downloaded into a new body. Her naked body is framed in medium close-up and lit in neon pink, while the amniotic pool is bathed in intense and unnatural white light. She opens her mouth wide in excessive emotion and writhes. "They Evolved" is stamped upon the screen. A strong generic image, this clip has many similarities in *mise en scène* with *Minority Report* (2002), chiefly in terms of the presentation of the "pre-cog" Agatha. Agatha is contained for much of the film within a pool of thick, viscous clear liquid inside a cavelike room, where she has visions of the future utilized by the "Pre-Crime" Division of the Washington, DC, law enforcement team. The medium close-up of Caprica Six is replaced by an extreme long shot of the rebirthing tank, its blazing white sarcophagean structure shown in stark contrast to the black and undefined depths of room. There is an uncanny sense of otherness pervading the text, where the humanoid Cylons inhabit an altogether artificial and unnatural world, coded as such by the stark lighting and use of color.

In turn, this is also the space that *BSG*'s Cylon Hybrid is located ("Torn" 3.06). Although she is not one of the twelve Cylon models, the Hybrid has a female face and appears human. Plugged straight into the basestar system with unwieldy black wires that mirror the leeching of human life by machines in *The Matrix* (1999) and permanently located in an immersion tank, the Hybrid is pale and young, and bears a distinct resemblance to Maria in *Metropolis*. The Hybrid also possesses an otherworldly, uncanny body made more distinct by the constant torrent of disjunctive and nonsensical words that emanate from her mouth. Fading from Caprica Six's download, "There Are Many Copies" appears on screen. It fades out as four copies of Number Eight are shown standing side by side. Finally, and most ominously, an image of an office appears on-screen. Dressed in somber clothing, Five, Six, and Eight walk into the room, looking authoritative. The image disappears and the words fly in onto the screen "And They Have a Plan." The opening credit fades to black. Silence pervades before the *BSG* logo appears and a voiceover begins, "Previously, on *Battlestar Galactica* . . ."

Season Three's montage can be split into two distinct sections: narrative history and recapitulation of the central themes of the coming episode (and more broadly the season). Similarly, this structure has been noted in *Buffy*'s opening sequences by David Kociemba, who points out that the sequences "construct the series' past, shape the viewer's present experience of the episode, and prepare the way for future narratives" (84). The opening montage sequence in contemporary television reverses the traditional serial narrative through nonsequiturs, for "the plot fragments are presented out of sequence; episodic and seasonal moments are presented in a new order that foregrounds not only the individual plot points but also their significance as metaphors for the overarching themes of the programme" (Freedman 165). In a highly condensed format the images create the bare bones of the show's mythology, allowing the casual viewer to grasp the basic premise of this episode. The opening montage sequence downloads the necessary information to the viewer, much in the same way a Cylon's memories are transmitted into another body. Having downloaded all the information required to watch the show from the opening sequence, the viewer has been automatically equipped to deal with basic narrative forms and character relationships, as well as having an understanding of the basic visual style of the text.

The textuality of television reveals an obsessive reenactment with the uncanny body, present in both visual style and narrative as well as in the formal structure of the long-running serial itself. Constant flashbacks begin episodes; montage sequences speak to the past, present, and future; narrative arcs are complex and circulative, while the weekly voiceover "Previously on *Battlestar Galactica* . . ." signals the significance of the past on present events. The preoccupation with the past is made explicit by Leoben in "Flesh and Bone" (1.08) when interrogated by Starbuck. Quoting the Book of Pythia, Leoben tells Starbuck, "All of this has happened before and all of it will happen again. Your destiny has already been written."

There Are Many Copies

The double is the most important form of the uncanny in *BSG*. In additions to its prominence in Gothic literature from the 1800s onward, the double is prevalent throughout over a century of horror film, and Robin Wood proposes that the "the figure of the doppelgänger, alter ego, or double" (26) is the privileged trope of all horror fictions created in the past century. Freud suggests that the double is "the uncanny harbinger of death" ("Uncanny" 357), and through a century of horror film and literature, doubles are irrevocably linked together. This is made clear in the gothic story "William Wilson" by Edgar Allen Poe. The protagonist Wilson discovers that when he has stabbed his double to death that he has killed himself:

It was Wilson, but he spoke no longer in a whisper, and I could have fancied that I myself was speaking when he said: 'You have conquered, and I yield. Yet henceforth art thou also dead—dead to the World, to Heaven, and to Hope! In me didst thou exist—and, in my death, see by this image, which thine own, how utterly thou hast murdered thyself. (117)

The Cylon body is particularly interesting in this regard, for death to a doubled Cylon body results in downloading and resurrection, creating an oppositional form of the uncanny. The constant return and resurrection of the double, after possible countless deaths, is where the true horror of Cylon body is made manifest. Horror for the Cylons is in the threat of being "boxed," as discussed in "Downloaded" (2.18). Boomer and Caprica Six are threatened with being boxed after exhibiting human characteristics and compassion for humanity. In being boxed, the Cylon's consciousness is downloaded into storage, and is not allowed to be resurrected into a new body. The inability to resurrect results in a form of absolute stasis for the unconscious, in effect it is death for the Cylon in question. In "Rapture" (3.12), this threat is carried out on the entire Number Three model, boxed by Cavil for seeking out the identity of the final five Cylons.

Freud's sources for his article on the uncanny are few and far between, and the only paper he regularly cites is Ernst Jentsch's "On the Psychology of the Uncanny." Writing thirteen years before Freud's exposition on the subject, Jentsch's essay explores the psychic conditions that constitute the feeling of the uncanny, and how they arise from an intellectual experience of uncertainty as to whether an object is animate or inanimate. Jentsch claims this is an uncertainty rooted in the opposition between the unknown and the known. He stresses one form in particular:

Among all the psychical uncertainties that can become an original cause of the uncanny feeling, there is one in particular which is able to develop a fairly regular, powerful and very general effect: namely doubt as to whether an apparently living being is animate and, conversely, doubt as to whether a lifeless object may not in fact be animate. (11)

Freud devotes a great deal of his paper to claiming that "intellectual uncertainty" is not a province of the uncanny, disputing Jentsch's suggestions concerning the potential uncanny quality of animating waxworks, dolls, and automata. However, this is not necessarily correct, as noted by Adam Bresnick: "While Freud categorically rejects Jentsch's argument, the text of 'The Uncanny' suggests that he is more uncertain about uncertainty than he initially lets on" (116). Indeed, the popularity of tropes of the (in)animate have proliferated throughout decades of horror in film and literature: waxworks, mummies, zombies, and puppets are just four examples.

Following Jentsch, it could be argued that tension and suspense are created when it becomes unclear whether the screen body is alive or dead. However, *BSG* moves beyond established tropes of horror in film and literature to offer up an uncanny mode of television viewing. In fact, *BSG* moves beyond this notion of the uncanny double suggested by Freud and the horror of the animation of the inanimate outlined by Jentsch. Paralleling *Blade Runner* (1982) and *A.I.: Artificial Intelligence* (2001), where the differences between "skin job" robots and humans are indecipherable to the human eye, *BSG* creates bodily anxieties not through the replication of the double alone, but through the fact that these doubles are identical, human in appearance, and have independent thought and distinguishable personalities. While they appear on the surface to be doubles, creating an initial moment of uncanniness, the bodies of the Cylons become horrific when it is realized that they are autonomous and cannot die: the body becomes only a vessel for the consciousness of the robot and is able to be disposed of. As Laura Roslin writes in her diary during "Occupation" (3.01), "It is simply not enough to kill Cylons, because they do not die. They resurrect themselves and continue to walk among us. It is horrifying." Through the continual resurrection of the Cylons, *BSG* opens up new uncanny questions around identity and the body. The renewal of the Cylons, their doubling, and their ability to discard useless dead bodies and return anew, speaks closely to central tropes of horror established in film and literature and then moves forward, creating a new paradigm for the televisual uncanny.

In her study of the assimilating cyborg collective the Borg in *Star Trek: First Contact* (1996), Linda Dryden points out that "the Borg disdain organic physical wholeness: the horror of their practices lies in their calculated replacement of human eyes, arms and legs with cumbersome, but effective technological implants and prosthetics designed to maximise their efficiency" (159). The Borg "are without emotion, terrible killing machines with no conscience: conscience, morality, indeed most human values derived from religion are regarded by the Borg as weakness" (159). The contrast between the Borg and the Cylons becomes clear in Dryden's quote, and in fact reinforces the humanoid

Cylon's uncanniness: it is their very human appearance, their acceptance of organic physical wholeness that makes them uncanny, and their subsequent replication truly horrific. Therefore, *BSG* offers a new televisual rendering of the uncanny, transforming traditional notions of the uncanny proposed by Jentsch and Freud. *BSG* presents endless doubles with the ability to regenerate through downloading. The televisual uncanny occurs initially through the presentation of the double, but it can be argued that then the real horror takes place when the double recognizes itself and does not fear its replication, for, as noted by Poe and Freud, the presentation of the double is often an uncanny sign of imminent death.

And They Have a Plan

One of the major plotlines in the first four episodes of Season Three is the imprisonment of Starbuck in a New Caprica detention center by Leoben. Leoben is obsessed with Starbuck after she interrogated him aboard *Galactica* ("Flesh and Bone" 1.08) and is determined to make Starbuck love him. Leoben has kidnapped Starbuck and keeps her prisoner in his modern and pristine New Caprica apartment, which is quickly revealed to be nothing more than a luxurious prison cell with iron bars at the doors. Throughout these four episodes, Starbuck repeatedly stabs and kills Leoben, only to have him to return again hours later. Through the Starbuck-Leoben plotline, the text draws upon the tropes of the horror genre of the rape-revenge film and fuses it with the uncanny recurrence of the Cylon body.

In "Occupation" (3.01), the pair sit at the table eating steak. Leoben cuts up Starbuck's steak as he will not provide her with a knife. She turns and stabs him in the neck with a metal skewer, and then repeatedly skewers him viciously in the chest until he dies. Female violence abounds in this plotline, and after killing Leoben (the insinuation is that this has been going on for months), Starbuck calmly sits down with bloodied hands, accompanied by extradiegetic classical music, and eats her steak. Starbuck has become a serial killer, although her constant execution of Leoben cannot be considered emancipatory, for Leoben continues to return from the dead, and patiently restarts his attempts to woo her.

Failing to make any romantic headway with a woman who kills him at every opportunity, Leoben produces a small blonde child for Starbuck, introducing her as Kacey ("Precipice" 3.02). He claims to have salvaged

Starbuck's ovary from a breeding farm on Caprica (alluding to events in "The Farm" 2.05) and inseminated it to create their child. After initially refusing to acknowledge Kacey, by "Exodus, Part 1" Starbuck begins to develop a maternal attachment to the child. In "Exodus, Part 2" Leoben locks Starbuck inside the apartment while he investigates the insurgency. As the humans begin to win the battle, the detention center is liberated, but Starbuck is knocked unconscious in the blast. After being rescued by her husband Samuel Anders, she returns alone to the cell for her child, and finds Leoben with Kacey. The final scene between the pair has aggressive sexual overtones, insinuating rape and murder. The threat of sexual violence is implicit throughout the episodes featuring Leoben and Starbuck. Although until this point, Leoben has continued to remain polite and well-mannered, the sexual dominance he so clearly desires is the end aim. Leoben refuses to release Kacey until Starbuck tells him she loves him, "and the rest." She kisses him and he kisses her back fiercely and deeply. With his mouth open he pushes her against the wall, overpowering her. As Starbuck kisses him back, she guts him with a knife, and murders him once more.

When Leoben devours Starbuck with his kisses, it is a clear violation. As such, the final violent moments of the relationship between Leoben and Starbuck can be read as a symbolic appropriation of the rape-revenge narrative present in horror film, articulated by such films as *I Spit on Your Grave* (1978), and *Ms. 45* (1981). Examining the horror film, Carol Clover argues that "female self-sufficiency, both physical and mental, is the hallmark of the rape-revenge genre" (143). Starbuck epitomizes female self-sufficiency, and her repeated execution of her obsessive and lustful male captor prepares her for when he exhibits his greatest weakness: when he is overcome by lust and at his most vulnerable, Starbuck stabs him, knowing he will be dead long enough for her to escape with Kacey. Starbuck creates a plan that trades upon both the iconography of the rape-revenge film and the mythology of the uncanny Cylon body. Indeed Leoben will return from the repressed, but it will be to an empty prison cell. However, he continues to haunt Starbuck's dreams, where sexual aggression is made ever more manifest. In "Maelstrom" (3.17) Starbuck dreams she is in her apartment on Caprica. She looks at the Eye of Jupiter painting on the wall, and then throws white paint over it. As she does so, Leoben approaches her from behind and she turns. They kiss violently and have sex on the apartment floor, covering their bodies in white paint, suggesting both the hostile culmination of Leoben's desires and Starbuck's inability to move on from her imprisonment.

In *The Pleasures of Horror*, Matt Hills points out that there is a perception that "in authentic horror anything goes. . . . By contrast, TV horror is not 'really' horror precisely because it cannot go all-out to scare audiences: types of graphic 'splatter' horror that are possible in novels and films are generally less permissible in made-for-TV horror" (115). While this is certainly the case to a degree, this does not preclude television from creating horror. Indeed, there has been a distinct evolution of late in terms of horror television. While the commissioning of these series does reflect network interest in capturing the post-*Buffy* audience, it can still be argued that the contemporary television series is growing increasingly obsessed with horror and the uncanny, as evidenced by the presence of *Angel*, *Carnivàle* (2003–2005), and *Supernatural* (2005–present) in the U.S., and *Afterlife* (2005–2006), *Hex* (2004–2005), and *Sea of Souls* (2004–present) in the UK. What must be acknowledged, as Hills points out, is that horror in television is negotiated in a series of complex and imaginative ways that present horror and the uncanny through a variety of narrative, stylistic, and iconographic tropes. Rather than relying on outright depictions of blood, gore, and bodily dismemberment, televisual presentations of horror, mediated through the uncanny, are present in *BSG* though the obsession with the disintegration and renewal of Cylon bodies and Starbuck's rape-revenge narrative. This complex televisual rendering of the uncanny and horrific body offers a far more stimulating and intellectual account of the ontology of horror and the uncanny than the unrestrained recent cinematic releases that revel in torture, rape, and murder, such as the *Saw* trilogy (2004, 2005, 2006); and the increasing turn to "torture porn" demonstrated by *Hostel* (2005) and *The Devil's Rejects* (2005).[2]

Furthermore, there is certainly not a one-size-fits-all approach to presenting horror and the uncanny on television. While *Supernatural* is the closest to traditional Western renditions of horror in presenting bodies bloodily opened up on-screen, demons, exorcism and the constant manipulation of off-screen space, *Carnivàle* speaks to horror films of the 1930s through its presentation of "freak" bodies, and *Charmed* (1998–2006), featuring the trio of witch sisters, draws on horror iconography in order to articulate a postfeminist discourse.[3] Likewise, *BSG* offers an ideal case study of the televisual uncanny. The anxiety around the textual body (penetration, death, rebirth, and resurrection) underpins narrative content and structure, as well as visual style. While hoping to go some way to furthering the legitimacy of close textual analysis as a methodology in television studies,[4] this chapter also argues that the Cylons' ability to evoke horror, through their own scenes of death and rebirth, suggests that Freud's study of dread and fright in art and literature has a place in the analysis of contemporary television aesthetics, almost ninety years after its first publication. Unsettling in narrative structure, theme, and presentation of the body, *BSG* is truly uncanny.

Notes

1. The original, longer version of the episode can be found on the DVD release of Season Two, where Thorne actually rapes Sharon before Helo and Tyrol can rescue her.

2. For an overview of the emerging prominence of the "torture-porn" genre, see Kira Cochrane.

3. See Alison Peirse, "Postfeminism Without Limits?"

4. For a discussion of the close analysis of texts in television studies, see Jason Jacobs, Karen Lury, Glen Creeber, and in particular Helen Wheatley (18–22).

10

"Humanity's Children": Constructing and Confronting the Cylons

Tama Leaver

"What science fiction should be . . . is a look at ourselves, an examination of humanity."

—Ronald D. Moore (quoted in Littlejohn)

In *Mind Children*, Hans Moravec, director of the Mobile Robot Laboratory at Carnegie Mellon University, foreshadows what he argues to be an inevitable "postbiological" future where the machines, computers, and artificial intelligences of today will culminate to form new life for which humanity *en masse* is the proud parent. When our "artificial progeny" arrive, Moravec sees little place for their stumbling, inefficient fleshy ancestors (Moravec 108). In the miniseries that reintroduced *Battlestar Galactica* to a twenty-first-century audience, the seductive Cylon agent who comes to be known as Caprica Six warns her shocked human lover, Dr. Gaius Baltar, that, after the Cylons were driven away from the human Colonies decades earlier, "Humanity's children are returning home . . . today" (M.01). In a key shift from the original 1970s series, the Cylons are no longer the product of an alien civilization, but rather humanity's own technological creations that have become self-aware and self-directing. As with Moravec's prediction, the existence of the Cylons immediately begs the question as to humanity's ultimate response and

responsibility to the Cylons they have created. Within the diegesis of
the new television series, such philosophical questions may, at first
glance, be less than pressing for the few surviving officers and crew of the
Colonial Fleet. Military training and the necessities of survival in combat
leave little room for speculation or ambiguity. However, from the outset,
the series has been dominated by questions of humanity's relationship to
and with the Cylons. Executive producer Ronald D. Moore has frequently
stated that he considers science fiction a genre that is about asking difficult questions about humanity and the present, as much as speculating
about possible futures (quoted in Lee). Rather than relying on the technobabble, exotic aliens, and unflinching moral certainty that characterize
much mainstream science-fiction television, Moore sees *BSG* as a chance
"to introduce realism into what has heretofore been an aggressively unrealistic genre" (Bassom, *Official Companion* 8). The ease with which
audiences achieve suspension of disbelief makes the bigger issues confronted by the show all that much more immediate and engaging.

In *Artificial Knowing*, Alison Adam examines the way that the scientific disciplines situate and construct artificial intelligence and artificial
life—that is, attempts to replicate either human-level intelligence or
biological-style organisms within a digital context. Adam argues that the
claims of artificial life narratives can meaningfully be divided between
what is termed a "weak view," whereby artificial life is treated as a
metaphor for biological life and thus useful in asking questions about
humanity, and a "strong view," which claims that artificial life is life and
should be examined on its own terms (151). In a similar fashion, the
Cylons can be read in two differing modes: either in a weak sense, where
the dynamics between Cylons and humans act as a metaphor for interactions within current human society; or in a strong sense, whereby the
seemingly genocidal ambitions of the Cylons posit a cautionary tale about
the potential of our technological creations to evolve beyond the control
of, or need for, human beings. As with most binary distinctions, weak
and strong readings often intertwine and are by no means mutually exclusive. This chapter examines the way the Cylons are constructed within
the narrative and production processes of *BSG* while simultaneously exploring some of the meanings and questions with which audiences are
implicitly asked to engage, whether the Cylons are read as metaphors for
current human society or for speculative figurations of artificial life.

Face to Face

In adapting the original *Battlestar Galactica* for a twenty-first-century audience, Moore realized that the premise of the seemingly peaceful human Colonies being almost entirely annihilated in a massive unforeseen onslaught would have an immediate political and cultural resonance for contemporary viewers. Moore has explicitly stated that in rewriting *BSG* he saw the show as an opportunity to "comment on things that are happening in today's society, from the war against terror to the question of what happens to people in the face of unimaginable catastrophe" (quoted in Bassom, *Official Companion* 12). In the miniseries and Season One, the characters were immediately gripped with an us-and-them mentality, the ragtag fleet of human beings fighting their mechanical enemies, who were quickly dubbed with the derogatory nickname "toasters." That said, despite the fact that the Cylons are clearly the aggressors in a war with all of humanity, Moore and the show's writers have consistently challenged easy binary divisions between good and evil or right and wrong; these characteristics never line up exclusively with one side. In what was supposed to be his retirement speech, Commander Adama highlights that complexity: "We decided to play god. Create life. When that life turned against us . . . we comforted ourselves in the knowledge that it really wasn't our fault, not really. You cannot play god then wash your hands of the things that you've created." No longer the product of alien civilization as in the 1970s series, in the new *BSG*, the Cylons are the technological creations of human beings and thus humanity is, to some extent, responsible for the actions of their "artificial progeny." That relationship is easy enough to ignore in the midst of ongoing battles between weapons-laden spacecraft. Yet, as Moore notes, *BSG's* writers have consistently revelled in the "chance to upend a lot of expectations about what the show is," and have never provided a black and white moral or ethical scenario (quoted in Lee). For the survivors of the Cylon attacks, those shades of grey are particularly evident not when they are fighting ship-to-ship in space, but when they capture humanoid Cylons.

In "Flesh and Bone" (1.08), a humanoid Cylon is captured and President Roslin orders that the prisoner be interrogated. The Cylon in question is the same model as Leoben Conoy, whom Commander Adama killed at Ragnar Anchorage during the miniseries. Starbuck, still recovering after crashing on a planet's surface during a dogfight with a Cylon raider, is sent to question Leoben. During her interrogation, Starbuck becomes increasingly frustrated and repeatedly tells Leoben that he is "just a machine," without a soul, and that since he's not human, there are no bounds on which methods she can use to extract information. Leoben is beaten and almost drowned after being forcibly submerged in water by the guards assisting Starbuck. The torture only stops when the president arrives and intervenes, only to then have the Cylon thrown out of an airlock into space, to die. As Moore has pointed out, this episode was informed by the 2004 Abu Ghraib incident in which a number of U.S. soldiers tortured Iraqi prisoners and photographed the abuse. The photographs then found their way into the mass media, causing a public outcry. In a similar vein, the episode's writer, Toni Graphia, has argued, "If people see the Cylons as just machines, they can do anything to them. But we also wanted to explore the Cylons' claims that they do have souls. We wanted to create some doubts in Kara's mind about this guy's nature" (Bassom, *Official Companion* 76). Despite Starbuck's extreme tactics, she does start to empathize with Leoben, and tries to intervene when President Roslin orders Leoben be killed.

In her first confrontation with an embodied, humanoid Cylon, even having tortured "just a machine," Starbuck shows significant signs that this physical encounter leaves her less certain about the exact nature of Cylons, and provokes questions about the ethical implications of killing a Cylon prisoner. In his final moments, without visible irony,[1] Leoben asks Roslin to be lenient on Starbuck because she has military training, in which "they teach you to dehumanize people." Intended or otherwise, it is a stark inversion to have the technological Cylon sympathizing with Starbuck, lamenting that her experiences have led her to "dehumanize" him. In Adam's weak sense, this moment is fairly blunt comment on military training and lifestyle, a culture that can lead to the violations at Abu Ghraib or the continued internment of those named enemy combatants at Guantanamo Bay.[2] In the strong sense, Leoben's human characteristics and subjectivity have a similar impact to Donna Haraway's sense of cyborgs, in which she argues that the ongoing physical and ontological interweaving of human beings and technology make the boundaries between the two blurred and porous (149–81). That uncertainty is reinforced by a final secret whispered by Leoben to President Roslin: "Adama is a Cylon." It is a secret the president spends a considerable amount of time exploring in the following episode ("Tigh Me Up, Tigh Me Down" 1.09). Ultimately, though, the clearest expression that physically confronting the Cylons has left Starbuck uncertain about their moral "human" rights (for lack of a better term) comes in the final scene, where Starbuck is seen praying to her gods, asking them to look after Leoben's soul. Ethical and moral questions about torturing Cylons are raised even more powerfully in Season Two, in a story arc featuring the arrival of the *Pegasus*. After the initial jubilation at the arrival of the *Pegasus*, it quickly becomes obvious that members of her crew have far less humane ideas about dealing with Cylon prisoners. It is worth noting that in the intervening episodes, one member of *Galactica*'s crew, Boomer, has been discovered to be a Cylon assassin and eventually killed, only to have another Sharon take her place. While Sharon is still confined to a prison cell, her romantic relationship with Helo and the assistance to the crew of *Galactica* position her as a sympathetic character. Thus, when the commanding officer of the *Pegasus*, Admiral Cain, instructs Baltar to examine their Cylon prisoner, he, presumably like the audience, is shocked to find another Six, clearly beaten and abused by her captors ("Pegasus" 2.10). The contrast between the tortured Six (Gina), wearing just a cloth sack, tethered to the floor, and covered in numerous dark bruises, and Baltar's virtual Six, whose appearance is consistently and explicitly the height of fashion and beauty, is vivid.

As Haraway, Adam, and others have convincingly argued, cultural understandings of technology are almost always situated in frameworks where gender has significance. Adam, for example, argues that in contemporary scientific discourses, "A gendered vision of the world is inscribed in the technology of AI [Artificial Intelligence]" (1). For the Cylon characters in *BSG*, not only do they exist within similar circuits of cultural meaning, but the dramatic impact of these meanings is amplified since the humanoid Cylons are, at the end of the day, necessarily played by human actors. Whereas Leoben's torture was informed by his masculinity, the extremely confrontational nature of Six's torture on *Pegasus* is likewise informed by gendered meaning. Within the diegesis of the series, Cally and others in the deck gang on *Galactica* are repulsed by members of the *Pegasus* crew boasting that they have taken turns raping Gina as a form of torture; despite having no love for the Cylons, Cally's reaction implies that she sympathizes with Gina through shared gender (and also implicitly, a shared sense of subjectivity, if not humanity *per se*). The reaction of Chief Tyrol and Helo is similarly informed by gendered meaning, as they run through *Galactica* immediately following this exchange, realizing that Sharon is about to also be sexually assaulted by

Pegasus' interrogator Lieutenant Thorne. This episode, with the persuasive performances by all the cast, leaves audiences in no doubt that rape of any sort of being is a horrendous act, and the threat to Sharon reifies her connection with the sympathetic crew members on *Galactica*. Furthermore, when apologizing for the attempted assault by the *Pegasus* officers, Adama refers to Sharon for the first time as "her" rather than "it." While this sequence certainly makes for uncomfortable viewing, the threat of rape and torture increases the apparent humanity of the Cylons since the protective reactions, in both viewers and characters, are informed by ideas of gender; in turn, gendered identities themselves only make sense in a diegetic manner by implying human identity for these characters as well.

In the following two episodes, Tyrol and Helo are arrested and sentenced to death after they accidentally kill Thorne while preventing him from raping Sharon. This quasi-judicial process demonstrates not just the differences in the idea of humanity between the upper echelons of *Galactica* and *Pegasus*, but also the readiness with which humans can apply the label of enemy to each other, not just the Cylons. While incarcerated on *Pegasus*, Tyrol and Helo are attacked by four members of the *Pegasus* crew, who begin to inflict their own version of torture ("Resurrection Ship, Part 2" 2.12). When this attack is eventually interrupted, Helo tries to explain that they had attacked Thorne because "He was trying to rape a prisoner," only to have this explanation shot down by Commander Fisk, who bluntly states, "You can't rape a machine." To most viewers of *BSG*, this statement seems almost ludicrous since Sharon (and Gina, for that matter) has complex characterisation behind her and, for all appearances, has as much humanity as any other character. The assaults on Sharon and Gina, ironically, put into question the humanity (in an ethical sense) of members of the *Pegasus* crew, while reinforcing the humanlike traits of the Cylons. Similarly, as a result of Helo and Tyrol's arrest, Adama comes very close to an all-out shooting war with the *Pegasus*, highlighting the fact that "the enemy" can be a transitory label, applied to other humans as readily as it is to the Cylons.

In those moments when the surviving humans and Cylons come face-to-face in the first two seasons of *BSG*, torture or abuse is not far behind. For Starbuck and the crew of *Galactica*, the moral certainties initially held are shaken by Leoben, creating questions about how easily the Cylons can be simply dismissed as machines. The two Eights—Boomer and Sharon—further complicate matters because confronting these Cylons is also about confronting lovers or confronting friends for various members of *Galactica's* crew. Leoben's claim that the military teaches you to dehumanize people proves an accurate description to apply to many officers onboard the *Pegasus* in the various scenes of rape and torture. These traumatic scenes all serve to highlight the fact that when the humans confront the mechanistic Cylons, they simultaneously tend to construct the Cylons as human, from empathy with Leoben's wish to live, to sympathy when Sharon is almost raped.

Given the military core of *BSG*, the role of abuse and torture is by no means absent in Season Three. In the opening episodes, the human resistance is sending suicide bombers against their oppressors, while the Cylons are torturing some prisoners and killing others. Similarly, both Cylon Three and Adama take their turn torturing Baltar later in the season ("A Measure of Salvation" 3.07; "Taking a Break from All Your Worries" 3.13). While not the most heart-warming comparison, these examples reinforce that human and Cylon alike are capable of great evil and great compassion; these are shared traits, not characteristics that mark two separate groups.

Reproducing Rights

One arena in which similarities between humanity and their technological descendants seems least likely is that of reproduction. Images of childbearing and birth are some of the most powerful symbols in any narrative, and this holds true in *BSG*. Indeed, the influence of technology in shaping, controlling, and sometimes usurping the reproductive abilities and rights of women is a divisive issue in contemporary society, and a trope commonly explored in science fiction (Kember 160). Margaret Atwood's *The Handmaid's Tale* famously sketches a dystopian future in which fertile women are reduced to baby-carrying commodities, and this could easily be the template for the situation Starbuck faces when she is captured by Cylons after returning to Caprica ("The Farm" 2.05). After being shot in a fire fight, Starbuck wakes in what she is told is a Resistance hospital, but which is in fact a Cylon facility. Her doctor is another humanoid Cylon who refers to himself as Simon. When treating Starbuck, Simon comments that she should "keep that reproductive system in great shape. It's your most valuable asset these days." Simon expands, explaining that since there are so few women left in the human race that can have children, the fact that Starbuck can bear offspring makes her an important commodity. Incensed, Starbuck responds, "I'm not a commodity, I'm a Viper pilot." Starbuck escapes and, while fleeing the hospital, stumbles across a room in which a dozen women are strapped to hospital beds, with masses of machinery and tubbing implanted in their bodies, connected to an array of machines. One of them, resistance fighter Sue-Shaun, is groggy and weak but wakes at Starbuck's prompting. They quickly realize that Sue-Shaun cannot be readily disconnected from the machinery, and so she begs Starbuck to kill her. She tells Starbuck that all of the women are being forcibly turned into Cylon "baby machines," and that she'd rather die; Starbuck reluctantly respects Sue-Shaun's wishes and destroys the machines, killing the women connected to them. After Starbuck is rescued, Sharon explains that these women were part of a Cylon experiment in reproducing with humans. Starbuck exclaims that what Cylons have done is unconscionable and all they have achieved is "to rape human women."

The treatment of women in "The Farm" clearly marks the Cylons as less than human, and less than humane, in that they are not just being violent, but are violating the rights of human women on a sexual and reproductive level. Starbuck's anger at the Cylons' raping these women, and Sue-Shaun's preference to die rather than be reduced to a "baby machine," reinforces the fact that these acts are worse than simply killing an enemy. The Cylons are seen to be treating human beings as less than human in forcing women to act as merely a means of reproduction. In this particular confrontation, the Cylons appear to be very different from their human foes. Their lack of humanity is gauged against the human rights that the Cylons have taken away or completely ignored. The idea of reducing people to "baby machines" against their will is thus diegetically positioned as a less-than-human act. While this episode does not at first glance leave much moral or ethical uncertainty, later events in the same season of *BSG* complicate this seemingly straightforward notion.

For the human survivors travelling in the fleet led by *Galactica*, the rights of women to control their own bodies and to have children at a time of their choosing, if at all, appears initially to be set in stone. Certainly these rights appear to have been part of Colonial law before the Cylon attack. However, when it becomes apparent that the doctor on board *Galactica* has been performing abortions, President Roslin is faced with a crisis when action is demanded by some vocal politicians. After much deliberation, the president makes a difficult decision:

Since assuming the presidency, I've made it my mission to maintain the rights and freedoms we so enjoyed prior to the attack. One of these rights has now come into direct conflict with the survival of the species, and I find myself forced to make a very difficult decision. The issue is stark. The fact is that if this civilization is to survive, we must, must repopulate this fleet. Therefore, I'm issuing an executive order. From this day forward, anyone seeking to interfere with a birth of child, whether it be the mother or a medical practitioner, shall be subject to criminal penalty. ("The Captain's Hand" 2.17)

While the president's rationale may appear justified—Baltar has calculated that the human race will soon be extinct if they do not have more babies—the end result is not that different from the decision made by the Cylons in "The Farm." While less visually compelling, the president's decision does force some women in the fleet to have children against their wills, reducing them in some ways to the status of a "baby machine." It is noteworthy, too, that in the following episode, "Downloaded" (2.18), when Sharon gives birth to Hera, her child is immediately removed and Sharon told a lie that her daughter died. This decision again rests with Roslin, who not only removes a human woman's right to control her own body in the fleet, but who also clearly does not consider a Cylon woman to have the right to raise her own child.

By the end of Season Two, the difference between the Cylons and the human fleet on the issue of reproductive rights is only a question of degree. The horror of having a "farm" of women forcibly connected to machinery in order to create babies that are human/Cylon hybrids is both visually and ethically more startling, but Roslin's decree removing a woman's right to control her own body achieves a similar end. Read with Adam's weak analytic frame, these similarities point out that the issues of a woman's right to control her own body is an issue very much alive in contemporary culture. Similarly, read with the strong analytic frame, within the narrative universe of *BSG*, the Cylons and humans appear both, at times, to regard women as reproductive systems first, and citizens second, leaving a provocative question mark hanging about the influence of technology over certain human rights. Far from marking the differences between the Cylons and humanity, the issue of reproductive rights is seen to be problematic in both cultures; in this example, confronting the Cylons is absolutely about also confronting ourselves (humanity).

The Shape of Things to Come

In *BSG*, the birth of a child with both Cylon and human parents signifies many things, but especially important is the implication that both symbolically and materially Cylons and humans could have a future together, to which both cultures can be parents, metaphorically and physically. Indeed, the coming Cylon/human child is explicitly referred to by the Cylons as "the face of the shape of things to come" ("Kobol's Last Gleaming, Part 2" 1.13). However, even before the first Cylon/human child is born—Sharon and Helo's daughter, Hera—her existence has a profound symbolic and corporeal impact. During Season Two, Roslin is dying from cancer. Having exhausted all conventional treatment, the president is almost dead when Baltar discovers that Hera's fetal blood has particular healing properties; when the president is injected with some of this blood, her cancer goes into remission ("Epiphanies" 2.13). It is later revealed that through having carried Hera, Sharon is immune to a virus that kills Cylons within days, but does not affect humans, due to the exchange of blood between mother and daughter ("A Measure of Salvation" 3.07). The meaningful connection between Cylons and humans, even if only in a physical sense, proves beneficial for both groups. Catherine Waldby calls this an "intercorporeal exchange," where bodily material is meaningfully and usefully exchanged between two people (240). The possibility for Cylons and humans to share biological material is significant since, as Waldby also points out, our "immune system marks the limits and bounds of the body" (248), and thus Cylon and human bodies both exist with very similar boundaries. Within the show's narrative, these intercorporeal connections blur the line between Cylon and human, emphasizing similarities, not differences. In a broader sense, this exchange also points to the porousness of the boundaries between different human bodies, and between humans and technology.

In particular, "Downloaded" (2.18) reveals the complexity of Cylon society by focusing on the emerging Cylon culture on Caprica. The story centers on Caprica Six and a newly resurrected Boomer, both of whom have spent considerable time among human societies, and both of whom also feel love for human men. Both are having trouble integrating into Cylon society, and have been spending time together and with a Cylon Three. After they are trapped together, Caprica Six realizes that the Three is afraid of her and Boomer, because they represent a new perspective, a perspective that challenges the moral certainty that informs most Cylons' genocidal attitude toward humanity. The Three laments that Caprica Six and Boomer have been corrupted by their time with humans, but Six quickly realizes that they are celebrities in a culture based on homogeny. The individuality of Boomer and Caprica Six highlights a Cylon society that is becoming increasingly complicated. Just as no two humans are the same, these two Cylons appear to herald a change of Cylon society, to one with many differing views. The question of how Cylons react to their individual experiences becomes even more potent in the final episode of Season Three, when four central characters on *Galactica* whom we have long known as human suddenly realize, to their complete surprise, that they are in fact Cylons. The revelation certainly confuses these newfound Cylons, but as a major battle looms, the awakened Cylon Colonel declares: "My name is Saul Tigh. I am an officer in the Colonial Fleet. Whatever else I am, what ever else that means, that's the man I want to be, and if I die today, that's the man I'll be" ("Crossroads, Part 2" 3.20). For Tigh and the other newly aware Cylons, their existence is not defined by their biological or technological origins. Rather, they are defined by their experiences and individual perspectives. Tigh's speech points out that being a person is as much, if not more, about actions rather than origins. In confronting the Cylons, Tigh and his companions suddenly find themselves looking in a mirror, which to a large extent symbolizes *BSG* in its entirety.

In Adam's weak sense, *BSG*'s clear references to the "War on Terror," to the treatment of prisoners, and to the rights of women to control their bodies, all speak loudly to issues prevalent in contemporary culture. In a strong sense, as artificial intelligence and artificial life look increasingly likely to emerge in some manner in the coming decades, the implication of *BSG* and other science fiction across various media is to experiment in thinking about how societies will react to our "artificial progeny" before humanity's children arrive. These two levels are never mutually exclusive, and both are layered into almost every moment of the series. The continual confrontations with the Cylons are also moments in which viewers must construct their own responses to the many cultural, political, and other shades of grey; or, as N. Katherine Hayles argues in *My Mother Was a Computer*, "an essential component of coming to terms with the ethical implications of intelligent machines is recognizing the mutuality of our interactions with them, the complex dynamics through which they create us even as we create them" (243).

Notes

1. On Cylon irony, see Matthew Gumpert, in this volume.

2. For more on the ethical and human rights questions raised by the U.S. prisoner camps in Guantanamo Bay, see David Rose, *Guantanamo*.

11

Hybridity's End

Matthew Gumpert

1.

Efforts to read *Battlestar Galactica* as political allegory tend to rely on binary oppositions that have become standard in the post-9/11 era.[1] Thus Alan Sepinwall: "The human heroes were set up as America; the robotic Cylons, who were created and trained by the humans . . . were stand-ins for Al Qaeda" (quoted in McLemee). *BSG*, to its credit, makes it difficult to think in terms of strict antitheses. Cultural critics such as Jean Baudrillard (8) and Paul Virilio (178) have suggested that 9/11 represents not a battle between civilizations, but civilization turning upon itself. This would explain the hysterical fear of an enemy, far from us, and different from us; hysterical, because the enemy, we would like to forget, may not be so different from us, and may already be among us. The perpetrators of 9/11, it was said, lived like us, looked like us, and could have been any one of us. *BSG* is dominated by this kind of hysteria, represented as such; there, too, the enemy is one of our own making; there, too, that enemy, imagined to be without, is repeatedly discovered to be within.

The revenge of the machine is a central fable in our popular culture. From the *Terminator* to the *Matrix*, from William Gibson's *Neuromancer* trilogy to *BSG*, the war between human beings and machines is represented as a battle of ontological essences; that is to say, a conflict between one form of being and another. This is a defensive mode of fiction: for this struggle between an "us" and a "them" is really a struggle within ourselves, projected outward. It is the struggle to understand what it means to be human. The fable of the machine helps us do that, while serving, paradoxically, as a veiled reminder that we do not know the answer. Hysteria, in psychoanalytic terms, is a forbidden fear or fantasy converted into physical symptoms, made visible on the site of the body (Freud, "Hysteria"). Thus, like any hysteria, the fable of the machine is a message pointing to the very fear it is designed to conceal, which is why it begins, typically, when the machine becomes, not too different from, but too much like us. The *Terminator* hearkens back to the moment when the machines are given sentience; at the center of Gibson's trilogy is the advent of artificial intelligence; the Cylons' war upon humanity, which marks the beginning of the series, coincides with their assumption of human form.[2]

It is because these machines are essentially human that they must be understood to be essentially alien. And so emerges a vast heterogeneous discourse of differences: the laws, legends, and prophecies, the jokes, epithets, and "facts" that, collectively, constitute knowledge, or what we know about something. *BSG* is saturated with such knowledge, which depends upon a familiar set of binary oppositions, all of which serve to define and defend the essential nature of the human. Their very pervasiveness belies their speciousness, betrays the fears and fantasies they hide. The more the show progresses, the more these oppositions come to seem inadequate, and even reversible. There are five particularly significant sets of binaries upon which the show builds:

1. Humans are free; Cylons are determined.
Hence the trope of the Cylon as computer; human emotions or decisions contrasted with Cylon "software" or "programming." Boomer, apparently following the directives of a program that has been hidden, even to herself, unexpectedly shoots Commander Adama ("Kobol's Last Gleaming, Part 2" 1.13). And yet only four episodes after Boomer shoots Adama, Cally shoots Boomer ("Resistance" 2.04), playing Jack Ruby to Boomer's Lee Harvey Oswald. Human beings seem as much the victims of forces outside themselves as Cylons. Both appear to be guided by greater powers, be it in the form of visions, hallucinations, or prophecies. Human freedom in *BSG*, in any case, is hardly absolute; much of the show thematizes the tension between secular democracy and either military law or religious dogmatism.

2. Humans are subjects; Cylons are objects.

Cylons are referred to as "things." Sharon says to Tyrol, "I'm not a person to them, I'm a thing" ("Home, Part 2" 2.07). They are also computers (Cylon death is referred to as "downloading") or, less respectfully, "toasters." Even the personal pronoun is sometimes refused, as when Adama contemptuously dismisses Sharon with the phrase, "Take *that* to the brig" ("Lay Down Your Burdens, Part 2" 2.20). Yet human beings in *BSG* can be as unfeeling as Cylons, who, in turn, appear to suffer like human beings, and earn their sympathy. Cylons even fall in love, with human beings, who, in turn, fall in love with Cylons.

3. Humans are moral beings; Cylons are amoral beings.

The "thingification" of the Cylon removes it from the realm of human feeling and justice. Boomer's love for Tyrol is termed by Roslin "software instead of an emotion" ("Home, Part 1" 2.06). Because Cylons do not possess feelings, they cannot be compassionate, nor do they deserve our compassion. Admiral Cain appears to sanction the attack upon Sharon by Lieutenant Thorne, when she asserts, "You can't rape a machine" ("Pegasus" 2.10). But that attack does elicit compassion. The relation between humans and Cylons is marked by acts of mutual kindness, as well as cruelty. Cylons wrestle with moral dilemmas, as do their human counterparts; Sharon explicitly asserts: "I have a conscience. And I know the difference between right and wrong" ("Downloaded" 2.18). Both are willing to commit egregious crimes in the name of god(s) or country. The Cylons contemplate the destruction of the human colony ("Exodus, Part 1" 3.03); four episodes later, the Colonials plot to destroy the entire Cylon race ("A Means of Salvation" 3.07). Carrying out such a plan, Helo protests, would mean "We're no better than they are."

4. Humans are original; Cylons are copies.

This is obviously true of the faceless Cylon Centurions, but even the humanoid Cylons are multiple copies of a limited number of prototypes. Apollo tells Sharon, in "Home, Part 1" (2.06), "You're all the same." Consider, however, Boomer's ontological disorientation when confronted with multiple avatars of herself ("Kobol's Last Gleaming, Part 2" 1.13). Cylon death as downloading is another symptom of this distinction, dramatized in the domestic dueling between Starbuck and Loeben, with Loeben repeatedly downloading to a new body every time Starbuck kills him ("Occupation" 3.01). But Cylons who look alike do not necessarily think alike. Cylons (like humans) appear divided in their sentiments, some seeking reconciliation with the enemy, others bent on extermination. Human differences, on the other hand, are limited by the constraints of military culture, and the unity forged through the presence of a common enemy.

5. Humans are organic; Cylons are inorganic.

Cylons are beyond the realm of life and death, more mineral than animal or vegetable. They are viewed either as abstract entities, like programs that can be downloaded from one computer to another, or as computers themselves, assemblages of wires and chips—as when Sharon inserts a computer cable into her arm in "Flight of the Phoenix" (2.09). At the same time, Cylons are clearly living, breathing biological entities. Even the virus that distinguishes Cylons from humans has the effect of blurring that distinction, not only because it renders them vulnerable, and therefore sympathetic, but because this is no computer virus, but an old-fashioned disease of the body. The central emblem of this knowledge based on binary opposition is Baltar's Cylon detector. The fact that its effectiveness is uncertain renders it, and the knowledge it stands for, problematic. Hand in hand with this dubious instrument of classification is the central fear that prompted its invention in the first place, and which renders suspect all of the oppositions listed above: the fear that one is actually a Cylon. Brother Cavil, in his capacity as Cylon messenger, tells the Colonials a truce has been declared, and that "Cylons and men will now go their separate ways" ("Lay Down Your Burdens, Part 2" 2.20). But they do not go their separate ways; on the contrary, BSG seems intent on showing us the inevitable convergence of their ways (and, indeed, the same episode ends with the occupation of New Caprica by a Cylon colonizing force).

2.

Cylons are like us; we are like Cylons. This could have been a liberating symmetry, an escape from the old notion of the self as something undivided, and distinct from other selves. That is how Donna Haraway views the advent of the cyborg. For the Cylons of BSG—even more than the Terminator, the Stepford wives, RoboCop, and the Borg, to name a few of their pop culture predecessors—are Haraway's cyborgs: hybrid beings, both human and machine, and therefore neither human nor machine, whose very ontological indeterminacy represents a challenge to the old essentialist notion of identity.

In the cyborg, Haraway asserts, the old dichotomies "between mind and body, animal and human, organism and machine" are obsolete (163); the cyborg does not seek "organic wholeness through a final appropriation of all the powers of the parts into a higher unity" (150). Long before genetic splicing and plastic surgery became commonplace, before human beings became inextricably fused to their iPods, Haraway suggests we are already "fabricated hybrids of machine and organism . . . we are cyborgs" (150). At the same time she suggests the cyborg is a fantasy for the future, an "ironic political myth" and "a creature of fiction" (149). Why did Haraway's liberating dream of the cyborg become the recurrent nightmare of popular culture?

Like Haraway, Homi Bhabha sees hybridity as an escape from the old unitary self, pitted against a unitary other. In hybridity, "we may elude the politics of polarity and emerge as the other of our selves" (38). For Bhabha, hybridity "entertains difference without an assumed or imposed hierarchy" (3–4). Such hybridity can only be achieved through struggle; it is part of the larger political struggle, Bhabha argues, between colonizer and colonized.

Many of the great tales of the revenge of the machine, from the *Terminator* to the *Matrix*, are stories of Colonial mastery, during the course of which a human resistance movement rebels against the rule of the machine. But *BSG* is more cynical than these other pop culture post-Colonial fantasies: it does not let us forget that, once upon a time, it was we humans who ruled over our machines as Colonial masters.[3] On the one side stand the Twelve Colonies of Kobol; on the other, a slave race, and, like all colonized peoples, the creation, in effect, of their masters. Thus the genocidal attack of the Cylons against the humans is also an act of revenge against Colonial rule. *BSG* perfectly illustrates the way Colonial regimes are inherently reversible. In "Lay Down Your Burdens, Part 2" (2.20), newly elected President Gaius Baltar orders the settlement of a planet called, with Colonial panache, New Caprica. But in its last few minutes the episode fast-forwards a year ahead: New Caprica is occupied by the Cylons, who call it their "colony."

When Cavil proclaims (falsely, it would appear) the end of the war between humans and Cylons, he is also speaking like a former colonized subject: "We got it into our heads," he says, "that we were children of humanity. We became what we beheld; we became you." A mistake: "We're machines, we should be true to that" ("Lay Down Your Burdens, Part 2" 2.20). Mimicry, for Bhabha, is the master principle in the formation of identity in the Colonial subject. The Cylons, like all such subjects, are dominated by "the desire to emerge as 'authentic' through mimicry" (88); they are "mimic men" (87), men like the colonized peoples of the British Empire who are "Anglicized" but not "English." But the desire to become what one imitates, as Cavil suggests, is doomed to fail; the mimic is never fully present, but a "part-object" (91), a "partial representation" (86). Between the always incomplete copy and the original, there is an essential difference, "a difference that is almost nothing but not quite" (91). Cylons, in just this sense, are always almost but not quite human. Certain scenes in *BSG* stand out as emblems of this post-Colonial take on *différance* (Jacques Derrida's term for the way meaning is always fated to be divided from, or catching up to itself): in "Epiphanies" (2.13), for example, Baltar, attempting to explain the healing properties of Hera's fetal blood, presents the molecular composition of human and Cylon blood as nearly identical, overlapping structures; between them a difference "almost nothing but not quite."

The mimicry of the Colonial subject is always viewed as mockery, or menace: a "part-object" like the Cylon is an attack upon our notion of identity. We gaze upon what we have created, and see something almost like ourselves, but not quite, gazing back at us. Thus the Colonial master "is threatened by the displacing gaze of its disciplinary double" (86). This would help to explain the motif of the scanning red eye as Cylon symbol, associated both with Cylon Centurions and Raiders (a reference, perhaps, to the baleful red eye of the computer HAL in Kubrick's *2001: A Space Odyssey*).

Mimicry, for Bhabha, "conceals no presence or identity behind its mask: it is not what Aimé Césaire describes as 'colonization-thingification' behind which there stands the essence of the *présence Africaine*" (88). It would be reassuring indeed if the Cylons were truly alien objects inhabited by some *présence Cylonienne*, absolutely distinct from the human. The Cylons are like us, but not quite; like us, in part, but which part? The *Cylon-in-itself* cannot be located anywhere. In this sense the Cylon is Gayatri Spivak's "colonized subaltern subject," who is always "irretrievably heterogeneous" (26). A resemblance that "hides no essence, no 'itself'" is, Bhabha argues, "the most terrifying thing to behold" (90), for it forces us to admit that *we* may have no essence, that the *human-in-itself* cannot be located. As Trinh T. Minh-ha puts it, "If you can't locate the other, how are you to locate yourself?" (217)

We first meet Brother Cavil as counselor to Tyrol, who harbors the secret fear that he is a Cylon ("Lay Down Your Burdens, Part 1" 2.19). "Oh, I'm a Cylon, too," says Brother Cavil, disguising the truth by parading it. What is clear, Cavil tells Tyrol, is that "you don't know your essential nature as a human being." When Tyrol discovers, in "Crossroads, Part 2" (3.20), that he is a Cylon, we can see that Cavil is right. But does he know that? It is far from clear, in any case, what Cavil's essential nature is; he proves an elusive and inscrutable interlocutor.

Can a machine be true to itself? This is another way of asking Spivak's question: "Can the subaltern speak?" (25). Both questions (naively) assume the presence of a self, or one self, to which one could be true, and give a voice. But as "mimic men," the Cylons are always elusive; it is impossible to say when they are being "true to themselves." Humans in *BSG* tend to be naive, straight-talking folk; their Cylon counterparts are more the ironic sort. Cavil's message to his human captors—the war is over—is delivered tongue-in-cheek, as if he himself does not believe what he has (perhaps) been programmed to say. The mimicry of the Colonial subject represents, for Bhabha, an "ironic compromise" between two languages competing within the Colonial sphere: one adopting the "synchronic, panoptical vision of domination," the other embracing the "diachrony of history" or "change" (85–86). It is the ever-ironic Cylons who are the advocates and the agents of change. Haraway's cyborg, too, makes irony its instrument of change (180).

Irony is inherently subversive. As a form of irony, mimicry is a threat to power, and the entire system of "knowledge," which underpins it. In response, power is intensified, and knowledge reinforced. Thus the very indeterminacy of the colonized subject works to perpetuate the Colonial regime: "The success of colonial appropriation," Bhabha writes, "depends on a proliferation of inappropriate objects" (86), which are neither sufficiently like nor unlike their models. Mimicry "coheres the dominant strategic function of colonial power, intensifies surveillance, and poses an immanent threat to both 'normalized' knowledges and disciplinary powers" (86). Hence the expansion of surveillance, and the normalization of knowledge: "The repetition of guilt, justification, pseudo-scientific theories, superstition, spurious authorities, and classifications [all visible in *BSG*] can be seen as the desperate effort to 'normalize' formally the disturbance of a discourse" (91)—the authoritarian discourse of Colonial rule. The results are all too clear in *BSG*: the hardening of polarities, the institutionalization of hatred, the formation of a "science" of the Cylons (evident in speculations on the nature of Cylon life, analyses of Cylon blood, and debates on the existence of Cylon consciousness), and in the proliferation of epithets, slurs, fears, and fantasies (the last two visible in the interspecial romances, rapes, and hallucinations that are a regular feature of the series). The Cylon, let us not forget, is also an "inappropriate object" of desire, or what we might call a fetish (Freud, "Fetishism"). One example may suffice: despite Cain's assertion, following Thorne's attack on Sharon, that "You can't rape a machine" ("Pegasus" 2.10), he certainly looked like he was raping something; one can only surmise that what Thorne was raping was, for him, not just a machine.

Perhaps the most obvious symptom of the existential crisis provoked by the Cylon is the fear that one is a Cylon (fear of being outed, either to others or to oneself). This fear is attached to many of the major characters in the series, some of whom turn out to actually be Cylons. (Hence Tyrol's doubts, which prove well-founded, and Baltar's, which remain unconfirmed.) Behind that fear there is a deeper one: the fear, springing from what Bhabha calls the "classificatory confusion" of mimesis, that one is neither Cylon nor human, because these very classifications are meaningless; and that there is, therefore, no difference between humans and Cylons. Closely connected with this fear is the so-called Cylon detector, *BSG*'s most explicit emblem of Colonial surveillance and science, or what Trinh T. Minh-ha calls "classificatory power" (216). But its most significant feature, one that is perhaps inevitable, given the fact that Colonial regimes depend on the continuing presence (or "partial" presence) of "inappropriate objects"—objects too close to, and yet not close enough to, their models—is that it is never entirely clear if it works. Thus the Cylon detector becomes a device for sowing classificatory confusion, instead of solving it.[4] By means of this instrument that vicious circle is perpetuated, without which no Colonial system can survive: paranoia demanding more surveillance; more surveillance producing still more paranoia.

3.

Must hybridity always be a failed proposition, a mimetic charade? With the birth of Hera, the half-human, half-Cylon baby, we appear to be confronted, not with "partial representation," but true hybridity and, consequently, complete classificatory confusion or clarity. In this creature, both human and Cylon (Cyman? Hulon?), there would be neither human nor Cylon, for the very difference between these classes would be erased.

That we are still in the realm of the hysterical is indicated by the Colonial reaction to the birth, which is viewed either as a transcendent miracle, or an apocalyptic catastrophe,[5] and by the increasingly significant role it plays in the first three seasons of *BSG* (and, we are to assume, in the coming fourth). In the panic that arises from the specter of this hybridity, the Colonials cling desperately to the old polarities, and the logic of the part-object: in "Epiphanies" (2.13), Roslin and Adama, advising the destruction of the fetus, refer to it as a "machine," or a "thing," while Baltar reminds them that this "thing" is "half-human," adding, "I suggest we keep that half in mind." That Baltar has his own hidden agenda does not detract from the force of his argument.

Bhabha imagines a form of being based upon difference without hierarchy (3–4). Haraway dreams of a world "in which people are not afraid of their joint kinship with animals and machines, not afraid of permanently partial identities" (154). Such utopian fantasies belong, one would think, in the realm of science fiction. But the futurism of science fiction is often a form of veiled nostalgia; and *BSG*, by seeming to go further than Haraway and Bhabha, in fact retreats, and assumes a defensive posture. The cyborg revolution becomes genocidal terror. Under siege, the old self—as something essential, undivided, and distinct from other selves—must be defended at all costs. *BSG* does this, paradoxically, by imagining a world without distinct and disparate selves, a world that will have transcended categories and types.

Hybridity, for both Haraway and Bhabha, is not an identity without essence but with multiple essences, identities that must be kept intact and distinct. But *BSG* indulges us in the fantasy, or the nightmare, of true hybridity, as the specter of the human-Cylon baby suggests that such perfect hybridity is self-canceling. The true hybrid, were it to exist, would erase itself at the moment of its coming into being; for in it those distinct essences, once separate but equal, would merge. That multipolar, collective self dreamed of by Haraway and Bhabha would collapse upon itself, become whole again, and one. Hybridity must therefore be lost at the moment it is gained, and return, in its very triumph, to a state of pure, undivided essence. The cyborg, Haraway insists, "is not innocent; it was not born in a garden: it does not seek unitary identity" (180). But that is precisely what is imagined in the birth of the hybrid Hera. True hybridity is a fantasy of wholeness retrieved: the return to an Edenic world where there are no distinct identities at war with each other, but only undivided of Identity itself.

This monolithic Identity is something both desired and feared in *BSG*, for it means the end of human identity as we know it, one that had always been sustained through a struggle against an antithetical Other. It is located, consequently, either in an irretrievable past or a utopian future. This nostalgic futurism, typical of so much science fiction, suggests the "splitting of discourse" that Bhabha sees as characteristic of Colonial regimes (91). Such regimes are schizophrenic cultures, both forward- and backward-looking.[6] Cylons and humans would appear to articulate these contradictory perspectives, the desire for and fear of a world without identities, or one Identity (whether it is desired or feared depends, of course, on whether it is viewed as Cylon or human). There are Cylons and humans who speak, optimistically, of a hybrid future; others, on both sides, panic at the prospect of losing the old parochial identities, and seem wedded to the past.

Hybridity in *BSG* is an anticipatory proposition: something that is going to happen, sometime, in the future. Even after her birth, Hera remains a mysterious figure, the implications of her hybridity yet to be realized. It may be that hybridity, as a fantasy of categories converging, is inherently anticipatory. It may also be that anticipation is a convenient strategy for any television series that wants to keep its viewers watching.[7] More to the point, deferral conveniently keeps true hybridity always one step away. It explains the general apocalyptic mood of the series, which is dominated, on both sides, by messianic visions, prophecies, and mythologies of predestination. Roslin believes she is an instrument of destiny, but so does Baltar's virtual Six. Consider this exchange:

> Baltar: Who are you?
> Six: I'm an angel of God sent here to protect you, to guide you.
> Baltar: To what end?
> Six: The end of the human race. ("Home, Part 2" 2.07)

In this prophetic utterance, the arrival of Hera would seem to presage either the destruction of the human race, or the fulfillment of its true purpose.[8] If we return to the notion of hybridity as both classificatory confusion and clarity, we can see that these two readings coincide, for Hera would indeed represent the end of the human race, just as much as she would of the Cylon race. True hybridity signifies the end of race itself: either the obsolescence of classes, types, and species, or their return as pure and unadulterated categories.[9]

And yet the spectre of a miraculous child whose coming will usher in a new era is a figure from our past, not our future: a sign of the pervasive nostalgia underlying the apocalyptic futurism of *BSG*. The central motif of this series, after all, appearing as a subtitle before each episode, is "The Search for Earth." It is the story of a race of exiles, trying to find their way back home. The fantasy of a utopian hybridity to come may really be nostalgia for a paradisiacal hybridity lost.[10]

This nostalgia is most obvious on the religious plane. The Colonials are a strangely archaic tribe, a "chosen people" driven by messianic visions hearkening back to the Jews, or perhaps the Mormons,[11] and steeped in the polytheism of ancient Greece and Rome (hence the Arrow of Apollo, the Tomb of Athena, and the Eye of Jupiter). The Cylons, on the other hand, are either skeptics or monotheists: more flexible, more modern, we might say, in their religious convictions. Cavil asserts, "There is no God" ("Lay Down Your Burdens, Part 2" 2.20), and mocks the Colonials' faith as primitive superstition. It is true that the Cylons are also prone to the messianic impulse. But the Cylons appear as messianic beings in their own right, next to their human counterparts. The death of a Cylon may be compared to the downloading of a computer program, but it also depicted in religious terms (hence the name given to the resurrection ships where Cylons are reborn in new bodies). Human life, in comparison, looks rather mechanistic, tied, as it is, to a particular body, a material frame whose destruction means death. Hence the juxtaposition of the old-fashioned birth of baby Hera with the epiphanic awakenings of resurrected Cylons ("Downloaded" 2.18).

On the technological level, of course, the Cylons are a superior race. It is the fact that the *Galactica* is itself a museum piece, about to be decommissioned, that renders it immune from the cyber-war that crushes the human race. But it also serves as a fitting symbol of the human dependency on old-fashioned force. Human beings believe in their machines. "We don't worship false idols," says Sharon ("Home, Part 2" 2.07). But the humans do, for that is exactly what the Cylons are: not just fetishes but idols, objects worshipped and feared by those who created them.

From the Cylon perspective, the ultimate nostalgia is to be found in the humans' stubborn adherence to the old ontological antinomies, in their persistent faith in classification itself—in types, classes, and categories—as a way of distinguishing one species of being from another: machines, gods, and human beings. To continue to believe in human beings is nostalgic, though it is equally nostalgic, of course, to believe in Cylons. It is the humans (most of them, anyway) who cling, understandably, to this notion: the Cylons (or at least some of them) appear to have surpassed it.

Notes

1. Executive Producer Ronald D. Moore has discussed the show's "political allegories" (see Aurthur). For discussions on *BSG* from a political perspective, see "Galactica Politica."

2. This form is a truth kept carefully guarded during the early days of the war; in "Litmus" (1.06) the great secret, that "Cylons now look like humans," is revealed, and met with considerable alarm.

3. The 2004 film, *I, Robot* (based on the 1950 collection of short stories by Isaac Asimov) shares this post-Colonial perspective.

4. Sowing "classificatory confusion" is the point of exercises like the "Battlestar Galactica Quiz" for March 21, 2007, on the Scifi.com "Battlestar Galactica" website, which asks: "Can you tell a Colonial citizen from a Cylon? Take our two new trivia quizzes and find out!" ("Battlestar Galactica"). Such questions rely on the distinction between two types of being; that these questions need to be asked, repeatedly, indicates the difficulty in maintaining that distinction.

5. On the one hand, fetal blood extracted from Sharon's womb puts President Roslin's cancer into remission ("Epiphanies" 2.13); on the other hand, Hera is regarded as a potential Cylon weapon. The ambivalence here, essential to all hybridity, is captured in close-ups of Athena's belly accompanied by foreboding music: this is an event pregnant with meaning.

6. Even on a stylistic level, *BSG* is a hybrid entity, a futuristic series that looks old-fashioned, borrowing from earlier science-fiction television series, including its own original 1978 avatar.

7. *BSG*, Moore insists, cannot go on forever: it has "a beginning, middle and end. Our main title every week says 'A Search for Earth,' and at some point you gotta find earth, or it becomes 'Gilligan's Island'" (quoted in Miller "Man").

8. Hera and Earth are increasingly linked as twinned elements of humanity's predestined end. See "Maelstrom" (3.17), "Crossroads, Part 1" (3.19), and "Crossroads, Part 2" (3.20).

9. The miraculous/apocalyptic birth that spells the end of one era and the beginning of another is a central motif in the cybernetic fantasies of popular culture. Many of the fables of the machine cited earlier, as well as other fantasies of hybridity such as *The X-Files*, *The 4400*, and *Heroes*, prophesy the coming of a messianic liberator who will

bring Armageddon (between humans and machines, or humans and aliens, or humans and genetically modified humans) to its predestined end.

10. That this is a nostalgic fantasy is suggested in Freud's description of what his friend calls an "oceanic feeling" at the beginning of *Civilization and Its Discontents*, the "feeling of an indissoluble bond, of being one with the external world as a whole" (11–12). Freud regards this feeling as a manifestation of the desire to return to that stage of infancy prior to the formation of the ego, when a line had yet to be drawn between us and the world.

11. See Michael Lorenzen: "The lost Tribe of Israel is central to *The Book of Mormon* in the same way that the lost colony of Earth is central to *Battlestar Galactica*."

12

Erasing Difference:
The Cylons as Racial Other

Christopher Deis

Battlestar Galactica is deeply concerned with questions of difference and the Other. Central characters from the original 1978 series, for example, have been replaced with actors of different gender and racial backgrounds in the newly imagined *BSG*. The recasting of roles like Admiral Adama (Edward James Olmos) and Boomer (Grace Park), combined with the creation of such characters as bridge officers Dualla and Gaeta, and President Roslin's assistant Tory, highlight creator Ronald D. Moore's commitment to creating a diverse cast for his space melodrama—a significant move given that while science fiction as a genre has nobly grappled with questions of diversity and difference, it has also been consistently critiqued for a lack of racial diversity.[1]

An examination of *BSG*'s individual episodes, as well as its overall story arc, reveals a willingness by the writers and executive producers to place questions of difference and of the Other as central to the epic storyline. In episodes such as "The Occupation" (3.01), "Precipice" (3.02), and "Collaborators" (3.05), the human protagonists are forced to use means that evoke current debates regarding America's "War on Terror" and the Iraq insurgency. Here the audience, presumably of the First World, finds itself made the Other by proxy (through what can be described as a type of forced empathy) when it is made to confront difficult questions regarding violence, resistance, justice, and freedom. Episodes like "The Woman King" (3.14) and "Dirty Hands" (3.16) grapple with questions of difference by centering episodes on such dilemmas as class inequality, cultural intolerance, xenophobia, and religious conflict.

Looking more broadly, *BSG*'s narrative—while superficially driven by a conflict of species difference between the Cylons and humans (artificial intelligence and synthetic life vs. human sentience and biological life)—can also be interpreted as one of conflict between monotheism and polytheism. The Cylons are seeking to understand humanity and the human soul, but are also simultaneously involved in a jihad against nonbelievers who neither understand, nor worship, the one ostensibly true God. Religious difference is a meaningful marker that drives the narrative.

BSG privileges differences of species, religion, class, and culture as essential for creating the dramatic situations that the show works to resolve internally. However, a deep internal tension exists in *BSG*'s narrative and in its treatment of these themes. While the show is anchored in many ways by encounters with and considerations of the Other, *BSG* does not overtly engage questions of racial difference among the human survivors. This is significant because race has historically worked to order societies, structure power relationships, and to determine which groups have access to resources and privilege. This omission is especially problematic given how deftly *BSG* has introduced and considered other questions of difference throughout its narrative.

Anticipating this chapter's conclusion, I advance three claims. First, I suggest that although racial difference and questions of the racialized Other are not overt categories of meaningful social difference between and among the human characters, *BSG* is driven forward by a conception of racial difference where the Cylons are a carefully constructed Other, and where the threat of genocide works to erase categories of difference among and between the human survivors. Second, I suggest that though superficially race is not a meaningful category among the human characters, it nevertheless does important work in *BSG* because the Cylon threat can be interpreted as embodying deep and long-held fears by white societies regarding miscegenation and racial passing. Third, I demonstrate the impact of the omission of an overt consideration of these questions on *BSG*'s overall plot and narrative.[2]

The first section of this chapter introduces questions of disaster and how cataclysmic events make more visible the social consequences of racial hierarchies. This section works to situate this claim within our understandings of science fiction and *BSG*. The second section considers how *BSG*'s paranoia surrounding Cylon infiltration (and its emphasis on Sharon's half-human, half-Cylon child) demonstrates the ways in which racial difference and racial passing are central to the narrative. Proceeding from this foundation, I consider the ways that the black body still symbolizes the Other. The external Cylon threat erases race and racial difference among the human protagonists, but a fear of the black male body in particular still works to create unity among the "raceless" crew.

Humanity in the Face of the Cylon Apocalypse

Humanity's responses to apocalyptic disasters, both human made and natural in origin, are standard tropes in science fiction and space fantasy. Disasters are a common motif because they allow a blank slate for the creative work and social commentary that lies at the heart of the best of science fiction. By placing humanity in a perilous situation, the disaster motif creates a laboratory rich with possibilities for exploring human nature. In *BSG*, this storytelling convention has allowed the show to ask difficult questions regarding such topics as the nature of justice, the limits of human rights, the right to abortion, the freedom of the press, and the difficulty of maintaining a democracy during wartime.

It is helpful to begin by asking a simple question: who survived the Cylons' genocidal attacks and why? The Cylon attack was swift, brutal, and without advance warning. While "Hero" (3.08) revisited a period prior to the *BSG* television series in order to reveal the military's fear of a (then) future Cylon attack, and Baltar's virtual Six hints that the surprise attack was long planned and inevitable, there was little, if any, advance warning provided to the humans. Survival in this instance was as much the result of happenstance as of preparation and intentionality. *BSG* provides a number of examples of the arbitrariness of survival at the moment of apocalypse. Helo and Sharon conduct a lottery among the human refugees in order to determine who they will transport to safety and who will be abandoned (presumably) to the Cylons (M.02)—ironically, this is also the moment where Baltar is spared the randomness of the lottery because of Helo's belief that Baltar's intellectual gifts could later help save humanity. In "Pegasus" (2.10), we discover that in contrast to the humanitarian approach taken by Adama, Admiral Cain, the commander of the *Pegasus*, abandoned large numbers of civilian ships, stripping them of supplies and drafting useful members of their crews because she considered a humanitarian mission as secondary to her military responsibilities. Such examples aside, though, given *BSG*'s dramatic and narrative complexities, an appeal to the randomness of survival is too simple and convenient a single explanation.

There are several clear hints that the Twelve Colonies were not utopias, but rather were individual worlds with "real world" problems of inequality and injustice. In "The Woman King" (3.14), with its emphasis on discrimination against the Sagittarons because of their rejection of modern medicine and science, there are suggestions that prejudice among certain ethnic or religious groups, and by extension for other groups, still exists. In "Black Market" (2.14), we glimpse the underground economy and the exploitive practices that drive and sustain it, as the criminal element has transplanted itself from the Colonies and into the fleet. In "Dirty Hands" (3.16), the viewers are exposed to the class inequality that oppresses the fleet's underclass of service workers. As noted by Moore during his commentary for the episode "Bastille Day" (1.03), one of the Colonies maintains an Apartheid-like racial caste system.[3] The leadership among the surviving humans does appear to possess a willingness to confront these problems as they act as trustees for the new human society, but the fact that these problems exist reveals a world in which human nature is not essentially unlike that of our present.

If we grant that there are class disparities in *BSG*'s universe which predate the attack, questions of inequality and opportunity still affect one's ability to escape, and how communities would decide who has value, and who is expendable and can therefore be safely discarded to their inevitable deaths (or enslavement), at the hands of the Cylon invaders. In our present, the contemporary American experience with disaster and near-apocalypse (for the victims) during Hurricane Katrina was a powerful reminder of how racial, social, and class inequality can impact one's chance for survival.[4] By extension, I propose that audience perceptions of the role that race and racial difference play in science fiction is influenced by their consideration of the way that disaster ostensibly works to remake society in both the short term and the long term, as well as how race maps onto systems of inequality. In a function of late twentieth-century liberal democratic, colorblind politics, the short-term narrative of humanity in the aftermath of disaster is one where racial differences will be superseded by the common good. The appeal of this line of reasoning and the differences that structured the world may be made less relevant in the moment of disaster: however, in the long term, the very inequality that typified a given society at rest will nonetheless be present at the moment of a society's reimagination, as it seeks the familiar in its efforts to reestablish and reinvent itself once the crisis has passed. In short, to the degree a society is structured by the existence and persistence of racial ideologies, it will retain, and perhaps return to, that familiar structure at its reformation.

There are a number of objections, of course, that can be made to the parallel of human disaster in the present with the Cylon apocalypse depicted by *BSG*, most prominently that the cases are somehow fundamentally different, or that one cannot make claims that race and racial difference are operative in *BSG* when there have been no explicit references to race as having social resonance for this new, human society. While not directly refuting these objections, I believe that they provide a useful entry point for a return to the question of science-fiction genre and the disaster motif because these objections point to the ways in which race is often deployed in science-fiction disaster films, as well as how some audiences can imagine race as no longer salient in a world that must be remade following disaster.

Racial Erasure and the Mulatto Cyborg

I also argue that audiences have difficulty with critically interrogating science fiction because race is in many ways erased from science fiction. In this genre, racial intolerance and humanity's triumph over racial prejudice are used as thematic devices, but the existence of fully realized, racially Othered characters is relatively uncommon. As Gregory E. Rutledge argues, one of the comforts of the imagined future is that the inconveniences created by such problems as racism and prejudice have been eliminated, with the category of Other transplanted onto aliens, cyborgs, or robots (238, 239).[5] In science fiction, these problems are often erased by an appeal to human progress (as in *Star Trek*) where humankind has outgrown such ostensibly petty differences, but in other instances, racism and racial inequality are corrected by removing people of color from the narrative. On this point, Sandra Y. Govan notes:

> Science fiction implies that the knots of terrestrial racism will eventually loosen because Terrans will have to unite against aliens, androids, or BEMs [Bug-Eyed Monsters] of the galaxy. Under these circumstances, humans become remarkable for their humanity, not their ethnicity. (44)

Although the imaginative intent behind the raceless future is benign, it could well give rise to a white future that reinscribes existing racial divisions (Rutledge 239). If, as W. E. B. DuBois famously observed, "the problem of the Twentieth Century is the problem of the color line" (xxxi), the problem of race has often been solved in the fictional future by eliminating people of color from the narrative frame. The deployment of white privilege, where the fact of race is a mere inconvenience that does not negatively affect life chances for the ingroup, has left majority audiences poorly equipped to see how race is coded in science-fiction entertainment.

The erasing of race as a meaningful category, and the work done by racial difference in science-fiction television and film (either through its presence or omission) is deftly addressed by Despina Kakoudaki. She argues that, in the disaster/apocalyptic motif, racial differences in society are massaged away by pairing together of characters from different racial backgrounds as a heroic duo. The storytelling convention allows the viewer to see a united human front against disaster, alien invasion, or war, as the typically interracial protagonists fight an enemy determined to destroy humanity. This union of the racially different, in the face of a visibly different Other, removes the lived day-to-day complexities of race in a multiracial society and allows the audience to escape to a more nostalgic and "simple" sociopolitical reference point (Kakoudaki 118, 124, 128, 143). This claim is especially resonant for *BSG*.

The war between the Cylons and the human survivors moves the plot forward, frames the narrative, and bounds the storytelling possibilities of *BSG*. The Cylon threat is part of a long science-fiction tradition of looking to the Other as a symbolic device through which to explore questions of tolerance, diversity, and inclusion. Race is coded for and read into *BSG* because the Cylons are powerfully evocative of the anxieties, paranoia, and fear regarding the racial Other, and in particular, the need to maintain "purity" among those currently identified as authentic humans. This narrative maps neatly onto what Randall Kennedy's *Interracial Intimacies* has documented to be an almost obsessive fear of miscegenation by white Americans, a fear that has been historically enforced by laws against interracial marriage and violence against those who violated those laws and social conventions. Leilani Nishime describes how the human-appearing robot is both an allegory for dilemmas surrounding racial inequality, as well as a proxy for racial passing. Nishime's argument for the ubiquity of the racial-passing narrative in science fiction

(34–36, 39) is a powerful analytic device for reading race back into *BSG*, and is especially valuable for our considerations of the Cylons' role in the series. On a practical level, *BSG* is driven by a need to protect human civilization from the Cylons. Security, safety, and the need to develop tools to protect human society from this genocidal threat dominate the narrative and figure prominently in the series.

"Water" (1.02) and "Bastille Day" (1.03) detail Baltar's attempts to create a machine that can be used to discover Cylon infiltrators among the surviving humans. In these episodes, a "Cylon detector" is constructed by the traitorous Baltar in order to preserve his value to Admiral Adama and President Roslin. This machine initially appears capable of distinguishing Cylons from human beings. However, as the machine is used, questions arise about its reliability, which is made more suspect and problematic given that any supposed truth it determines is subject to Baltar's often skewed and self-serving interpretations ("Resistance" 2.04). The device gives the appearance of security and safety from an outside threat—but not coincidentally, the nuclear weapon that Baltar demands as a key component of the Cylon detector comes to figure prominently in the near destruction of the human fleet and in guiding the Cylons to New Caprica.

Baltar's device speaks to a deeper truth in our efforts to read race critically in *BSG*, and to map onto the Cylon Other the work that race does in *BSG*'s human society. Baltar, ostensibly one of the smartest surviving humans in the fleet, is the only person equipped to recognize the Cylons with this device. Baltar's machine is a neat solution to an untidy problem because other humans have to rely on cruder measures, such as torture, to elicit unreliable confessions from suspected Cylons. In keeping with the suggestion that *BSG* is centrally driven by the Cylons' efforts at racial passing, the use of Baltar's Cylon detector to determine "racial identity" is a clear allusion to the pseudosciences of phrenology, race science, and eugenics that were central in the West's race-making projects.[6] Like the practitioners of race science, the ability to detect a "passing" Cylon is an arcane art exclusive to trained and learned "intellectuals."[7]

The dual themes of miscegenation and racial passing are also made manifest by the erotic appeal of the Other and of sex, consensual or otherwise, across the metaphorical color line dividing humans and Cylons. Baltar's relationship with the Cylon Six is one of several human-Cylon relationships among the human survivors. Although Boomer/Sharon's status as a Cylon is unknown at the beginning of their relationships, both Tyrol and Helo have been involved with different versions of the Eight (and continued to love her once her Cylon identity is revealed), with Helo having fathered a Cylon-human child. The first episodes of Season Three partnered Starbuck narratively, though not romantically, with the Cylon Leoben, in his effort to understand the nature of love. Additionally, the Cylon Cavil sexually exploits Colonel Tigh's wife, Ellen, to gain an understanding of human pleasure and sexuality in "Occupation" (3.01).

These pairings work for the melodrama by being central to the plot advancement of the series and by sharing a common theme of the taboo's appeal in violating norms of purity and separation that govern boundaries surrounding miscegenation and interracial relationships. These relationships risk sanction by the humans (and often the Cylons) if the true nature of the pairings is discovered, and evoke a sense that these relationships are somehow wrong or unsettling from the viewer's perspective. This idea is especially resonant in "Crossroads, Part 2" (3.20) during which several key characters discover that they too are apparently Cylons. In a range of emotions, from denial to acceptance to anger, these trusted, responsible, and empathetic characters have now discovered that they are the Other and represent a new face of what was a familiar enemy. These characters have been outed; the audience's expectations and understanding of the Cylon Other have been disrupted; and the characters themselves have to incorporate these new identities into their psyches (or not).

Historically, prohibitions against interracial relationships were part of a larger regime of power and social control. White men in the antebellum American South had free access to the bodies of black slaves, while conversely a fear that black men would seek out white women would help to legitimate Jim Crow and its racial regime. However, as Grace Elizabeth Hale has noted, in these same racially ordered societies, disgust and fear of black and brown bodies coexisted with a deep fascination regarding the bodies of the racial Other (199–239). *BSG*, in its theoretically raceless depiction of humanity, has appropriated this dual tendency of fascination and revulsion to the mixed-race body. For example, "Downloaded" (2.18) highlights the human leadership's fear of a human-Cylon child (Hera) and their worry about the broader consequences of her existence. The Cylons in "Exodus Part 1" (3.03), "The Farm" (2.05), and "Litmus" (1.06) reveal their deep fascination with the idea of biological reproduction; they see the creation of a human-Cylon hybrid as the key to their process of self-discovery and improvement as a species. Moreover, Hera, a mulatto, and the product of an "interracial" relationship, is imbued with fetishistic attributes. In examples ranging from metaphysical (Hera has appeared in visions and dreams of the central characters), to the almost magical (her blood has temporarily healed President Roslin's terminal cancer), Hera is symbolically portrayed as a child of destiny and a key to resolving the human and Cylon conflict.

(Not) Erasing Race: The Black Male Body

Any consideration of the questions of race, difference, and the Other would be incomplete without an attempt to interpret the more overt and racially evocative moments that have been present in the *BSG* narrative. The explicitly racialized bodies of black male characters in *BSG* have been provocatively depicted, and a duality exists in the show's consideration of race and racial difference, where race is "erased" in the series, yet black male characters are often depicted in a fashion that is stereotypical and essentialized.

By the end of Season Three, three black male characters have been featured prominently in either *BSG*'s overall story arc or in an individual episode: Phelan, a criminal overlord ("Black Market" 2.14); Simon, a Cylon who symbolically rapes a central character ("The Farm" 2.05); and Bulldog, a potential human traitor and Cylon infiltrator who harbors a "dark" secret about Admiral Adama's past ("Hero" 3.08). Problematically, there are no counterbalancing characters or images of black men in *BSG*, and the one recurring black female character, Dualla,[8] is a supporting character in the overall story. While conceding that Bill Duke's character Phelan adds richness to the *BSG* universe, the character merely fulfills the tired trope of the black male in popular culture as criminal, pimp, or hustler. Bulldog and Simon are more compelling objects of study, because, while certainly not progressive in their depiction of black men, they speak in a particularly lucid fashion to the overall work that race does in *BSG*.

The black male occupies a particularly perilous location in a white racial imagination, one that is focused on a fear of racial mixing and racial passing, because this psychological and historical framework is simultaneously both fascinated by the mythology surrounding black male sexuality and afraid of what it perceives to be the almost bestial, black male body (Maclean 141–48; Van DeBurg 148–49). "The Farm" (2.05) offers a clear portrayal of this dynamic. Simon conducts medical experiments on Starbuck's reproductive system with the apparent goal of extracting ova and breeding Starbuck with the Cylons. In a very personal and compelling performance, Starbuck, the white, blonde heroine is paired with Simon in a series of interactions where she is tied down, semi-nude in a hospital gown, experimented upon, and violated by the tall, handsome, powerful, black, male Cylon. And adding to the racially provocative coding of this episode, it is during this encounter that Simon, heretofore unknown to the audience, emerges as the only black character among the Cylon models depicted so far.

While Starbuck is not penetrated by Simon sexually, she is symbolically raped, penetrated surgically in her abdomen (and, likely, also penetrated medically through vaginal examinations while unconscious). The pairing of a black woman (Starbuck's companion in the hospital, Sue-Shaun) and a white woman in a similar circumstance suggests the writers' keen awareness of the racial subtext present in the episode, and a desire to diminish its potentially offensive interpretation by audiences—an effort that makes the allusion to interracial rape more resonant, rather than less. Fueling this racially charged narrative, another model of the Cylon Simon returns in "A Measure of Salvation" (3.07), where he is one of the few surviving members of a Cylon crew infected by a virus. This Simon is captured by the humans and is shackled and bound at the wrists, arms, and neck prior to his interrogation and (presumed) torture. In keeping with the narrative of the black male rapist and the white victim, Simon has, as the metaphorical black rapist, been punished and given his "just rewards" for violating the white heroine (Bederman 46; Hale 232–35).

The racialized Other does the work of cementing societies together by erasing difference between and among members of the dominant group. As Howard Winant and others have convincingly argued, because race is a social construct that is both made and formed, certain differences are privileged and made important (skin color or phenotypical difference), and others are homogenized away, such as the "ethnic" differences between members of the ingroup (Winant 20–21).[9] The erasing of difference by an external or outside group fits neatly with the raceless society of *BSG* because the Cylon threat makes less salient the racial differences among the human crew. In "Hero" (3.08), the work done by the Cylons in making a raceless society is further reinforced by the arrival of Bulldog, a pilot and friend of Adama and Tigh who was believed lost in a covert mission prior to the second Cylon war. Bulldog is the third black male character to feature prominently in *BSG*, and he embodies a deep distrust and worry on the part of some whites in American society regarding the loyalty, civic pride, and trustworthiness of black citizens.[10] Because the racial outsider creates unity and community for society, he is by definition racially marked. It is not coincidental that the racial outsider thought to be a Cylon (a "real" outsider in the *BSG* narrative) is also one of the few black characters on the show, and by extension embodies the outsider in racially ordered societies. While most of the main characters on *BSG* have been suspected of being Cylons at one point or another, this marking of Bulldog as the Cylon Other is noteworthy because his status as a suspected Cylon involves combining subtext (that the Cylons are coded as a racial Other) with the visible text (that in the "real world" people of color are a real and visible Other). This makes Bulldog distinct, when a suspected Cylon is played by someone (the actor Carl Lumbly) who is a "real world" Other.

Bulldog heals the rift between Adama and Tigh following the Cylon occupation. He symbolizes the need to erase the divisions within human society as embodied by the animosity between those who collaborated with the Cylons, and those who chose to resist. These tensions are crystallized by the rift between the two following the difficult choices made at the end of Season Two and the beginning of Season Three ("Collaborators" 3.05, "Unfinished Business" 3.09). The arrival of Bulldog provides an opportunity to restore their friendship. When Bulldog falls under suspicion as a Manchurian-candidate figure and possible Cylon collaborator with intentions to kill Adama, the war hero confronts Adama in order to discover the degree of Adama's culpability for Bulldog's capture by the Cylons. At the episode's climax, Tigh saves the life of his estranged friend Adama. Here, the wound between the Tigh and Adama is salved and the fissures in the presumed raceless human society are symbolically healed through the cathartic experience of confronting the black hero Bulldog, possible traitor and Cylon agent. Bulldog, later found innocent, fulfills the work done by racial difference by binding together the dominant group, negating the differences among the humans, and through a cathartic process of suspicion, rejection, and acceptance. He symbolically projects the possibility of future unity for the fractured crew. In a powerful and telling moment that speaks to a return for *BSG* to its raceless status quo, Admiral Adama publicly welcomes Bulldog back into the military at the end of the episode.

Concepts of race, and the work done by racial difference, are operative in and drive forward the *BSG* narrative. While maintaining the façade of a raceless future where humanity is united against a common threat, *BSG* has transplanted difficult questions regarding inclusion, fear, and the Other onto the Cylon antagonists of the show. This tension has consequences for the narrative because a choice to move the lens away from the humans and onto the Cylon Other represents a lost opportunity for explicitly exploring human nature and human society in a time of crisis. As Jacob Clifton asserts, one of the consistently missed opportunities for *BSG* is the question of "the day to day" with which humans must grapple as they struggle to recreate a sense of normalcy in the face of disaster (147). How do we live? How do we maintain our hope? How do we negotiate our humanity? What of our civilization will be recreated and what will be corrected in this process of recreation and rebirth? In the next and apparently final season of *BSG*, a focus on these questions will, I hope, become more prominent as the human fleet nears Earth and has to confront questions of how this collection of human survivors will remake their civilization.

At the climactic ending of Season Three, Tigh, on learning he is a Cylon, states, "My name is Saul Tigh. I am an officer in the Colonial Fleet. Whatever else I am, whatever else it means, that is the man I want to be, and if I die today that is the man I will be" ("Crossroads, Part 2" 3.20). This internal struggle and commitment to who or what we may be, despite our problems and inconsistencies, is a mantra that can guide *BSG* toward a more overt exploration of race and difference, concepts that have so far remained subtly coded in *BSG*'s narrative. By erasing its ostensibly raceless society, *BSG* will mature and come closer to achieving its full and rich potential as a laboratory for exploring human nature.

Notes

1. See Elisabeth Leonard, *Into Darkness Peering*.

2. In this chapter's consideration of these questions, I apply an interpretive approach influenced by "oppositional reading" with its attendance to how race and power are coded and deployed in popular culture. See Celeste Condit, "Rhetorical Limits"; bell hooks, *Reel to Real*; Linda Steiner, "Oppositional Decoding"; and Thomas Nakayama, "Show/Down Time."

3. Moore's podcast is unclear as to what specific colony has this arrangement. Moore's reference to Tom Zarek as a "Nelson Mandela–like" figure implies that it is likely Sagittaron, a colony that, as noted by the *Battlestar Wiki*, enslaved its labor class and where Zarek had his early beginnings as a revolutionary and "freedom fighter."

4. For example, Hurricane Katrina made clear how individual survival during the event was a function of luck, of resources, and of State response. See Spike Lee's film *When the Levees Broke: A Requiem in Four Acts* (2006). Also see Chester Hartman and Gregory Squires, *No Such Thing*; Michael Dyson, *Hell or High Water*; and David Troutt, *After the Storm*.

5. See also Ziauddin Sardar and Sean Cubitt, *Aliens R Us*; and Jenny Wolmark, *Aliens and Others*.

6. See Elizabeth Ewen and Stuart Ewen, *Typecasting*; and Warwich Anderson, *Cultivation of Whiteness*.

7. For a discussion of how race was "made" during Jim Crow segregation through "commonsense" notions of racial difference, see Mark Smith, *How Race Is Made*, 66–95.

8. Eric Greene too has noted briefly the "overwhelming Whiteness of the show" (21).

9. Also see Michael Omi and Howard Winant, *Racial Formation*; Matthew Frye Jacobson, *Whiteness*; and David Roediger, *Wages of Whiteness* and *Working Toward Whiteness*.

10. This belief has been described as "modern racism" or "symbolic racism." See Lawrence Bobo, "Whites' Opposition to Busing" and Donald Kinder and Lynn Sanders, *Divided by Color*, 291–94.

III

Form and Context in Twenty-First-Century Television

13

When Balance Goes Bad:
How *Battlestar Galactica* Says
Everything and Nothing

Chris Dzialo

Battlestar Galactica's self-consciously balanced narration—while not difficult to comprehend—is sometimes maddening to interpret. For example, as a secular Democrat watching *BSG*, I often experience a state of conflicted déjà vu when I identify with and root for Laura Roslin. After all, she attempts to steal a presidential election and allows her religious views to influence much of her policy (i.e., contravening Adama by sending Starbuck to retrieve the Arrow of Apollo because of her prophecies in "Kobol's Last Gleaming, Pt. 2" 1.13) à la George W. Bush, who many argue also stole an election and who has launched wars using veiled religious rhetoric. Similarly, Cylons at times are framed as ruthless and genocidal terrorists (obliterating the Twelve Colonies in the miniseries, for starters), but when we learn that a Six has been tortured and sexually abused by the crew of the Pegasus (2.10), the sympathies of both Gaius Baltar and the viewers are very much engaged. Such configurations—in which contrasting issues from contemporary culture are mapped in split, contradictory directions—abound in the series.

The rhetorical structure of "balance" through which *BSG* often speaks insists there are two or more legitimate sides to every story, leaving something approaching satirist Stephen Colbert's "truthiness" to be constructed dialectically by the audience at home. "Balance" conflates and substitutes "neutrality" for "objectivity."[1] As discussed later in this essay, global warming as framed by the corporate news media is perhaps the most pressing example of the rising frustration with this trope. Ultimately, then, BSG might be another signifier of America's reliance on and dissatisfaction with the idea of balance—particularly with a balance that is not so much the mean between two extremes, as the mere illusion of difference between two poles that are actually quite similar in the first place (i.e., Democrats and Republicans).

How do I make such claims? How, after all, does one account for correspondences between a televisual text and the culture that gives form to and is formed by such a text, without (a) positing overly simplistic and deterministic, knee-jerk linkages between culture and text, or (b) losing oneself (pleasurably or otherwise) in a sea of contingency? Too often in academia we are caught between saying "something" but endlessly qualifying it out of existence, or saying "nothing" with conviction. My approach is to employ a framework allowing the concurrent use of several theoretical constructs from psychoanalysis and cultural studies. As a fan of BSG, I will be privileging the instances from the series that matter most to me—astute viewers will be able to find many contrary examples to support their own, perhaps contrasting, claims. Thus, and admittedly at the risk of qualifying myself out of existence or creating a "balanced" structure of my own, I'm as much writing my understanding of the series and its contexts as I am reading them.

Luckily BSG presents the perfect, slippery text for such an analysis. Straddled uncomfortably over a changing cultural zeitgeist, BSG garnered critical acclaim and high viewership during the beginning of its run, immediately following the close November 2004 presidential elections. The show's ratings, however, have gradually started to slip (along with the approval numbers of the president). As I see it, BSG's self-consciously balanced narrative resonated with a polarized body politic from 2004–2006, but at the present moment (mid-2007) seems to be struggling to enunciate a less balanced form in order to find its audience in these arguably more unified times, when a sizeable majority appears discontented with George W. Bush and the war in Iraq—at least if the stinging rebuke to the Republicans during the 2006 midterm elections is any indication.

Through looking at several different moments in the series I hope to chart the widening gap and change (and eventual disavowal) in its rhetorical structure of balance. First I'll examine how the discourse on abortion, in both the show's narrative and in one of its commercials—cleverly disguised as a pro-life PSA—taunts the viewer during Season Two with the idea of a conflation of messages as a source of pleasure. Here what might appear to be unconscious symptoms revealing societal anxieties and desires regarding abortion and technology are actually only smokescreens, and do not say anything about these issues except how we can talk about them only through a balanced rhetorical structure. In the second section, I will analyze the growing dissatisfaction (in *BSG* viewers and the body politic at large) with this structure at the beginning of Season Three, evidenced by the less ambiguous deployment of human suicide bombers and Cylon occupiers. Such plotlines seem unavoidably to draw tight, deterministic parallels with current events and prevailing attitudes, making "neutrality" impossible. Finally, I'll chart the show's attempts at the end of Season Three to crystallize and give meaning to the sense of cultural aimlessness produced by the loss of the formerly familiar and comfortable—but now inadequate—structure of balance.

Cylons on a Tightrope

During the second season of *BSG*, a perplexing commercial might have given pause to viewers as they fast-forwarded their DVRs. In this advertisement,[2] a fetus floats serenely in a womb as lilting violins play. Patricia Clarkson's voice intones: "Life. Fragile. Peaceful. And innocent. What starts as microscopic matter, one day, has the power to change [pause] everything." We are finally cued to the fact that this is not a pro-life commercial when the music turns sinister, and the iconic red Cylon pulse glows ominously along the vertebrae through the translucent fetal flesh. Metallic spines stretch mysteriously through the ether, until they finally reveal themselves to be part of the *BSG* logo—suspended in what is either amniotic fluid or the emptiness of space.

At first the urge might be to search for the symptomatic meaning here. For Sigmund Freud, the psychological symptom indicates an underlying pathology, and stands as "a sign of, and a substitute for" what one really wants but doesn't think he should have ("Inhibitions" 5). In this way the patient unconsciously manufactures the symptom, as a result of more-or-less conscious repression (9), and develops a physical manifestation (a nervous tick, for example) instead of acting out on his or her repressed desires or fears. This is similar to how Boomer, rather than committing suicide by shooting herself in the brain, instead allows the bullet to graze her cheek in "Kobol's Last Gleaming, Part 1" (1.12). She wants to live, she wants to die—but she represses these competing urges and winds up with a gash in the cheek as the sign and substitute for the conflict between her life and death drives.

If we take society to be the patient,[3] we might therefore read the *BSG* commercial as a symptom—a festering boil—of the repression of our fears (and desires) regarding reproductive technology. The dark music in the commercial, and the way in which we are reminded of narrative elements from the series—such as the Cylon baby farm, in which human women are chained to hospital beds and used in attempts to create a Cylon-human hybrid ("The Farm" 2.05)—are symptomatic of our fears over technology. Conversely, the sense of power and prestige created by the impressively rendered phallic spines of the *BSG* logo echoes our desire for more technological control over our bodies. For Freud (and Sharon), symptoms do not carry only one meaning but at least two. In *The Interpretation of Dreams*, Freud insists there are no limits to the upper number of determinants or meanings a symptom may have, resulting in the "overdetermination" of these tricky manifestations (608).

The problem with such a reading of this commercial is that, for Freud, symptoms do not occur in the conscious, even if they form in part through conscious repression ("Inhibitions" 5). Yet this advertisement—which along with *BSG* and other televisual elements form a "supertext" (Browne) or "flow" (Williams)—clearly has an intentional goal: to sustain and increase viewership of the series. Of course marketing attempts often miss their mark, and inevitably reveal unconscious, latent anxieties and hopes. With this commercial in particular, however, I think employing only a Freudian symptomatic reading falls too readily into the advertisement's snare, and what is more, obfuscates the dominant cultural construct at work. A look at the multitude of competing cultural determinants reveals why.

On the one hand, the language of conservative anti-abortionists is deployed through the voice-over narration, suggesting we should cherish life in its most "innocent" form. However, the notable use of Patricia Clarkson as narrator recalls for many viewers the often politically liberal films and television shows making up her "star text" (see Dyer)—tipping the scale a bit the other way. Viewers might recognize her distinctive voice (even if they can't consciously name her) as belonging to the fiery and gracefully middle-aged redhead in films like *Far from Heaven* and *Goodnight and Good Luck*, as well as *Six Feet Under* (in which her character at one point even curses "George Fucking Bush"). Ideologically, this work is diametrically opposed to anything approaching the pro-life movement. In addition, the innocence she speaks about is revealed to be bastardized, as the baby is a human-machine hybrid, an abomination. The commercial begs a question: perhaps such a monster should be aborted?

On the other hand, *BSG* is narrated from the point of view of the Cylons as well. In this sense, the statement "What starts as microscopic matter, one day, has the power to change [pause] everything" has both positive and negative connotations, and perhaps even a hidden imperative. Humans and Cylons must change, after all, if they're to avoid destroying one another. The child of the Cylon Sharon and human Helo could be that microscopic seed matter, that good cyborg from Donna Haraway's "Cyborg Manifesto" who will allow us to reach our full potential—a cyborg whose blood, in fact, saves Laura Roslin's life by sending her cancer into remission, at least temporarily. Thus it is not that the commercial starts on a positive note and ends on the negative; rather, there is a self-conscious attempt to achieve a total cancelling-out, in order to make interpretation more pleasurably challenging and thereby act as a hook for the series.

Therefore it may be more accurate and interesting to view this commercial as an intentional strategy employing what only appear to be overdetermined (unconscious) cultural symptoms in order to sell a product. (If we only employ an overdetermined, Freudian, symptomatic reading here, we're then confronted with a tangle of competing elements, perhaps leading us to hypothesize that Patricia Clarkson wants to save our android children, or some other non sequitur.) In this sense the marketing executives are forging a link between different cultural forces with a specific goal in mind. Such a link is not necessary or timeless, but exists only fleetingly and contingently. This is akin to the concept of "articulation" in cultural studies. As Stuart Hall defines it, an articulation is

> a linkage which is not necessary, determined, absolute and essential for all time. . . . It enables us to think how an ideology empowers people, enabling them to make some sense or intelligibility of their historical situation, without reducing those forms of intelligibility to their socio-economic or class location or social position. (quoted in Grossberg 141–42)

What this concept allows us to do as cultural analysts is to bring intentionality and causality back into the mix without being simplistic or reductive. Thus we can conjecture that what only superficially appears to be an overdetermined, unconscious symptom is rather a fleeting yet consciously articulated cultural construct. *BSG*'s advertisement, then, is asymptomatic of the apparent fears or desires presented (i.e., over abortion and technology) because these are too self-consciously presented, and the cancelling out of each element by another makes such a reading moot. The process of this particular articulation, however—that is, the way in which it deploys intentionally provocative, charged elements—is indeed symptomatic, and reveals both pleasures and anxieties over the persistent cultural trope of balance.

Such moments of articulated balance are endemic to Season Two. One episode in particular ("The Captain's Hand" 2.17) deals explicitly with abortion, religion, and the presidency. Roslin, an advocate of reproductive rights, is about to grant asylum to a seventeen-year-old girl desperately in search of an abortion (the young woman's people, the Gemenons, object on religious grounds). To American viewers, Roslin's position as a pro-choice religious prophet initially seems contradictory. The issue flips again, however, when Roslin decides to allow this abortion but ban all others, due to the overriding necessity for the dwindling human population to restore itself. Effectively, this switches and conflates the whole abortion debate— ideally, Roslin would like to allow abortions but pragmatically she finds herself preventing them. Of course in the actual debate on abortion, the opposite is the case: ideals of human life are trumpeted by the pro-life camp ("all human life is sacred") and the realities of practical existence ("women and their bodies are damaged by driving abortion underground") privileged by the pro-choice side. By reflexively articulating such moments as these, the series treats all sides of the issue—providing a familiar, polarized structure while ensuring no one is offended (especially not advertisers and their customers). CNN's *Crossfire*, a program in which one pundit from the right and one from the left debate one another, is an obvious corollary to this, and interestingly was cancelled shortly after comedian and guest Jon Stewart implored cohosts Tucker Carlson and Paul Begala to "stop hurting America" during his appearance on October 15, 2004.

Global warming, as framed in the news around this time, perhaps best exemplifies this polarized structure. As a 2004 article from the *Columbia Journalism Review* put it, "Reporters must often deal with editors who reflexively cry out for 'balance,'" and global warming was the perfect issue to balance (Mooney 28). Until fairly recently, the small minority of scientists (many with ties to the automobile and oil industries, or to the Bush administration) who opined that global warming is not due to human activities received almost as much press coverage as the vast majority who said otherwise. The entrenched structure of journalistic balance putatively designed to ensure objectivity, in this case, led arguably to greater confusion instead:

> The question of how to substitute accuracy for mere "balance" in science reporting has become ever more pointed as journalists have struggled to cover the Bush administration, which scientists have widely accused of scientific distortions. . . . Journalists have thus had to decide whether to report on a he said/she said battle between scientists and the White House—which has had very few scientific defenders—or get to the bottom of each case of alleged distortion and report on who's actually right. (Mooney 28)

Similar to the way global warming is framed by the mainstream press, in the second season of *BSG* the categories of the aggressor and the aggrieved seem to be hopelessly artificial constructs as well, mapping evenly across Cylons and humans. Far from being unwitting and unconscious symptoms, the articulation of this purposefully overdetermined structure of balance seems replete with purpose; namely, to maintain high ratings in order to keep the series on the air.

Contrasted with *Crossfire* and other "news" sources, *BSG* is of course (relatively) more fictional. Also, as a fan of *BSG* I believe that the show is not hurting but helping America—precisely by parroting and simultaneously problematizing and calling attention to this structure. One example of this tension at work is the way in which humans and Cylons are often framed in distinct ways through the series' visual style, even if both are usually treated in an ostensibly neutral manner via the narrative. The opposite is found to be the case with the original version of the series by Lane Roth, who argues this balance ("ambiguity") occurs in the aesthetics, but notably is not expressed through the narrative:

> The clearcut conflict between man and machine, which is assigned moral coordinates of good vs. evil in the storyline, lacks correlative signifiers in *Battlestar Galactica*'s visual design. Basic shapes, particularly the circle and the triangle, recur throughout the text

without systematic correspondence to either human "good guys" or mechanical "bad guys." Nowhere is this ambiguity so conspicuous as in the spaceships, the most intricate sets and models, which function significantly in the narrative as means of life support, transportation and combat. (80–81)

Thus in the original series, the story tells us the humans are good and the Cylons are bad. Cylon ships of the current series, on the other hand, are much more organic than their human counterparts—they are actually alive, and in the case of Cylon Raiders, operate through the use of visible blood, tissue, and organs. Most of the other Cylon vessels have curvy exterior lines and chic, modlike interiors, which on the whole vary greatly from the humans' unapologetically boxy military-order vessels. Additionally, Cylon characters are often framed in a smoother, glowing, lower-contrast high key lighting like a halo, unlike the humans who very often are lit with harsh, unflattering, high-contrast lighting. The existence of such unbalanced aesthetic motifs suggests a growing annoyance with the structure of balance—a structure that is cracked apart much more drastically in Season Three.

Cylon Vertigo

When the third season of *BSG* premiered on October 6, 2006, with the bluntly titled episode "Occupation" (3.01), the United States was gearing up for the midterm congressional elections, widely considered to be a referendum on the war in Iraq. Few would have foreseen that Democrats would capture both chambers of Congress, doing so in the House by exceptionally wide margins. Al Gore's *An Inconvenient Truth* (2006) based on his PowerPoint presentation illustrating the threats of global warming, received wide release in June 2006 and became the third-highest grossing documentary in U.S. history. Calling into question the validity of journalistic structures of neutrality in front of millions of Americans, Gore compares the results of two studies, in which 928 peer-reviewed scientific articles (Oreskes) and 636 popular press articles (Boykoff and Boykoff) on global warming are analyzed. The shock and disgust of both the on-screen and off-screen audiences are palpable when Gore reveals that 0 percent of the peer-reviewed scientific articles—but a full 53 percent of the popular press articles—cast doubt as to the (human) causes of global warming. As Thomas Kuhn has convincingly argued, science too works according to constructed, value-laden paradigms. However, as the comparison between the two studies referenced above suggests, the scientific paradigm may well be less susceptible to this particular rhetoric (substituting balance and neutrality for objectivity) than the paradigm of popular journalism.

In this context, and from just the first twenty minutes of *BSG*'s third season, one can sense a difference between the first two seasons and the third. The narration now seems more certain, with clearly demarcated good guys and bad guys. Now, humans attempt to eke out an existence on a distant, barren planet but are discovered and subsequently occupied by the Cylons—some of whom, in a twist of the "white-man's burden" discourse, believe their purpose is to "save humanity from damnation" as Brother Cavil puts it in "Occupation" (3.01). Intercut with and over scenes of insurgent bombings and prisoner torture, former President Laura Roslin writes a letter read in voice-over:

> Our insurgency has been striking back against the Cylons whenever and wherever possible. Although at times these attacks seem like futile gestures, I believe that they are critical to morale, to maintaining some measure of hope. But in order for the insurgency to have a more meaningful impact, we need to strike a high-profile target.... The Cylon occupation authority continues to exert complete control over the city and we remain at their mercy. The Colonial government, under President Gaius Baltar, functions in name only. In recent months the Cylons have been recruiting and training humans in an attempt to establish a human police force. It is hard to think of anything more despicable than humans doing the dirty work of the Cylons. Led to believe they were merely taking the civilian security out of the hands of the Cylons, the members of the human police have since become an extension of the Cylons' corporeal authority.

Here, in intricate detail, the series' humans can easily be substituted for and mapped as present-day Iraqis and even Iraqi insurgents, and the Cylons their American occupiers. It is difficult to fathom this sort of discourse occurring in the mainstream U.S. media near the start of the war in 2003 without protests and boycotts; in the present moment, though, no one bats an eye. To the contrary, we might welcome the opportunity for an exegesis (and perhaps, by extension, forgiveness) of what the nation—now including traditionally red states and even more and more soldiers themselves—perceives as a mistake.[4] In other words, there is little room for overdetermination of meaning here when the parallels and point of view are drawn so assuredly.

However, this seemingly straightforward allegory may not be intentionally articulated. Ronald D. Moore insists during an interview conducted before the conclusion of Season Three,

> We never want to go into direct allegory for today's events because there's nothing really interesting about that. . . . Science fiction gives you the opportunity to mix and match the elements and the circumstances. You can deal with the deeper themes and issues because you've scrambled the chess pieces. (quoted in Miller, "Man")

While this aptly describes the first two seasons of the show, it seems wishful thinking for the third—which ends by putting President Gaius Baltar (arguably a new stand-in of sorts for George W. Bush's stand-in, Nouri al-Maliki) on trial for complicity in allowing the Cylon occupation. Initially, we are led to believe a conviction for Baltar is a foregone conclusion. He did, after all, nearly cause the destruction of the entire human race, and accepted the terms of the Cylon occupation rather easily. While he is acquitted (following a 3-2 decision) as a sort of everyman who was unavoidably put into an impossible situation, he nonetheless is forced to live in exile.

We have conflicting data, then, regarding the articulation of these moments. The show's creator says in essence that it is his intent to present an overdetermined, balanced, and nonallegorical narrative. Yet from Roslin's words and other narrative elements, it is hard to see what other determinants or meanings could explain these formations other than a close, clear-cut, and confidently moralistic mapping of the Iraq war. Instead of wrapping and conflating cultural elements, in Season Three they are allowed—purposefully or otherwise—to shine through. Any attempts to bury, confuse, or balance the narrative elements seem afterthoughts—as, for example, when in "Occupation" (3.01) Brother Cavil preaches about saving humanity from damnation through "any means necessary," leading Sharon to retort (under the menacing sound of Cylon raiders patrolling overhead) that "we're here to find a new way to live in peace." Such platitudes hardly serve to disrupt any sort of global good vs. bad, humans vs. Cylons binary set up by the narration. For critic Virginia Heffernan, the apparent Iraq allegory is broken when Roslin refuses to justify the bombing of innocent human civilians as collateral damage in a conversation with Baltar ("Precipice" 3.02). For me, however, the allegory is reaffirmed when a few seconds later Roslin angrily reminds Baltar of the continued torture of human prisoners, thus effectively reinscribing her original position and the binary opposition at hand.

Once the humans are evacuated off the planet, life in the fleet apparently returns to normal. The series ratings slip as well. Is this merely due to poor writing? Certainly several of the episodes (such as the especially melodramatic boxing tournament episode, "Unfinished Business" 3.09) lose the narrative momentum generated by the Season Two climax and Season Three opener. Yet I think an attentive reading, in general, reveals a move from articulated, "false" symptoms fitting the dominant structure of balance (Seasons One and Two) to articulated and direct allegory (first half of Season Three) speaking within the more unified cultural structure. Finally, in the second half of Season Three, there is a different type of symptom, in which the series apparently struggles to find a new structure within which to speak in order to avoid the tedium of preaching to the converted—as Moore's fears would seem to indicate.

A return to the psychologist's couch is in order. If the Freudian symptom is caused by many different causes or determinants (leading to the symptom's overdetermination), there is on the other hand a complete lack or vacuum of such causes (an "underdetermination") for Jacques Lacan's more poststructuralist idea of the symptom (Dean 24). This is seen in the conception of *jouissance*,[5] which for Lacan is akin to the orgasmic bliss and loss we try to instill in the Other (Dean 183–84). Put differently, *jouissance* is that endless pit of desire we want other people to have for us. For Lacanian scholar Colette Soler, this is where the Lacanian symptom comes to the rescue, serving as a coagulating agent of sorts mixed into the messy underdeterminations of *jouissance*:

> There is not subject without a symptom. Its function is to fix the mode of the privileged *jouissance* of the subject. It is the symptom that makes the singularity of the subject, subjected otherwise to the great law of the want-to-be. . . . A symptom snows in, nails in, *jouissance*. (72)

And thus the symptom creates, constructs, pours, writes meaning into the endlessly contingent vacuum of *jouissance*. In this light, the symptom is not a festering boil or nervous tick, but a desperate attempt to make meaning out of nothingness.

So it is, too, with the last half of Season Three. During the first and second seasons, its balanced structure resonated with viewers. Now, however, America is at least relatively less polarized, and such a structure is no longer appealing. *BSG* has therefore given up its balance, but has also tired of preaching to the converted with its Iraq allegory. The final episode of Season Three ("Crossroads, Part 2" 3.20) presents the most direct example of the show's struggle to create provocative meaning— made difficult by the glaringly empty loss or *jouissance* of a missing cultural trope to work with or against. What now look like (new) "symptoms" are thus again intentionally articulated, but this time they are only symptomatic of the attempt itself to create meaning out of meaning's lack.

The last few minutes of this episode best illustrate this phenomenon. As the narrative unfolds, four characters (Tyrol, Anders, Tigh, and Tory) incessantly hum an unknown song to themselves:

"There must be some way out of here,"
Said the joker to the thief.
"There's too much confusion here,
I can't get no relief."

Each winds up in the same spot in the ship at the same time, and all come to the conclusion that they must be Cylon sleeper agents. A twangy, guitar-infused cover of Bob Dylan's "All Along the Watchtower" plays as Starbuck—whom we thought was dead—pilots a Viper fighter through a nebula and exclaims to a very confused Apollo over the wireless that "I've been to Earth. I know where it is, and I'm going to take us there." We zoom out from *Galactica* and the encroaching Cylon fleet to reveal the entire Milky Way galaxy. Then, we zoom back, to the same general area but with one important difference: Earth. Specifically, North America—with the state of Florida (itself the site of so much contestation, hanging chads, and razor-thin balance) jutting out prominently.

Through the articulation of preexisting symptoms ripped literally from our culture (the Dylan song, and perhaps the 2000 Florida election debacle), *BSG* makes surprisingly literal the link between culture and text.

This is especially odd given that the series seems to be an originary myth about our distant past. But by having the characters speak Dylan's words while the camera zooms in on North America shortly thereafter, *BSG's* rhetoric has in effect shifted completely from veiled, contrasting, and incessantly balanced overdeterminations (working within/against a definite cultural trope of balance) to completely indexical moments of synecdoche, of direct citation in attempts to concretize something— anything—out of a lack of such a structure. Such narration is, viewed from a certain vantage point, akin to grasping at straws.

Seen from a different perspective, however, it may be that this is *BSG's* only way to articulate itself at this moment. Employing the already overdetermined and familiar lyrics "there's too much confusion here" (which may stand in for the viewers' confusion over the narrative, the producer's confusion over how to "speak" their series, or everyone's confusion over the new cultural landscape) is paradoxically the most fitting way to cancel out or close down the underdetermination of America's current state of uneasy *jouissance*. Essentially, we are now borrowing from the digested, comfortable, and popularized confusion of the late 1960s. I am embarrassed to admit that the first time I heard the song, however, was when it played on *BSG*. Now I can't get enough of it.

As I was writing this chapter, the immigrant handyman who works at my apartment complex asked if I was an "American boy"; I finally realized that indeed I am. Usually when asked their nationality, many Americans (including myself) confuse the question and reply with our lineage (Irish, Mexican, French, African). This is particularly the case, subconsciously, when we wish to instill a sense of desire or friendship in the other— something made increasingly difficult for Americans who do not agree with their president's and Congress's disastrous foreign policy decisions but who still love their country. *BSG* ultimately lends materiality to this confusion and tries, however vainly, to crystallize and work through it via reference to a previous generation's mantra: "There must be some way out of here." We will see, as *BSG* prepares for its fourth and (apparently) final season, and as the U.S. (apparently) prepares to leave Iraq, if this is the case.[6]

Notes

1. While the reader might find all of these terms to be loaded and unstable, it would seem that "balance" and "neutrality" are arguably *more* problematic—especially when used as a substitute for "objectivity" or "accuracy." One may be "neutral" yet not "objective." Often when one is most "objective," after all, "neutrality" becomes impossible.

2. As of printing, the commercial is available online at http://www.youtube.com/watch?v=YB5OgidhfLQ (entitled "Battlestar Galactica Baby Commercial").

3. Whether this jump from "unconscious" and "patient" to "text" and "society" is legitimate or not has been a source of debate. Compare Colette Soler and Tim Dean for two radically different viewpoints.

4. See Noam Levey on red states and Paul Yingling on soldiers.

5. For the English version of Roland Barthe's *Le Plaisir du Texte,* Richard Miller translates *jouissance* as "bliss"—which doesn't fully capture the full sense of the French infinitive *jouir* (which in slang means "to come"). As Stephen Heath puts it, "English lacks a word able to carry the range of meaning in the term *jouissance* which includes enjoyment in the sense of a legal or social possession (enjoy certain rights, enjoy a privilege), pleasure, and, crucially, the pleasure of sexual climax." He stresses that for Barthes *jouissance* "shatters—dissipates, loses—that cultural identity, that ego" (9).

6. I would like to thank Edward Branigan, Anna Everett, Jennifer Holt, Ryan Medders, Constance Penley, and Alta Peterson for their insightful comments and questions on various versions of this essay; Joe Palladino (who actually has a *BSG* character named after him) and Michael Sluchan for their help in tracking down answers to my more idiosyncratic questions; and C. W. (Toph) Marshall and Tiffany Potter for their expertise and efforts in assembling this collection.

14

"This Might Be Hard for You to Watch": Salvage Humanity in "Final Cut"

Kevin McNeilly

1.

For North American viewers in the aftermath of 9/11, *Battlestar Galactica* matters exactly because it's secondhand TV. The new series not only reconceptualizes the original late-seventies series, by getting its figurative hands dirty, but also incorporates into its visual and narrative fabrics a rethinking of the cultural politics of the television screen and of mediatization. It takes a second look at how television bears witness to disaster, if it still even can. Open-eyed and radical, the new version of *BSG* calls directly into question the possibility of any redemptive, meaningful practice of image-making. It's quintessentially late television, facing up to the posttraumatic disorders of contemporary American culture, while also recognizing and confronting the all-too-human shortfall of its own critical self-conception. Its unnerving depictions of existential duress—produced as the vestiges of a decimated humanity seek to relocate themselves—interrogate the complicity of technologies of depiction in human ruin, even as they comb through those same ruins to uncover whatever potential might remain for renewal, for better life.

One of the indicators of this roughening, a hallmark of *BSG*'s visual style throughout three seasons, is motile, handheld camera-work. The series eschews a stable perspective, preferring the feel of embedded points of view, and the textures of improvisational immediacy and documentary presence that a handheld camera offers. We're reminded in every scene that perspective is contingent and temporary, that someone is taking these pictures, making these images. The aperture constantly jiggles, drifts, redirects its attention, pulls, and readjusts its focus. Of course, it makes no sense when ostensibly enormous spacecraft deep in space are photographed with a handheld camera, or when we look along with the camera through the cockpit glass of a speeding Viper: such perspectives, despite the realistic visual style, are patently impossible. They produce what Geoffrey Hartman scathingly laments as television's "derealization of ordinary life" ("Tele-suffering" 434), a stylistic semblance of the documentary camera's capacity to "build in some resistance by counteracting the glossy or ghostly unreality of seemingly realistic yet increasingly surrealistic TV programs" (439). The point, however, is not to expose the viewers' capacity to be duped by illusion—that the *Battlestar Galactica* is a crafted plastic model in a dark studio space, or that the cockpit is merely a plywood and paint mock-up with a camera operator filming beside it, although these are viably realistic, if ironic, viewings. Rather, the documentary textures of *BSG*'s visuals serve as reminders of a corporeal, human materiality that informs the whole aesthetic of the program. The handheld, quasi-documentary camera introduces into the screen-image material traces of hands and eyes—two key tropes, the tactile and the visual, that pervade nearly every episode.

But in this context, human hands remain dirty, and you can't trust your eyes. The clean accessible visuality of the late seventies original series has diminished, its ideals crumbled, its self-confident American sheen worn off. This diminishment—represented in the conversion of *Galactica* into a museum, complete with artifacts from the original series (M.01)—refuses to figure itself as loss, and comes instead to represent dirt and decrepitude as markers of human endurance, and of the emergence of a new ethics: a self-awareness to counterbalance the smug anthropocentrism that appears to enable humanity's downfall at the hands of the Cylons. Those Cylon hands—whether the glistening metallic claws of the Centurions or the manicured fists of the twelve new models (an implicit pun, since Six is played by supermodel Tricia Helfer, epitomizing hyperreal body image)—initially enact a material presence that is decorporealized, as apparitions or simulacra rather than the messy actualities of flesh. But as the materialization of a hygienic, perfected human image—"they evolved," the opening credits remind us—the Cylons are also utterly deadly; they inflict their vision of existential hygiene on humanity to clean up the mess from the universe, an utterly genocidal vision.

The Cylons want alternatively to exert dominion over their former masters, in the eugenic work of their maternity "farms" or in their government of New Caprica, or to wash their hands of humanity entirely. It's significant that one of their key means of networking aboard a basestar is to immerse their hands in a liquid-filled tray, or that Hybrids and the resurrected copies are immersed in amniotic baths; such baptismal imagery suggests both rebirth and the purgation of sins. Moreover, it points up an embedded contrariety between the hygienic, networked absolutism of the Cylons and the abject, dissolute plurality of the human remnants: the unwashed visual textures associated with *BSG* contrast the Kubrickian white haze illuminating the interiors of Cylon vessels. The correlation between hand and eye, flesh and image, toward which the documentary textures of *BSG* gesture, puts at issue (as a form of viral or contaminated visuality) the possibility of salvage or salvation as redemptive. It bears remembering that two episodes in Season Three deal with contagious diseases and viruses among both Cylons and humans: "A Measure of Salvation" (3.07) and "The Woman King" (3.14), respectively. The virtuality of networked television, of clarified seeing, cannot in the troubled vision of *BSG*'s creators be perfected or virtuous, if humanity means to survive its traumas, and to find meaning in survival. Claims to perfection and virtue present an essential and overwhelming danger, threateningly akin to the persistent trauma both to and within human culture described by Maurice Blanchot in the aftermath of the Holocaust, "that the disaster acquire meaning instead of body" (41), that delusively clear, abstracted representations forgo the unruly and necessary presence of lived human experience. The danger is that we come to our demise overly mediated and mediatized. Humans need instead, as the visuals of the program repeatedly imply, to encounter and to address the difficult sight of their own unwashed state. "This might be hard for you to watch," reporter D'Anna Biers (later revealed to be an embedded Cylon) tells Colonel Tigh (the most conflicted of viewers) in the episode "Final Cut" (2.08). Exactly: hard watching is what *BSG* is all about.

2.

To explain this challenging viewership in practice, I want to walk critically through that episode. In "Final Cut," figurations of hand and eye, of the manual and the visual, shape the unfolding narrative of human destiny, on an individual as well as a collective scale. The episode invites us as nascent self-aware spectators into a critical disruption of the hygienic rationality of the screen, of the frame itself, to get our metaphorical hands (our means to grasp what's going on before our eyes) a little dirtier. The first scene of "Final Cut" opens from the perspective of an editor-reporter, D'Anna Biers, as she cuts together her own head-shot commentary with taped footage apparently retrieved from the personal videocam of a victim of the "*Gideon* Massacre" on which she's clandestinely reporting (and which viewers first witness in "Resistance" 2.04); we see a computer screen boxed at an angle in a console, on which the film image—with corners cut, like paper objects in this culture—is playing. The redundancies of the frames, coupled with skewing, with the horizontal surface-lines of refilmed videotape and with the instability of doubled cameras, remind us we're watching not only images but also the viewing of those images by others, screening their visual reception. The image of D'Anna Biers—whom actor Lucy Lawless claims is a deep-space Christiane Amanpour (Bassom, *Two* 54)—speaks directly into the camera, claiming an irrefutable facticity for what we're witnessing secondhand, on our screens: "This recently discovered footage from what's become known as the *Gideon* massacre appears to show *Galactica*'s marines firing indiscriminately into a crowd of unarmed civilians." Public knowledge, a mix of rumor and testimonial ("what's become known"), is put at stake by the seemingly intimate access we have, via television ("appears to show"), to atrocity. The perspective reels sideways (the horizon now parallel to the "cut corners" of the inner screen) as the cameraman falls; a child approaches, bends to look into the lens—and not the victim's face, remarkably—and mews "Daddy?" A traumatized humanity, on small scale, looks out at us. Viewers are reminded of our complicity, that our eyes, too, are liminally enframed by the television screen. Our eyes, perhaps cynically but certainly critically, are opened to the contrivance of image-making and of entitlement to what we see.

Mark Verheiden's script for "Final Cut" is pervaded by vocabularies of the visual and the tactile—often to articulate a distrust of human sensation, or its difficulty. D'Anna Biers is met on *Colonial One* by a fawning

President Roslin, who coos, in an obvious effort to ingratiate herself, "Miss Biers, it's nice to see you." (The pretense is immediately undermined by Adama, who cuts to the chase: "Where did you get the tape?") Seeing clearly, in other words, is never "nice," and Roslin isn't asking to "see" anyone or anything rigorously. But she quickly changes her approach, telling the reporter she wants a documentary representing the military more faithfully, provisionally to assuage popular unrest: "I want to put a human face on the officers and the crew who protect us against Cylons and guard our freedoms, every day. . . . Show us what the men and women of *Galactica* are really like." Rhetorical spin mixes in her speech uneasily with the call for documentary realism (as well as with a self-consciousness about television: "*Galactica*" after all could refer to the fictional space vessel, or it could implicitly refer to the program, which also aspires to stylized realism). Not unexpectedly, D'Anna doesn't trust her: "You might not like that face when you see it." That distrust emerges throughout the episode in Colonal Tigh's poor, indiscriminate vision, which is literally written on his face when he declares at the screening of the "final cut" that he's "seen enough," or when earlier he snaps into the camera, "Would you get out of my face!" (Notably, a year later, in "Occupation," 3.01, he'll lose an eye and wear a patch, as if to reaffirm his blinkered perspective.) To let go of skepticism, we can't ever claim to have seen enough, if we're unable in the show's terms to get to the "real face" beyond screening appearances.

Tigh complains that the resulting documentary "show[s] us with our pants down and our asses hanging out." But Adama suggests that such visual candor isn't so bad: "She put a human face on the guardians of the fleet. Warts and all. I'm proud of it. You [D'Anna] can show it to the entire fleet." Tigh's reference is more exact than it appears, since part of D'Anna's footage—not included in her "final cut"—involves Kat, high on "stims," shaking her naked backside at the camera. That scene, too, involves bodies in a specific manner: Apollo is drying himself off after a shower, and D'Anna and her cameraman intrude into the "officer's head" to interview him; his body is ogled, both by D'Anna and her camera, before she quips, "I think we've seen all we need to see here." (Slightly later, she'll joke to Apollo that "I hardly recognized you with your clothes on.") Aside from its voyeurism, the intrusiveness and incisiveness of D'Anna's camera confronts the imagery of bodily hygiene and clarified sight, the idealized shine that the unkempt visuals of documentary form tend to dull. How much do we really need to see?

This is also the moment when the camera and sound recorder inadvertently pick up clues to the plot against Tigh's life over his responsibility for the *Gideon* massacre: a glimpse of would-be assassin and massacre-participant Lieutenant Palladino with a book of Caprican poetry, coupled with a nearly inaudible voice in the background—"Lighten up, Palladino!"—a declaration that contrasts sharply the lines from the poem of the Caprican bard Kataris scrawled on Tigh's mirror: "From the darkness you must fall." The camera enables a close attention to which the human eye and ear might aspire but can't always manage; D'Anna will reexamine the footage and realize what Palladino is up to; critically acute human (and even Cylon) viewership becomes possible only when mediated by visual technologies. The "human face" that the documentary camera demands is responsive and, to a certain extent, belabored. Palladino will eventually confess as he holds Tigh at gunpoint: "I can't eat. I can't sleep. I see their faces. Those weren't Cylons we tagged. Those were real people." Disclosure, on-screen, is never painless. "Does this ever get any easier?" D'Anna asks Dualla after an averted Cylon attack (which turns out to be a relay mission by the Cylons for D'Anna's recordings); "No ma'am," she replies, "It gets harder."

This harder, critical self-scrutiny is figured in a screening-room set piece (which recurs in other episodes, such as "Maelstrom," 3.17), in which we watch characters watch video of themselves, and comment on it. "Final Cut" begins with an embedded screening, but significantly the episode also concludes with a viewing, set in what appears to be a theater on Caprica: four Cylons are screening the documentary, remarking on the tenacity of the remaining humans and evaluating the film as an anthropological document (as opposed to the puff-piece that, despite Adama's "warts and all" approbation, it becomes). The transition from Adama and Roslin previewing the material to the Cylons' screening is accomplished by identifying the "objective" camera of the show with the television screen itself, in close-up, and then pulling back to reveal the Cylons in an audience elsewhere; appropriately, as an in-joke, a version of Stu Phillips's militaristic theme music from the original late seventies movie and series (instantly recognizable to longtime fans) swells in the soundtrack to D'Anna's "documentary" in an outright ploy (contrary to any appearance of documentary objectivity) to elicit empathy among the audience in the fleet. What become immediately apparent as the perspective pulls back are the editorial and aesthetic manipulations, the music among them, that contribute to the film's "reality" effect. Six asks to see the footage cut from the original, footage we saw D'Anna procure by sleight-of hand from Adama, who wants it censored. We see the pregnant version of Sharon partially obscured behind a translucent polyethylene curtain, which is messily drawn aside just as the documentary camera is jostled and then its lens covered by a shadowed hand. The Cylon audience now knows something they shouldn't about survival and the possibility of blending human and Cylon bodies.

The camera operator is depicted as unwanted interloper, his or her lens picking up visual indiscretions, information to which the nonprivileged should not have access. This reinstantiating of cognitive boundaries had already become key in episode director Robert Young's cinema. By the time he came to work on *BSG*, eventually directing three episodes other than "Final Cut," ("Six Degrees of Separation" 1.07, "Unfinished Business" 3.09, and "The Son Also Rises" 3.18), Young already had a career as a renowned documentarian and filmmaker.[1] His earlier work as a cinematographer was characterized by a closely proximate camera style that carries over into his direction for *BSG*. The opening sequence of the 1964 film *Nothing But a Man* (directed by Michael Roemer) intercuts close-ups on the faces of African American railroad workers with rough hewn black-and-white images of labor; the camera tracks intimately throughout the film, following the actors' movements and scrutinizing with glamourless rigor the blemished contours of their faces, discovering the "human" aspect of black American life. This insistence on the humanity of others—Young isn't African American—recurs throughout the film, and looks forward to the fraught humanism of "Final Cut," where an ethics of human plurality—deploying visual media to produce community in difference—is exactly what's at stake. This visual tactic develops further in *The Eskimo: Fight for Life*, Young's 1970 collaboration with ethnographer Asen Balikci, a film Young understands as key to his work.[2] Again, Young's film centers on the persistence of the human, and in the recognition of a resilient humanity in adversity of the Netsilik Inuit. Balikci's opening voice-over emphasizes the work's elegiac character as "salvage anthropology," a document of a lost way of existence: "This is a record of their very last migration as I observed it while living amongst them at their winter camp." The resonances with *BSG* are striking: the cinematography is proximate and personal, as Young repeatedly attends to the faces of the Netsilik in their abject and unvarnished beauty. The migratory people endure, we're told, against conditions that are nowhere "more severe to man." The access gained by Young's camera doesn't so much transgress the boundaries of ethnographic propriety, intruding where he shouldn't be, as dramatize the difficult copresences of observer and observed, a severity of witness that implicates the viewer in the image itself, not as bystander but as engaged or proximate other.

"Final Cut" is preoccupied with literalizing the human experience of representation—an articulation dramatized at various thresholds between the visual and the material, thresholds at which the visual and the visionary touch upon their realization, intersect with their embodied manifestation. The sensory work of eyes becomes enmeshed with a virtual tactility, the promise of contact. Such thresholds, as permeable contact zones, are figured metonymically in various forms of screens. In one scene from the subplot, we witness a visit by Helo to Sharon's cell in *Galactica*'s brig. The camera's initial point of view, notably, is at eye-level with Helo, but from inside the cell, proximate to the grille through which visitors observe prisoners. We're not identified with Sharon, who is lying on a cot behind our virtual position, but we're framed by the rectangular limits of the cell, looking out. Helo looks past us, not at the camera, presumably frantic about Sharon; he grabs a telephone receiver (another hallmark of *BSG*'s preoccupation with decrepit technologies) and calls out to her; importantly, his fingers permeate the vertical bars of the grille as he shouts.

What we witness is actually a desperate (if enervated) attempt to tear at barriers, to get through, physically. Helo's hands (perhaps in an allusion to the shot of Orson Welles's fingers pushing through a manhole in *The Third Man*) try to break the fourth wall of the screen before him. When our point of view shifts (as Helo shouts off to his right, "Give me your light, now. Something's wrong"), we don't identify with his perspective, but are taken into closer proximity (reminiscent of Young's tight cinematography), to the agonized Sharon, who raises her bloodied hand in front of her eyes as flashlight beams play across her; she sees the evidence of something wrong, a breach of visual and corporeal hygiene in the uncontrolled smears of bodily fluid. The scene suggests the real possibility that disrupting the clean, representational planes of television, putting a human aspect on what we see, also endangers our comfort zones, liminally violating the limits of our privileged intimacy with these images, our closeness: we're meant to recognize that something's wrong with keeping safe distances as we watch.

That this scene is immediately preceded by Helo's on-camera interview for D'Anna Biers's documentary reinforces the interpretation of the cell's grille as a displaced screen through which Helo wants to reach. Framed in a screen within our screen, he speaks into the camera, breaking the frame, addressing his potential audience directly. Moreover, what he says assumes added resonance as we watch him try to help Sharon:

> D'Anna (off camera): What's been the hardest part for you?
>
> Helo: They try to turn off the human part of you because that's what'll get you killed, but . . . [pause] . . .when you're out in the field it's not that easy. Nothing's that easy.

The dialogue stresses the difficulty of human existence, and the necessity of embracing that difficulty—that life can't be clean and easy, if it's life. It's important to hear the disturbing technological metaphors in Helo's language: humans are treated by military commanders as if they were machines, as Cylons in other words, who can turn vital aspects of themselves on and off.

When Helo calls for light, he echoes a claim made by the Lithuanian philosopher and theologian Emmanuel Levinas (cited by Hartman as a warning about television) that juxtaposes visuality and tactility within the idea of light itself: "The interval of space given by light is instantaneously absorbed by light" (quoted in Hartman, "Trauma" 263). What Levinas means here is that seeing can produce a troubling illusion of immediacy that dissolves any potential encounter with human difference—with lived experience—in the clean lines and surreal glamour of visual representation. It is troubling because such a seductively unremarkable viewership amounts to an annihilation of any vital human plurality, which is what the Cylons, in *BSG*'s fictional universe, appear to want. "Television," for Hartman, "is a mechanism that brings us images from far away while making itself as invisible as possible. To be effective it cannot relinquish this magical realism" ("Tele-suffering" 1). This hyperbolic presence— that television viewing is overly absorbing—obfuscates trauma, inviting us habitually to repress and to misdirect necessary difficulty, substituting anesthetic pleasures for challenging critical work: we gawk at images rather than engaging them.

But this view of television as dire distraction actually emerges from a misreading of Levinas's warning about light, since what the philosopher seeks (if we go back and read what he says in his essay) is actually a redemption of the sort at which *BSG*—through mouthpieces like the all-too-human Helo—recurrently gestures:

> Life could only become the path of redemption if, in its struggle with matter, it encountered an event that stops its everyday transcendence from falling back upon a point that is always the same. To catch sight of this transcendence, which supports the transcendence of light and lends a real exteriority to the exterior world, it is necessary to return to the concrete situation wherein light is given in enjoyment—that is, to material existence. (Levinas 66)

This sounds abstract, but the "transcendence" of which Levinas hopes to catch sight—going beyond or transcending the closed boundaries of egocentrism and self-satisfaction—consists in a materialization of what is wholly other than the self-satisfied human ego, a tangible recognition of human plurality, of the humanity of others. In this light, transcendence manifests at the threshold of the visual and the tactile, a threshold explicitly thematized in the grille through which Helo's fingers pass. The potential for redemption, for helping ourselves and others to salvage whatever humanity remains to *BSG*'s refugees, inheres liminally in human touch. But how can television touch us, bridging its screen-bound, hygienic distances, its dehumanizing detachment? How does it put on a human face?

In "Final Cut," this practice of difficult cognition is explicitly associated with reading and books. In Tigh's quarters, the threat on his life (a quotation from the poet Kataris, "From the darkness you must fall") is scrawled in red ink across his mirror; the shot in which the text is revealed, moreover, positions Tigh and Ellen in that same mirror, in a visual palimpsest, their images overwritten by the line. Not only does this mimesis produce an embedded picture of the screen itself—as if captioned or subtitled—but it also locates the written word, the poetic word, on the virtual surface of that visual threshold. Writing occurs in the medial zone between body and image, between the material and the representational. Books and print media recur throughout the program as images of archaism, artifacts of an unnetworked, material technology. Adama is depicted in his quarters either as reading or as working on his model ship, a physical representation of bygone wooden vessels. Even electronic technologies are dated and subsistence level: wireless communication happens over static-laden radios; officers use Bakelite telephones to speak, as far from a clean-lined Star Trek communicator as can be imagined; the DRADIS resembles a 1980-era video game. The graphic becomes tangible, bound up in touch and materialized corporeality, in other episodes, notably "Maelstrom" (3.17), in which Starbuck faces her own death, crossing spiritual and visual thresholds such as the mortal "hard deck" (the point where her Viper will not be able to escape the planet's gravitational field), or such as the imagined doorway—a visual echo of the threshold through which we glimpse Sharon in sickbay in "Final Cut"—to her mother's bedroom, where Socrata Thrace lies on her deathbed, clutching a scrapbook of Starbuck's papers and drawings. "I can't believe you kept all this," Starbuck whispers as she flips through the pages, memory appearing to materialize through her visionary experience. The paint and wax that throughout the episode re-form into images of the "Eye of Jupiter," the turbulent storm through which Starbuck later plunges in flight, smear and blot over surfaces: skin, drywall, steel decking, paper. The physical barriers through which vision and visuality invite us sometimes perilously to pass are screens upon which what is other and unknown (figured here as death) inscribes its difficult presence.

In both material and poetic forms, print media in *BSG* indicate a refusal of clarified, unproblematized seeing, and a resilience set against the conforming clasp of television itself. Adama, riding in a Raptor, comes upon copies of a magazine, *Caprican Life*, that Racetrack tells him were "left over from a civilian run." She's "been meaning to throw them out," but Adama instead tells her to "put them in a safe place. Hold on to them." Life sustains itself and survives through tangible, readable memory, seen and held.

Palladino's book of poetry appears to provide a vital clue to solving the mystery, saving Tigh's life and catching the supposed bad guy; D'Anna's active reviewing of the tapes seems to present a model of critical scrutiny, through which a better, ethical cognition might be achieved. But notably nothing is resolved: Tigh remains unpunished either by law or by vigilante justice for his complicity in the massacre, which Adama is keen to obscure in terminological quibbles: "What happened aboard the *Gideon* was a tragedy, but it was not a massacre." Palladino's guilt, in his nightmarish visions of victims' faces, stays unreconciled. Transcendence, on and through the aesthetics of television, doesn't simply mean closing the question of humanity's meaningful survival, "seeing the end" as Adama and Roslin put it, and finally arriving at a mythical "Earth" intact and welcomed. Rather, instead of *telos*, of absolution or of resolution for their unfolding narrative, the transcendence promised and delivered by television involves the critical encounter with that unresolvability. It means relearning how to *read* the television screen. It inheres in the unwashed, confrontational poetics of difficult watching, of watching as active reading. The facing that television itself enables takes on aesthetic value as it presents not glib closure but difficult renewal, not salvation attained so much as beautiful, awful salvage.

In *Thinking Past Terror*, her critical response to 9/11, Susan Buck-Morss seeks with measured hope a new understanding of "the global" (a term arguably transposed into *BSG* as "Earth," as the imagined home of a salvaged humanity) that necessarily depends on reimagining the function and character of communications media:

> To speak of the global is to speak about media. And, of course, a mediated community is not a community in the traditional sense of living together, working together. The collective spirit produced by media is fairly superficial. Empathetic identifications are instantaneous, but they can just as instantaneously disappear. Without language in common, the global public sphere will have to rely heavily on images. It will be a visual culture—or musical, perhaps, but not dominantly print. (132)

Like Hartman, Buck-Morss decries the false, ghostly identifications that superficialty, the pervasive surface of screened images, tends to produce. But she does not share Hartman's disdain for audiovisual media. She continues to affirm the need "to reject essentialist ontology and return to critical epistemology, making judgments regarding visual and textual culture in all its aspects, including the difficult but crucial distinction between the aestheticizing of politics and the politicizing of art" (74). This means that, even in spite of her claims about the end of print culture, Buck-Morss retains a thorough grounding in critical textuality, in active interventionist reading as opposed to passive viewing. Her echo of Walter Benjamin's famous warning against "aestheticizing" politics—which Benjamin understands as fundamental to militaristic fascism, the artful obscuring of political participation in spectacle (Benjamin 269–70)—is also an affirmation of the political value of art, of the aesthetic. She calls for a critical aesthetics, which as what she calls "epistemology" addresses not so much who we are (a form of "essentialist" ontological claim belied by human plurality and difference) as how we do things. Taken in the context of *BSG*, this call affirms the possibility of a kind of television that functions as ethically and aesthetically challenging, and of a difficult and touching beauty that appears at the tactile thresholds of our shared screens. "When you finally face it," Starbuck's spirit-guide tells her in "Maelstrom" (3.17), "it's beautiful." Sometimes it might be hard for us to watch, but the palpable critical pleasures of that challenge are exactly what make *BSG* worth watching.

Notes

1. Robert M. Young, the director who works on *BSG*, has been misidentified in numerous online databases as television director Robert W. Young. Robert M. Young cofounded YOY Productions in Los Angeles with Edward James Olmos, and has collaborated with the actor on a number of socially committed films, as well as on *BSG*.

2. *BSG* producer David Eick emphasizes the importance of this documentary in his podcast commentary for "Final Cut."

15

"Long Live Stardoe!"
Can a Female Starbuck Survive?

Carla Kungl

"Starbuck is dead! Long Live Stardoe!"

—Dirk Benedict

Sherrie Inness's *Tough Girls*, which examines television, movies, and comic books, illustrates some of the problems that arise for strong women: they are portrayed with ambivalence by a media not exactly sure how much toughness is too much, depicted so that "they do not challenge gender conventions too dramatically" (5). While the number of tough women in films and on television has increased in past years, it is hard to draw any conclusions from this fact, especially concerning their acceptability to mainstream audiences; Inness merely concludes that we need to study the construction of such images because of what they say about "changing gender identities" in the United States (9).

The phrase "changing gender identities" is apt, and well-suited for a chapter like this, which is concerned with the replacement of a male Starbuck on the 1970s *Battlestar Galactica* with a female character of the same name. The phrase certainly suggests that one of the longstanding goals of the women's movement has come true—that women are taking over men's roles in a way that reidentifies those roles. But for many, the phrase might take on larger meaning as well: that men and women can (and do, in this particular case) literally change identities. Such a move is frightening for some and clearly so for many fans of the original *BSG*, who were horrified at the new *BSG*'s creation of a female Starbuck instead of casting a man in the role.

Certainly female characters have been placed in roles normally played by men before the new casting of *BSG*; in science-fiction series, Captain Janeway in *Star Trek: Voyager* comes most immediately to mind. But on the new *BSG*, seemingly new territory has been claimed: a woman is playing what was a specific man's role.[1] Despite the utopian nature of much science fiction, which tells us we can imagine the future differently, the virulent outpouring of anger about this move on websites and message boards suggests a fear that belies this dream and delves deeply into a more primal controversy. For many, this casting implies the worst of imagined feminist platforms come true: there is literally no difference between men and women.

There is no doubt that Katee Sackhoff's Starbuck is a tough girl; the question is, why does she have to be? She is, simply, a Viper pilot, like so many other men and women on the show—indeed, she is the best pilot, man or woman. But beyond the regular toughness needed to be a woman in the military, this female version of the loveable rogue created by Dirk Benedict is portrayed as tough in character. When given background traits like empathy or insecurity, she runs the risk of being seen as too weak, too feminine, and thus the character walks an impossible line: either despised for weakness when she exhibits emotions or despised for not being feminine when she doesn't.

Thus, while at its heart this chapter examines this double bind for tough women in Hollywood, as outlined by Inness's work, it also moves beyond that discussion to take into account the unique situation that recasting a male character as a woman creates. Because producer Ronald D. Moore wanted to take the show in a new direction ("Making Starbuck female was primarily done to mix things up"),[2] he helped create a maelstrom of controversy and alienated a standing fan base, whose anger was vociferously expressed; in their eyes the replacement of the apparently sacrosanct Benedict is beyond repair.

Three seasons later, the show is highly acclaimed, and the fact of Starbuck's female sex, beyond a few overtures in the first few episodes, has not been made an issue, either by producers or media outlets. Sackhoff's Starbuck, from what these first three seasons have shown us, is not afraid of being on either end of the "toughness" binary, exhibiting strength *and* vulnerability, a humanity that successfully moves women characters onto new ground.

Starbuck as a woman had a rough beginning, however, as part of a series that featured many characters and plotlines being "reimagined" (as Moore describes his show). Fans of the original show, in addition to original stars and producers, had long been engaged in a fight to get a more traditional remake on the air. For instance, Richard Hatch, who played Apollo on the original *BSG*, was so inspired by fans he met at conventions that he created and self-financed a 4½-minute trailer depicting a more faithful reincarnation of the show, *Battlestar Galactica: The Second Coming* (1999). Its popularity led him to believe that a series that picked up where the original left off would be successful. While he never had any rights to the franchise itself, he was in discussions with both Universal Studios (which owned the television rights) and original producer Glen Larson (who owned the movie rights) about getting something made. The vocal and dedicated *BSG* fan base was excited that both a movie and a series might be forthcoming. They had helped keep the show alive—through fanzines, at conventions, and later, with websites and message boards—and thus felt as if they knew best what the franchise should look like. Needless to say, when Moore's reimagined *BSG* came out, fans were furious that what they called "the integrity" of the original show was not being maintained. Sean O'Donnell, leader of the fan club Colonial Fan Force, wrote after its release that "Richard's trailer captured what fans really wanted—a continuation of the original. . . . What's airing in December has nothing to do with that. Sci-Fi Channel is pushing out something with the *Battlestar* name, but the feel is more Beverly Hills 90210 Galactica, or Melrose Place in Space" (Jardin). A major reason for the "soap opera in space" criticism, and the item that got the biggest condemnation, was the recasting of Starbuck as a woman. And an outspoken critic of this move was Dirk Benedict himself. In a *Dreamwatch* article from May 2004, Benedict lashed out at the show's producers and network executives for "caving in" to moneymaking over creative artistry, believing that recasting Starbuck was primarily a ploy to make money. This echoes a common sentiment on message boards—that the producers had to be politically correct and put more strong women on the show. But Benedict's reprisal is more startling than most because he blames the feminist movement itself for allowing such a sex change to be conceivable. After waxing poetic about the past and the construction of his Starbuck, he begins to lament the new politically correct era in which he (and Starbuck) now live:

There was a time—I know I was there—when men were men, women were women and sometimes a cigar was just a good smoke. But 40 years of feminism have taken their toll. The war against masculinity has been won. Everything has turned into its opposite, so that what was once flirting and smoking is now sexual harassment and criminal. And everyone is more lonely and miserable as a result.

Witness the "re-imagined" *Battlestar Galactica*. It's bleak, miserable, despairing, angry and confused. Which is to say, it reflects, in microcosm, the complete change in the politics and mores of today's world as opposed to the world of yesterday. (Dirk Benedict Central)

Perhaps Benedict more than anyone had a right to be dismayed with this casting. As the title of his article, "Lost in Castration," suggests, he was personally affronted by what he called the "Gonads Gone!" mentality that turned his character into "Stardoe" (whence the title of this article). If it were just Benedict who had problems accepting this character, then we could dismiss the rant above as just that, a rant. But there was a huge segment of fandom that absolutely hated the thought of this change.[3] The anger over this move felt by so many suggests more than just one man's castration anxieties. In this new world, the clear-cut boundaries between women and men have become murky—women have more power and command more respect than they used to, the men seemingly less. As Benedict describes the sex roles in the "female driven" *BSG*: "The male characters, from Adama on down, are confused, weak, and wracked with indecision while the female characters are decisive, bold, angry as hell, puffing cigars (gasp) and not about to take it any more." This swapping of traditional roles, of which Starbuck's sex is a part, represents a much bigger battle.

In an essentialist way of thinking, "signs" like masculinity and femininity are inherent and natural, and as such precede any socially constructed meaning. In such a system, "man" and "woman," as Diana Fuss explains, are "stable objects, coherent signs which derive their coherency from their unchangeability and predictability" (3). While an essentialist believes in innate differences, a constructionist assumes that cultural influences shape our meaning-making; being indecisive, to use the example above, is not inherent to being female but instead a trait that cultures have demarcated feminine.[4] Part of the anger over Starbuck's sex change stems from the shock that this change gives to those who believe that the biological differences between men and women are strict and hence preclude real equality. Benedict, for one, doesn't believe that you can just take a woman and put her in a man's role:

> Women are from Venus. Men are from Mars. Hamlet does not scan as Hamletta. Nor does Han Solo as Han Sally. Faceman [Benedict's character on *The A-Team*] is not the same as Facewoman. Nor does a Stardoe a Starbuck make. Men hand out cigars. Women "hand out" babies. And thus the world, for thousands of years, has gone round.

Notwithstanding the lack of transition in this argument, the point he makes resonates for many, especially those threatened by what is seen as encroachment of women into men's positions and of women exhibiting masculine qualities.

"Toughness" is one of those areas thought to be the province of men, and therefore, tough women like Starbuck upset our society's notions not just of femininity, but of masculinity as well. As Inness points out, a woman displaying toughness undermines the belief that gender roles are fixed, and this idea

> throws into question the whole foundation upon which our culture is based. If masculine attributes, such as toughness, and feminine attributes too, are conceived as free-floating signifiers that refer to either a male or female body, our whole culture is destabilized because it is based on what are perceived as the essential differences between men and women. (180)

Clearly this is the assumption upon which Benedict and others base their notions of our society. Brian Attebery, describing why conservative science fiction meant to reach broad audiences typically upholds the sexual status quo, notes this fear: "When women, too, can be adventurous, autonomous, and audacious, then the carefully constructed masculine self loses its foundation" (8). Hence, there is much more at stake than a person on a science-fiction television show. A character like Starbuck, which through its very existence redefines both womanhood and manhood, cannot—should not—work.

Time has proven Benedict wrong, not just about Starbuck but about the show as a whole. The series received a Peabody Award, and the Sci-Fi Channel has announced not just a fourth season of *BSG* but a possible series spin-off called *Caprica*, which could trace the development of the Cylons. Even the Colonial Fan Force has been forced to admit that the new series is "garnering excellent ratings" while maintaining their stance that there are still "a significant number of people who would like to see a reunion movie based on the original 1978 series" (BattlestarGalactica.com). Even Richard Hatch soon accepted a role on the new series; though it does not match his original vision, he now speaks glowingly of it. Critical reviews are often shaped by one's assumptions that the remake will be awful before the surprise— that it isn't—is given away: "Battlestar Galactica: it may sound silly or pretentious. It isn't. It's just good" (Strachan); "Galactica not your father's sci-fi" (Tilley); "Battlestar hype justified after all" (Strachan); "Jettison expectations; 'Battlestar Galactica' is serious drama, not kiddie sci-fi" (Owen). And so on.

Starbuck as a woman works too. With the baggage such a role carries, it cannot have been an easy role for Sackhoff. Over the seasons, Sackhoff has managed to create a character that is not battened down by comparisons to a predecessor, effectively moving this character out of the "battle of the sexes" milieu and into sheer good storytelling. There were several attempts in the series' first few episodes to draw the parallel, to give the female Starbuck similar characteristics to the male version. Most notably, she is masculine-looking, with her muscular body and short hair, and she holds down a traditional man's job.[5] She also loves a good cigar, plays cards, flouts authority, and can be sexually aggressive. At first glance these characteristics seemed an obvious ploy to tie her to the original, and their inclusion points to the difficulty of simply dressing up a woman in a man's body. Such portrayals do not make believable characterizations, and, to be effective, they need to go beyond surface details.

This is where the double bind for tough women like Starbuck occurs. Because her outward "masculine" toughness is her overriding trait, she runs the risk of being reread as too feminine for this persona when she exhibits weakness or other traits traditionally scripted female. For example, she feels pity for Leoben, the Cylon whom she has tortured and who has been shot out an airlock, and she prays for his soul ("Flesh and Bone" 1.08). She has a one-night stand with Baltar, and instead of asking for slaps on the back from her comrades, she feels pretty bad about herself

("Kobol's Last Gleaming, Part 1" 1.12). Starbuck walks an uneasy line, construed not as merely human for exhibiting a wide range of human emotion, but as unnatural—too manly or too womanly.

Sackhoff's Starbuck succeeds in escaping this trap better than most tough women in science fiction. Certainly the seeds of character traits she inherited from the original Starbuck seem to fit her character as she has grown. For instance, his bluster and boasting are given a background: Sackhoff says her character "has a sense of bravado that masks her insecurity, traits that she believes existed in the first Starbuck in the original 'Battlestar'" (Mason). Similarly, Moore has said that her character trait of sleeping around isn't just a "sexed-up" version of Benedict's womanizing, but is a true aspect of who Starbuck is: "She does it because she wants to do it, and because of the nature of the show it meant that was going to be a deeply screwed-up character. A person who actually has all these attributes is really damaged in a lot of fundamental ways, so it made her more complicated and interesting" (quoted in Peterson).

Moore also notes the difficulty of trying to put a woman on equal footing as a man, even in (or perhaps especially in) science fiction: "You can dress them up in leather, S&M outfits, and you can fetishize them as objects, but if you just have sex with them, if it's just like they're people and you allow their sexualization to be co-equal with men, it flips the fans out" (quoted in Peterson). Sackhoff notes the same general tendency: "Granted, it's fun to watch, but if you realistically sit down and talk to any man, does he really think a woman can do the s— we do on television? No . . . They still will always say a man can do it better" (quoted in Tilley).

This is true even for a tough girl like Starbuck. One might hope that a series set in the future would not have to deal with gender inequality, that the utopian world of science fiction would dispense with such a basic ideological stumbling block. But Inness suggests that placing tough women in the future serves as an effective means of containing them: women in science fiction or postapocalyptic narratives (which is perhaps a more appropriate description of *BSG*) operate at a safe distance from the present, mitigating their ability to challenge the status quo, and thus "even the toughest women [are] limited, confined, reduced, and regulated" (178). She lists several ways this is done, all of which we can pick out in Starbuck's characterization: not only by setting her in the future, but by emphasizing her femininity or maternity; by playing up her sexuality, which in our society often is tied to subordination and thus reduces her toughness; and lastly, by placing her in situations where despite her toughness she is rescued or saved by still tougher men (179). We see aspects of the complicated nature of Sackhoff's Starbuck in two very different episodes that focus on her ability to be tough: "You Can't Go Home Again" (1.05) and "The Farm" (2.05). "You Can't Go Home Again" features Starbuck marooned on a planet and running out of oxygen; "The Farm" is one of the darker and more frightening hours of television, as it considers the right of women in a futuristic world to control their own bodies. And it is in this episode, and the continuation of its storyline in the beginning of Season Three, that Starbuck extends the limitations of toughness that Inness describes and moves her characterization beyond many we've seen for tough women.

"You Can't Go Home Again" is a fairly standard hour of science-fiction television, but it is notable in a few ways: one, it focuses on primarily one actor, and two, it features a tough girl pilot who is not saved by even tougher men, one of the ways Inness suggests that women from postapocalyptic settings are made less threatening. Starbuck's Viper and a Cylon Raider crash on a planet without breathable air, and though *Galactica* does everything it can to reach Starbuck, her fellow pilots cannot find her. Starbuck figures out how the organic-mechanical Raider works ("Every flying machine has four basic controls: power, pitch, yaw, and roll. Where are yours?") and gets it to fly. Knowing that a Cylon ship approaching *Galactica* will be shot down, Starbuck spells out her name on the undersides of both wings and wags them at Apollo to get his attention.

The episode is also notable in that it contains several allusions to the original series: the attention to one actor and large parts of the plot correlate to "The Return of Starbuck," a *Galactica 1980* episode; the wiggle of the wings imitates a trick that the original Starbuck and Apollo do to be recognized in "Hand of God" from the 1978 series; and, drawing the parallel between characters even closer, when Adama asks Starbuck if she needs anything while she is recuperating in sickbay, she answers, "A stogie would be nice." In part because it alludes so heavily to the original, this episode is worth exploring because it shows that even early in Season One, the show is willing reformulate what a female character can contain, and in the process eradicate one of the methods of "containment" of strong women observed by Inness. Starbuck is not saved by anyone but herself, and the focus shifts from the passive "wait to be rescued" attitude so ubiquitously displayed by women in popular culture, to an active display of courage and intelligence. Not that getting rescued isn't Starbuck's first thought—"Okay, okay, get to higher ground. Then they see you…then they rescue you"—and one could easily imagine the heroes of this piece being the male pilots braving harsh conditions and low visibility to rescue their comrade, who just happens to be female. But the show moves beyond the expected when it comes to women's characterization. When Starbuck does need to be rescued ("Rapture" 3.12), she is rescued by another woman, Dualla.

Starbuck's sex is a key part of the dark second-season episode "The Farm," in which Starbuck is an unwilling participant in a Cylon-human breeding program. Since Cylons cannot reproduce biologically on their own, they take human women to impregnate, removing their ovaries and attaching the women to machines, though Sharon claims that if women chose to cooperate in the breeding program, they would get to live a more normal life and perhaps choose their mate. Sharon's own pregnancy is explained as a success because the parents—she and Helo—are in love. Starbuck escapes the breeding farm and it is destroyed, but Sharon suggests there are "hundreds, maybe thousands" of such farms in existence (though this seems unlikely, given the implicit logic of the show).[6]

Raising issues of who can be a mother, and under what circumstances, not only makes this episode politically charged but adds another layer to Starbuck's characterization as a woman. Reducing her to her biology, the Cylon Simon, impersonating a human doctor, tells Starbuck that her reproductive system is her "most valuable asset" since "finding healthy child-bearing women your age is a top priority." Starbuck angrily refuses the role of mother; when told she is "a very precious commodity" to the resistance, she shoots back: "I'm not a commodity; I'm a Viper pilot." Her fierce rejection of possible motherhood can be traced in part to the assumption of an abusive parent, a storyline explained in Season Three ("Maelstrom" 3.17). Motherhood's negative depiction in this episode also undermines another of the mitigating factors that Inness suggests exists for tough girls in postapocalyptic worlds, playing up a female character's maternity or femininity. Thus, though Starbuck as a woman is vital to this plotline, Starbuck remains tough, not "feminized" by motherhood. Indeed, the episode ends with Starbuck flying back to *Galactica* to resume her job as a pilot.

However, when Starbuck is kidnapped on New Caprica and made to live with Leoben at the beginning of Season Three, this storyline is picked up again. Starbuck is made to believe that the Cylons succeeded in their breeding program and is presented with her "daughter" ("Precipice" 3.02). And this time, despite her initial disbelief, she embraces the role of mother, quickly believing the lie and trying to care for her child. When uniting her with her supposed daughter turns out to have been a ploy to manipulate her, perhaps into having another child, Starbuck is crushed. For several episodes, she exhibits a recklessness and carelessness about herself and others that reflects what is for her the death of her child.

These several episodes expand Starbuck's character. It's hard to argue that Starbuck's willingness to mother a child works as a reversal of her "tough" characterization, though she does accept a mothering role, however surprising it may have been for the viewers. Starbuck clearly remains tough in conventional ways as well: we see her kill Loeben several times—violently and angrily, with a chopstick to the jugular in one instance—juxtaposed with scenes of tenderness toward her supposed daughter, especially after the child has been injured due to Starbuck's indifference.[7] What this does show is the Cylons' keen understanding of human nature: that it is a natural reaction to care for a child who is weaker than you and needs you, especially in times of duress. What it shows is that *BSG*'s producers and writers are willing to create a fully human character, complicating the role of the tough girl and expanding its definition.

Indeed, the notion that motherhood automatically makes one less tough might be rethought. Inness suggests that mothering softens tough women in the popular imagination because it reminds viewers of what is considered women's "essential nature" (179). But as a soldier actively fighting in a war, Starbuck inhabits a particular category in which warfare and motherhood are metaphorically and symbolically connected.[8] Klaus Theweleit, concluding the collection *Gendering War Talk*, states succinctly: "*WAR* ranks high among the male ways of giving birth" (284). This symbolic relationship between mothering and war, as "a male appropriation of the specifically female capacity for bearing and producing children" (Ramazani 27), speaks to the "tough" nature of both acts (though this appropriation is often cast in a negative light). The rigid boundaries that denote war as a male activity and mothering as a female activity break down under an analysis in which gender—composed of culturally designated traits as opposed to being essentially aligned with one's biological sex—becomes a focus. Illuminating the weakness of the gendered stereotypes that order the "myths of war," Miriam Cooke asks, "Is a soldier a soldier if he is afraid, weak, and vulnerable? Is a mother a mother if she is fearless, strong, and politically effective?" (177).

Inness herself devotes very little discussion to the subject of mother-hood in reducing the effect of toughness. Her primary example is Ripley from the *Alien* series, whose actions as a mother-figure "tone down her tough demeanor" (111). At the same time, Inness considers Ripley one of the few science-fiction characters who has truly expanded women's roles, in large part because Ripley "is shown as being capable of love" and thus becomes "a more complex character" (109). Inness reiterates throughout her study that television exhibits contrasting messages that can paradoxically both reinscribe and challenge existing stereotypes; Ripley and Starbuck seem to be characters able to break down the simple binaries that delineate much of society's thinking about what is appropriate female behavior.

Uncovering other ways that Starbuck is tough, beyond her physicality, is vital to understanding the success of her character. While Inness suggests (and Benedict would agree) that physical toughness in women makes society uneasy, toughness that goes beyond mere strength is not necessarily coded masculine. In describing how women can be tough without using violence, Maria Derose writes, "Tough women are powerful in many ways, partly due to their violence, but also including their determination, their drive for independence, and their sense of self-identity" (67). In the world of *BSG*, one exhibits toughness when one consistently fights back against oppressors, Cylon or otherwise; when one returns to a battle zone to save one's child; when one faces one's fears about dying and about what lies beyond. Starbuck, because she is tough in so many ways, slips out of the double bind for tough women more successfully than most.

Sackhoff is now merely bemused by the negative reaction to her person and to her character. Her mother reads the message boards for her and only tells her about the really outrageous postings. Sackhoff knows that fans of the original *BSG* and Benedict "still talk crap about me and that's fine. I'm developing a very thick skin" (quoted in Nguyen). Perhaps Dirk Benedict should be proud. He writes of his own renegade characterization of Starbuck, which disregarded what others thought would be best: "It was best for the show, best for the character and the best that I could do." Certainly Sackhoff and her version of Starbuck do the same.

Season Three's ambiguous ending suggests that the difficulty surrounding strong female leads remains. Starbuck appears to die earlier in the season ("Maelstrom" 3.17), and Sackhoff's name was significantly absent from the opening credits of the last three episodes. In the final moment of the season, Starbuck appears to a weary and disbelieving Apollo, flying her Viper (which he saw explode) next to his, telling him she can lead the crew to Earth. We'll see what they manage to do with her when Season Four begins, but her early death could mean that television is still not sure what to do with the tough girl. One hopes that this plot twist won't undermine the trail Starbuck has blazed.

Notes

1. Other "sex changes" in this series include Boomer (played by Grace Park) and Admiral Cain (played by Michelle Forbes).

2. Quoted in "Code sigma957," April 29, 2006, <http://sigma957.suddenlaunch.com>.

3. A reviewer at "Ain't-it-Cool-News" described Sackhoff as "some crazed Dirk Benedict breeding experiment gone wrong. With huge boobs and raisin nips and chomping a cigar, she has all the charisma of the typical PRICE IS RIGHT contestant" ("Harry checks out"). A fan on the message boards at the *Battlestar Galactica* fan club writes, "They should never have called it Battlestar Galactica. It is a insult [sic] to TOS [The Original Series] and its fans. What's next, a remake of Star Wars making Han Solo into a girl who sleeps with Luke. Yes, it could be done and it could be done well. Does it make it right?" Even more conspicuous is the "Save Starbuck's Genitalia" online petition. It reads a little tongue-in-cheek (its site is http://www.petitiononline.com/nopeepee/petition.html), but its message is that "Starbuck's lower region is fine the way it is"; as of this writing it has 543 signatures.

4. The role of essentialist/constructionist thinking in feminist theory is especially persistently debated; these are methods of constructing reality and are much more complicated than typically simple reductions can communicate. Diana Fuss's short book provides an excellent initial discussion.

5. Not coincidentally, Starbuck grew out her hair, sporting a much more traditionally feminine look, when she married and set up house with Anders on New Caprica.

6. Such a number would imply that there might be dozens of farms on each of the former Colonies, implying a much greater survival rate for humanity than the series otherwise suggests.

7. Moore, in his podcast commentary of this episode, describes his thoughts on this scene: "She's been holding this child at a distant-arms-length, and when the child is hurt and you think you might be the parent, that there's a moment where you sit on the other side of that hospital bed and you accept the coffee cup from Leoben and suddenly you're just a parent."

8. See Miriam Cooke and Angela Woolacott's collection *Gendering War Talk*; Vaheed Ramazani's "The Mother of All Things"; and Susan E. Linville's "The Mother of All Battles."

16

Authorized Resistance: Is Fan Production Frakked?

Suzanne Scott

As convergence culture increasingly affects media production and con-sumption, fan-producers are contending with both intricate new story-telling matrices and the persistent cycles of consumption these narratives encourage. As Henry Jenkins notes in *Convergence Culture: Where Old and New Media Collide*, convergence is "both a top-down corporate-driven process and a bottom-up consumer-driven process" (18) that occupies an increasingly conflicted position as "media producers are responding to these newly empowered consumers in contradictory ways, sometimes encouraging change, sometimes resisting what they see as renegade behavior" (19). Given that creator and executive producer Ronald D. Moore has emerged as such a visible proponent of fan-centric new media content, *Battlestar Galactica* is an ideal property to interrogate what types of fan production can flourish or founder under emerging convergence conditions. From webisodes to podcasts, from download-able deleted scenes to creator blogs and vlogs, *BSG* has aimed an unpar-alleled wealth of fan-oriented content at its audience and, whether one chooses to view this as a dialogic departure from the producer/consumer binary or merely a tech-savvy marketing ploy, it is an integrated media model that is rapidly gaining popularity.

Jenkins makes an important distinction between "prohibitionist" and "collaborationist" corporate approaches to our increasingly participatory culture (*Convergence* 169). While we can firmly root the *BSG* creative team and its corporate overseers in the latter camp, undoubtedly due in large part to Moore's long history with fan franchises like *Star Trek*[1] and his intimate knowledge of how fandom functions, we must make a distinction between the prohibitionist attempt to "shut down unauthorized participation" (*Convergence* 169) by fans and *BSG*'s unique collaborationist approach, namely one that produces content like fans, for fans. There are a number of ways to read *BSG*'s collaborationist stance. It may be that the production of web content both validates fan practice and "authorizes" fan production, to a degree. More critically, the content being targeted at the *BSG* fan community could be viewed as ultimately reinscribing textual "authority" to the show's creators. In both cases, *BSG* encourages fans to consume authorial/authorized content that frequently performs the textual work we associate with fan narratives: exploring alternate narrative trajectories, extrapolating minor characters' backstories, and so on. These authorized supplements come at the expense of letting fans explore those narrative fissures through their own textual production. This begs the question: is *BSG* fan production frakked?

While *BSG* features a highly involved, diverse, and creative fan community, this essay proposes that the glut of fan-oriented content released by the series' producers and corporate partners could have a counterintuitive effect, increasing fan consumption of this material and thus reinforcing the producers' creative authority. As *BSG* was one of the first television series to embrace the continuous dissemination of varied new media content (from podcasts to vlogs), in addition to dabbling in transmedia storytelling techniques[2] (most notably the webisode series and Dynamite Entertainment's *BSG* comic books), it serves as a critical locus through which broader questions about the shifting nature of fan production can be broached. As DIY (do-it-yourself) fan production comes under temporal and creative threat by DIY (download-it-yourself) content from series' creators, certain types of fan texts will be impacted more than others. Specifically, those fan texts that aim to actively engage with canonical narrative[3] must contend with both *BSG*'s (appropriately) militaristic narrative structure, the mounting rigors of what Matt Hills dubs "just-in-time fandom," or fan production that seeks to keep pace with broadcasting patterns (*Fan* 128), and the unprecedented influx of fan-oriented content for consumption.

Though the multifaceted definition of fan productivity outlined by John Fiske could and should be addressed in a convergence context, the following analysis employs a purposefully narrow definition of the types of fan production impacted by convergence culture. Fan production, within the parameters of this argument, is loosely defined as fan-produced narratives that aim to engage directly with the unfolding canonical narrative. The overtly authorial nature of the content being provided to fans by Moore and his creative colleagues, though surely distributed with good intentions, potentially discourages (and perpetually invalidates) fans' textual productivity. This potential discouragement of textual productivity is coupled with an encouragement of certain forms of enunciative productivity, defined by Fiske as "fan talk" ("Fandom" 38) that "can occur only within immediate social relationships . . . and the popular cultural capital it generates is thus limited to a restricted circulation, a very localized economy" (39). We clearly must amend Fiske's description of the "restricted" circulation of analog fan talk to incorporate the online forum/message board, and accordingly consider how enunciative productivity by fans is increasingly serving a widespread economic/promotional function for *BSG*, Sci Fi, and parent company NBC Universal.

This argument begins with a brief examination of *BSG*'s narrative structure and a closer analysis of how "The Resistance" webisode series, Moore's episodic podcasts, and Dynamite Entertainment's comic book series function within that structure to dissuade or promote fan productivity. The ultimate aim of this essay is not to imply that fan production is frakked, or that *BSG*'s creative and corporate overlords are wielding fan-oriented content to purely promotional, nefarious ends. Rather, it will examine an expanding media trend that *BSG* was one of the first franchises to champion, providing audiences with ample, diverse, fan-oriented content to consume. Whether this content dissuades fans from producing their own texts is something that cannot be quantitatively measured. A far more viable criticism to launch against this influx of fan-oriented content, and one that is retained as an analytic constant for each of the cases to follow, is that this stream of content has the potential to become authorial and canonically validated, an alternative to the consumption of fan narratives that do similar textual work, thereby making fan-produced texts that seek to engage with the *BSG* canon more difficult to produce and less likely to be consumed.

Lay Down Your (Temporal) Burdens

From *BSG*'s inaugural episode, "33" (1.01), time is constructed as an oppressive and potentially destructive force second only to the omnipresent Cylon threat. As dwindling food ("The Passage" 3.10), water ("Water" 1.02, "Bastille Day" 1.03), or fuel reserves ("The Hand of God" 1.10) are posed as races against time, just as perilous as the race toward Earth, one might argue that *BSG*'s frequently rigorous pacing plays a clear-cut narrative purpose by masterfully building tension. However, such a strict narratological control over time, with relatively few temporal ellipses within episodes, between episodes, or even between seasons, poses a series of creative problems for fan-producers looking to engage directly with the *BSG* canon. As fan-produced texts are commonly theorized as striving to "resolve gaps, to explore excess details and underdeveloped potentials" (Jenkins, *Poachers* 278), *BSG* poses an inflexible canonic source despite its seriality, science-fiction premise, and active fan community.

The notable exception to *BSG*'s taut temporality is the expansive narrative gap embedded in the Season Two finale ("Lay Down Your Burdens, Part 2" 2.20). Jumping from the inauguration of Gaius Baltar as president of the Twelve Colonies to "one year later" creates a narrative gap that represents an expansive playground for fan production. Innumerable narrative tidbits begged for further exploration by fans over the long hiatus between Seasons Two and Three: when and under what conditions did Starbuck and Anders get married? How did Gaeta come to serve as President Baltar's aide? What in the name of the gods could have prompted Adama to grow a mustache? Though I have yet to come across a fan text that adequately answers that last question, there were countless fan texts that revelled in the opportunity to author the unwritten year on New Caprica before Season Three commenced. While the earthbound nature of New Caprica closed off the possibility for certain narrative tropes (e.g., Starbuck having access to a Viper would be implausible), it opened up the possibility to explore not only the missing year of narrative time, but the few plotlines that the canon had left conspicuously unresolved (such as the revelation of D'Anna as a Cylon).

The trouble with *BSG*'s new media content model is that it erodes the temporal gaps that occur within the show's narrative diagesis. Perhaps more importantly, it increasingly does so during the hiatus between seasons when more elaborate fan texts are likely to flourish. Not only did the webisode series begin actively and authoritatively filling in that lost narrative time a month prior to the Season Three premiere, but three Writer's Room podcasts were released in the gap between Seasons Two and Three. In addition to Moore's promise of more podcasts over the current extended hiatus between Seasons Three and Four, the forthcoming *Battlestar Pegasus* "movie" has been described as either "extended" or "extra" episodes for Season Four (scheduled to begin broadcast in January 2008). Airing in the fall of 2007 and scheduled for DVD release the following day, the two-hour event, according to Moore, "offers the opportunity to set up something for the fourth season that had not been told to the audiences and that the characters themselves hadn't realized" (quoted in Owen, "Cliffhanger"), with the ultimate aim of giving "the fans something to see and [keeping] the show alive" (quoted in Miller, "Man"). Undoubtedly, the *BSG* fan community will be keeping the show alive by using the nine-month hiatus between Seasons Three and Four to build narratives of their own, but more disquieting, the frequently strict equation of fan involvement with fan consumption obscures the constraints these additional texts place on fan producers.

Hills's description of "just-in-time fandom" emphasizes that "practices of fandom have become increasingly enmeshed within the rhythms and temporalities of broadcasting" (*Fan* 178), and cautions that a simple reading of this as "a techno-evolution towards fuller 'interactivity' . . . neglects the extent to which this eradication of the [analog fanzine] 'time-lag' works ever more insistently to discipline and regulate the opportunities for temporally-licensed 'feedback,' and the very horizons of the fan experience" (179). Extrapolating the definition of "feedback" to include textual production by fans (which can function in a similar fashion, reflecting pleasures taken in and frustrations with the source text), the "time-lags" between the events in weekly serial installments, or in the months between seasons are something to be prized creatively by fan authors looking to explore and elaborate on the canon.

The widespread interfandom jargon of one's fic being "Jossed" (or invalidated by new canon material, a term derived from *Buffy the Vampire Slayer* creator Joss Whedon), or for elements of a still-incomplete fanfic to be negated or rendered implausible by the development of the canon text, speaks to the creative stakes in authoring fan texts that strive for fidelity. In the case of *BSG*, fan producers must strive both to remain faithful to the television series' episodic content and to navigate the various streams of content deriving from *BSG*'s producers, such as podcasts that point toward resolutions or provide alternate narrative trajectories with reasons they were discarded. The conditions under which *BSG* fan authors can write within the canon and have their work validated and consumed by other fans are far from ideal. No longer is being "Jossed" by the televisual text the lone concern for participants in contemporary just-in-time fandom: being "Moored" by an abundance of "authorized" convergence content is also a threat. For those fan producers looking to forge collaborative relationships with the ever-expanding *BSG* canon, there is a continuously diminishing amount of time for their narratives to be consumed and embraced by other fans before being replaced by authorized content.

Given the recent announcement that the upcoming season will be *BSG*'s last, it will be interesting to see how fan authors react to the post–Season Four drought, following the flood of content to which they've grown accustomed. Ironically, the "death" of a show like *BSG* can often breathe new life into fan-authored texts, as audiences turn from official to unofficial narratives. Given that being "Jossed" is conceptually reliant on an open canonical source text, the conclusion of Season Four of *BSG* might eradicate this creative roadblock for fan authors once and for all. However, just as *Buffy the Vampire Slayer* fandom continued to function after the televisual canon's closure and was ultimately reinvigorated by the 2007 release of Joss Whedon's "Season Eight" comic book series, we could see a similar cycle with *BSG* and the proposed prequel series *Caprica*. Ultimately, while fan production is reliant on the regular consumption of a source text, it is the frequency of consumption through the multiplication of supplemental texts that stands to affect the types of texts fans are able to produce. It is precisely this model that Moore has been central in popularizing, thus producing the eponymous challenge that fan texts will continue to face as other producers adopt *BSG*'s model.

Collaborators (and Other Dirty Words)

Released as a ten-part serial on Scifi.com in the month prior to *BSG*'s Season Three premiere, the webisode series "Battlestar Galactica: The Resistance" narratively picks up sixty-seven days after the occupation of New Caprica that concluded Season Two. Both the marketing objectives and the narrative objectives of the webisodes are clear: in addition to promoting the Season Three premiere, the webisodes laid the narrative groundwork for its first story arc, detailing the early stages of the Cylon resistance movement formed by Tigh and Tyrol. Focusing on a pair of minor characters from the *BSG* universe, former Viper-jock Duck and former *Galactica* deckhand Jammer, each of the two-to-four-minute episodes detailed their personal motivations to join and betray the resistance, respectively. The content of the webisode series (e.g., the murder of Duck's wife Nora, Jammer's recruitment by the New Caprica Police) directly informed a number of key narrative developments in Season Three, most prominently Duck's suicide bombing in "Occupation" (3.01), the death order carried out in part by Jammer in "Precipice" (3.02) and "Exodus, Part 1" (3.03), and Jammer's execution in "Collaborators" (3.05). As the webisode series was conceived after filming for Season Three had commenced, it mirrored the process of fan production and narrative (re)construction, beginning with elusive or ambiguous facets of the canon text (Duck's mention of Nora before the suicide bombing, Jammer helping Cally escape execution) and providing context retroactively. However, since the webisodes aired prior to the Season Three premiere, they functioned to answer fans' questions before they were given the opportunity to ask, settled debates before they were allowed to grow lively.

Offering a motivational speech on recruiting members for the resistance movement in the webisodes' debut, perhaps Tigh puts it best: "Talk to [Duck], make him understand that we need him. Throw in some poetic crap about the struggle for liberty against the Cylon oppressors, whatever it takes. We need more people or this resistance movement is going to die in its crib." Tigh's innate comprehension of how frequently that "poetic crap" is used to delineate between us (good) and them (bad) echoes much of the scholarship on active audiences and fan cultures.[4] As discussed at length by Hills (*Fan* 29–30), there is a scholarly tendency to immediately equate fan practice with (good) "resistant" consumption, and extol fan activity that overtly flouts its textual or ideological "resistance." Accordingly, the fan texts that frequently garner the most scholarly and popular attention are slash fiction/art/vids. The idealized resistant fan, juxtaposed with the mindless consumer, is a dialectic that Hills justly critiques, as it "falsifies the fan experience by positioning fan and consumer as separable cultural entities" (*Fan* 29). As patently "resistant" fan productivity[5] is under little threat from a media model that encourages consumption of materials that reinforce the canon, it is perhaps more interesting to explore how the webisodes themselves restructured the producer/consumer resistance paradigm so often ascribed to fan production.

Just as their content turned static notions of heroism and villainy on their respective heads, the webisodes brought longstanding fan debates into the corporate sphere. *Newsweek*, equating Moore with *Star Wars'* Rebel Alliance struggling against NBC Universal's totalitarian Empire in the title of an October 2006 article, cheekily paid homage to George Lucas's notoriously firm ownership rights over fan-produced texts (Hontz). Reframing fandom's longstanding "collision" with producers over their creative content in corporate terms, industry-wide debates were sparked about the primary function of webisode content. Central to the conflict, NBC Universal claimed them as promotional materials, and thus refused to pay residuals to the creative team involved in their production (Hontz). As Moore clearly conceived of them as key narrative texts aligned with the television series (or, collectively, a full episode in their own right), the press coverage of his resistance toward the network and its parent company further served to frame Moore as a producer for the people.

As fan texts that actively avoid resistant relationships with the *BSG* canon, adopting a collaborationist approach, are ironically those that come under threat from the "collaborationist" media model that Jenkins's describes, we must assign the term multiple meanings. Much like *BSG's* increasingly conflicted use of "collaborator" as a negative term and continued interrogation of what constitutes collaboration ("Collaborators" 3.05), collaborative fan texts (though often academically marginalized when equating valuable fan production with resistance) prove an ideal site to gauge the central conflicts of convergence culture. While slash or AU fan texts are typically the nexus of prohibitionist contempt or legal censure, collaborationist fan production forces us to question our typically utopian readings of industrial collaboration with fan culture. Thus, when considering the *BSG* webisodes' revolutionary collaboration with the televisual canon, one has to be mindful of the creative restrictions that come along with this breed of narrative expansion, and to what extent fans' collaboration is hindered as a result.[6]

Act(s) of Contrition?

Frequently labeled as a podcasting "pioneer," Moore describes his weekly episode commentaries as giving fans an opportunity to "see how the sausage is made." Quick to deny their content as a mere "PR thing," Moore's podcasts allow him to, in his own words, "put the show to bed" (quoted in Miller "Podcasting"). This creative tucking in includes elaborating on discarded potential plot lines, justifying narrative choices, and generally allowing fans an unparalleled peek into *BSG*'s creative process. Though Moore has gotten flack from professionals and fans alike for the podcasts' amateur aesthetic (with their frequent aural interruptions by household pets, garbage trucks, and the chatty but occasionally insightful contributions of "Mrs. Ron"), it is precisely this combination of intimacy and authority that makes the podcasts fascinating texts in their own right. Given that Moore himself has stated that he doesn't listen to podcasts as part of his own consumption process and is "surprised" to find that anyone listens to them (quoted in Dahlen), it only seems fitting to focus on what dialogues the podcasts open/close for fans before speculating on what impact the podcasts have on fan productivity.

The thread for fans to discuss Moore's weekly podcasts in the Television Without Pity forums is aptly titled "Chain-Smoking & Apologies," reflecting both Moore's habit of lighting up during his podcasts and his propensity toward honest reflection on various episodes' strengths and weaknesses. The dialogue between fans that the podcasts promote (encouraging close analysis of the text, and closer analysis of Moore's response to the text) clearly falls under Fiske's enunciative form of fan productivity. The debates sparked by the podcasts frequently touch upon their dichotomous nature, with Moore alternately constructed as fanboy conversationalist and omnipotent author-god, and the information relayed framed as deepening or limiting one's analysis of a particular episode. While fan sentiment ranges from the grateful acknowledgement that "at the end of the day, it's just fabulous that we get them at all" (Bourgeois Nerd, post 98),[7] and assertions that the podcasts "validated the nature of being a fan and participating on message boards" (wisteria, post 14), Moore's "military view of leadership" is a frequent topic of conversation. Though Bourgeois Nerd applauds that Moore feels, "ultimately, the failings of his subordinates or his mission (the show) are HIS responsibility" (post 98), others deride the frequency with which Moore's "leadership" is equated with a single, "proper" reading of the text.

Making a distinction between wanting to know how the sausage is made and being told there's only one way to make a sausage (and that Moore is the one man to make it), poster stillshimpy found herself/ himself "questioning the sausage aspect" after "just flat out disagreeing" with one of Moore's commentaries (post 212). Others, like Ankai, feel more strongly: "When [Moore] says 'you're not thinking about that' and 'the audience feels,' I don't feel so much invited [into Moore's way of seeing things] as shoved around . . . like this is not just what he presented, but how we're meant to see it" (post 112). While these complaints are rare, they lay bare the tenuous positioning of the podcast commentaries for fans. In the case of a controversial episode such as "Maelstrom" (3.17), Moore's commentary on Starbuck's apparent death sparked fan outrage. There were those who felt as though Moore's understandably cagey commentary was nothing more than an attempt to "mindfrak" loyal viewers/listeners, further confirming the desire for authoritative answers as the podcasts' primary allure. Likewise, there were a large number of fans, appalled by Moore's nonchalant retelling of the writers' flippant decision to kill Starbuck, who lost their faith in his sausage-making abilities. Though these anxieties were ultimately assuaged by the podcast for "Crossroads, Part 2" (3.20), the fact remains that fans' consumption of the podcasts is intimately bound up with the acceptance of Moore's word as law and the occasional desire to flout that law.

That Moore's podcasts open up dialogue not limited to the textual content of the show, but to the creative process that generates it, is surely a boon to enunciative modes of fan productivity such as online forums. In terms of fans' textual productivity, the degree to which Moore's commentary puts these practices "to bed" along with each episode is still up for debate. Though some, like *BSG* podcast enthusiast stillshimpy, enjoy Moore's discussions of "various pieces of cut story . . . [and] why it is he thought they were not necessary, or failed to work," because it helps "sort of reshape an episode in my mind, or change a view on it when I understand where it might have gone, but didn't and why" (post 47), fan authors could easily indulge in similar reshaping through the textual production of new narratives inspired by Moore's comments. However, as the podcasts strive to provide a sense of creative closure (for Moore and fans alike), they prove narratively inflexible, thus making reshaping by fans more difficult. Similar to the case of Lucas definitively stating that Boba Fett was a man after female fans took the character in as a potential feminist touchstone in *Star Wars*' overwhelmingly masculine universe (Brooker 202–4), Moore's podcasts are guilty of "preempting important lines of fan speculation," despite their potential to "sustain new fantasies" (Jenkins, *Convergence* 115).

The Son Also Rises (From the Dead)

BSG has more recently embraced transmedia storytelling techniques in its forays into comic books. Described by Jenkins as a story that "unfolds across multiple media platforms, each with a new text making a distinctive and valuable contribution to the whole" (*Convergence* 95–96), the *Battlestar Galactica* comic book series (featuring a story arc that purportedly takes place midway through the television series' second season), the *Zarek* series (exploring the trajectory of Tom Zarek from childhood to his imprisonment on the Astral Queen), and the forthcoming *Battlestar Galactica: Season Zero* (set approximately two years before the 2003 miniseries) all function to tug at the margins and expand the middle of the *BSG* canon. Though this certainly points toward a "more collaborative model of authorship" (Jenkins, *Convergence* 96), it is still unclear to what extent this model undermines or buoys the collaborative model between source text(s) and fan texts. While the *Zarek* series and *Battlestar Galactica: Season Zero* serve to write in narrative events that predate the television series, and provide insight into characters' backgrounds and motivations for their behavior on the television series (much like *The Resistance* webisodes), the *Battlestar Galactica* series poses a more intriguing case for fan consumers and producers alike.

Preceded by an authorial note that "the events of this comic book series take place . . . after the return from Kobol in episode 207 and before the arrival of *Pegasus* in episode 211,"[8] the *Battlestar Galactica* comic features a story arc replete with narrative bombshells . . . provided that one chooses to absorb the comic narrative into its preordained place in the *BSG* televisual canon. The comic's central mystery surrounds the "Returners," a medivac ship teeming with dead loved ones (most notably, Zak Adama, son to Bill, brother to Apollo, and fiancée to Starbuck), and their connection to a prophecy contained in the Sacred Scrolls and to a Cylon plot. Over the course of the comic arc (issues 1–9 of 12), we're presented with a number of plot details that have a profound impact on a rereading of Season Two and the *BSG* narrative universe as a whole: the psychological ramifications of an anomalous partial Cylon download (issue 5), the return of a fleet of antebellum-model Cylons who retain their loyalty to the Twelve Colonies (issue 4), a viral infection that incapacitates three-quarters of the fleet (issue 2), and ultimately the discovery that the Cylons made countless prototypes to the current twelve Cylon "skinjob" models (issue 9). Writer Greg Pak's insistence that all involved are "working hard to make sure that the comics fit right into the continuity of the show" (ClashTV), is perplexing, but would seem to encourage a more flexible construction of the *BSG* canon.

A recent interview with *Zarek* and *Season Zero* writer Brandon Jerwa also stresses continuity and canon in the comics' ultimate aim to "give the fans more." Noting that Jerwa echoes a similar statement by Pak that "every aspect of the comic universe is run directly through Ron Moore's office," and that the writers of the comics are "presented with a pretty extensive list of points from the office" (quoted in McCarty) requesting revisions, we can view the comics' use of Moore's authorial signature in a number of ways. Despite their collaborative approach to authorship, transmedia franchises are most successful when "a single creator or creative unit maintains control" (Jenkins, *Convergence* 106), and accordingly, we might view this approval process a simple measure taken to ensure cohesion between the franchise's various properties. If this is the case, and it appears that consistency between the television series and comic series is something that is pointedly stressed by all involved, we need to consider what function the comic series serve (for the producers and fans of the show alike), and what impact they might have on fan productivity.

The *Zarek* and *Season Zero* series pose a straightforward case of the comics serving to (literally) ink in the blank narrative margins of the television series, potentially canonized in the process. The *Battlestar Galactica* series is concurrently more and less canonical than other *BSG* comics: though it supposedly occurs within the diagesis of the television series, there has been no evidence to validate its occurrence retroactively. As the comic employs a wide variety of typically fannish narrative tropes (reviving characters thought dead, emphasizing simmering love triangles and interpersonal conflicts), it is perhaps the best example of authorized *BSG* content to examine as an inspirational source for fan productivity. Its potential, importantly, has less to do with the comic's content than its claim to a place within the televisual narrative. If we're to believe Pak (and by extension, Moore), that such an unconventional plot can nest between episodes, the narrative possibilities for fan authors looking for a place to write within the canon are virtually limitless. Moreover, how the comic collaborates with *BSG*'s Season Two retroactively has the potential to inspire fans to look backward as well as forward, a move that is wise given Season One's relative lack of authorized content.

Unfinished Business

Quoted at length in a 2005 *Newsday* article framing fanfiction as "modern folklore," Moore was put forth as a champion of fans' right to write: "I always loved it when writers went into strange nooks and crannies and turned the universe upside down in ways that we couldn't. 'Wouldn't it be great if Kirk and Spock were lovers?' We can't do that, but it's great that somebody can" (quoted in Werts). While his acknowledgement and encouragement of fan production should certainly be lauded, Moore's impulse is to herald slash fanfic as a standard of textual play is striking for several reasons. Not only does Moore emphasize fans' narrative contributions as being those that clearly diverge from canonical narrative, but by authorizing fan production in the "strange" narrative fissures, those that take narrative to places that the canon textually or ideologically can't go, Moore ultimately only engages with overtly resistant fan texts. Certainly, the production and theorization of slash has been central to both our cultural conception of what fan production is and why it's commonly conceived as a resistant practice, and it has been a key factor in placing media makers in prohibitionist or collaborationist camps. The above analysis of the conditions under which *BSG* fans are producing texts, however cursory, suggests that collaboration is increasingly relevant for critical engagement when approaching fan production in the age of convergence. While prohibitionists still embody the most visible and hostile opponents of fan production, we must meet the shift toward collaborationist models such as *BSG*'s with a healthy dose of skepticism and pay close attention to its evolving impact on how formerly collaborative or canonical fan production is being increasingly forced into resistant practice.

Notes

1. As the anecdote goes, Moore (a self-proclaimed *Star Trek* fan) received his first writing job on *Star Trek: The Next Generation* after slipping a spec script to one of Gene Roddenberry's assistants while touring the set (Ken P.).

2. See Jenkins, *Convergence* 93–130 for a more detailed discussion of transmedia storytelling through an analysis of *The Matrix* franchise.

3. I'm thinking of "Gen" fanfiction or EU (extended universe) narratives in particular, as opposed to slash fanfiction or overtly AU (alternate universe) endeavors, which typically have more tenuous connections to canonical narrative.

4. See Cornel Sandvoss, *Fans* 11–43 for a more detailed account of this tendency, in particular Sandvoss's discussion of Fiske's *Understanding Popular Culture*.

5. In *Using the Force: Creativity, Community and Star Wars Fans*, Will Brooker contends that slash and genfic play "exactly the same game with the primary texts" (133), consequently reading all fan texts as both resistant and collaborative to varying degrees. While this is a valid claim, Lucas's prohibitionist stance toward any and all types of fan production (133) differs greatly from Moore's collaborationist stance. Thus, though slash and gen might play the same fundamental narrative game, it is still necessary to examine who is enforcing the rules and how. The case of *BSG* poses a structural reinforcement of how fans are allowed to play, rather than framing Moore as a referee.

6. Instances when fan production is overtly encouraged, such as Sci-Fi's creation and promotion of their "BSG Videomaker Toolkit" (www.scifi.com/battlestar/videomaker/), retain a conflicted collaborationist stance, as the resultant fan texts are required to attach a promotional clip to their creation, turn over all rights to Sci-Fi, and are ultimately used to promote the show <www.scifi.com/battlestar/videomaker/terms/>.

7. All posts cited in this and the following paragraphs originate from the "Chain-Smoking & Apologies: Podcasts" board at *Television Without Pity*: <http://forums.televisionwithoutpity.com/index.php?showtopic=3149128>.

8. This note is amended in issue 2 to position the events of the comic taking place between "the return from Kobol and the arrival of the Pegasus," due perhaps in part because the *Pegasus* arrives in episode 2.10.

17

Of Duduks and Dylan: Negotiating Music and the Aural Space

Eftychia Papanikolaou

It occurs several times in every episode: the high-pitched shrill sound every time a door opens or closes on *Galactica* must be the most easily identifiable sound in the series. Diegetic music[1] is rare in *Battlestar Galactica*. Rather, diegetic sounds are of utmost importance—produced by humans, machines, and, of course, doors. The aural landscape of the series, however, bursts with nondiegetic (background) music. This essay will focus on the novel ways Bear McCreary's groundbreaking soundtrack for the series underscores or subverts the narrative of *BSG*.

A protégé of the legendary Elmer Bernstein (1922–2004), McCreary holds degrees in Composition and Recording Arts from the Thornton School of Music of the University of Southern California. On his personal website (http://www.bearmccreary.com/; hereafter, McCreary) he regularly provides eloquent commentary on the thematic ideas that permeate the score, and gives background information on the genesis of the music. On the unconventional music profile of the series, he notes that the producers felt that

> orchestral fanfare had been done to death in science fiction. Beyond that conceptual premise, the reality is that orchestral bombast

in the score would ruin the carefully constructed sense of realism in the writing and production. (McCreary 9/13/2006)

Thus, Richard Gibbs, the composer for the 2003 miniseries, created an exceptionally original musical backdrop, which McCreary has taken to new levels of sophistication.[2] Previously successful science-fiction television series, such as *Star Trek* or *Babylon 5*, typically feature nondiegetic music that serves as an auditory evocation of the visual narrative. One is reminded, for example, of how battle scenes in *Star Trek* are accompanied by sweeping orchestral sounds that equal in intensity the projected epic images—usually underscoring their triumphant nature with the trumpet, the musical instrument that most commonly symbolizes earthly battle. To that effect, the music that Stu Phillips and Glen A. Larson created in the late seventies for the original *BSG* series adheres closely to that premise. Over Phillips's richly orchestrated main theme, a memorable trumpet fanfare emerges, a symbol of military victory and heroic apotheosis.[3] Similarly, nondiegetic music for scenes of an intimate nature usually resemble those of traditional Hollywood soundtracks, where music aims to satisfy the audience's expectations through a fixed and tightly controlled—and controlling—system of musical significations. Soundtrack music may be a "signifier of emotion itself" (72), as Claudia Gorbman has maintained, and it signifies "not only according to pure musical codes, but also according to *cultural* musical codes" (2–3). In other words, music appropriates identifiable cultural signifiers, presented through a codified musical vocabulary. As a result, the viewer/listener— or, *perceiver*, in Anahid Kassabian's term—can read explicit cultural meaning or symbolism into the music.[4]

Music in *BSG* assumes a slightly different role. Unconventional instruments permeate the aural landscape with versatility that eschews stereotypical cultural encoding. Glass harmonica and glass marimba,[5] Portuguese guitar, Indian sitar, Balinese gamelan,[6] bagpipes, Uilleann pipes (mellow-sounding bagpipes associated with Irish music),[7] erhu (a kind of two-string bowed Chinese fiddle), and, most importantly, duduk. The Armenian duduk, a type of double-reed aerophone and an inherently melodious instrument, lends its wailing, velvety sound to several scenes in *BSG*. Thus, although the plot avoids historicizing the narrative, the musical discourse highlights music of non-Western flavor.[8] With the exception of instruments such as the Uilleann pipes (with their overtly recognizable Celtic sound) and the duduk (whose sound may carry unequivocal ethnic significations),[9] it is almost impossible for the perceiver to construct any culture-specific meaning—partly due to the composer's and performers' imaginative and unidiomatic use of the instruments' properties. Since the story implies that Caprica and Earth do not share cross-cultural signifiers beyond those implied archetypal ones, no musical signifiers associated with life on Earth can or should be immediately identifiable, since no collective memory of that planet exists. For the same reason, diegetic music is rare in *BSG*. When it occurs, it bears an uncanny resemblance to what we would recognize as contemporary pop sounds, although they carry no identifiable cultural context.

An auditory staple of all episodes involves nondiegetic music that emphasizes percussion. For example, bass drums accentuate moments of intensity, while snare drums and Japanese taikos underline battle imagery. In addition to percussive sounds, the soundtrack is replete with eerie ostinato patterns (repeated rhythmic or thematic ideas) that provide a counterpoint to the visual narrative, while unusual rhythms acquire an emblematic status. Especially recognizable is the 9/8 rhythmic motive of the main titles, which recurs in a leitmotivic fashion whenever Cylons reappear (especially Six).[10]

An evocative addition to the soundtrack is the use of exotic vocal sounds in a multitude of languages: Sanskrit for the text of the opening credits (from the Gayatri Mantra), Italian ("Tigh Me Up, Tigh Me Down" 1.09), Latin ("Kobol's Last Gleaming, Part 2" 1.13), and Sinhalese ("Scattered" 2.01). Most often, however, a textless vocalization floods the nondiegetic fabric, in a style that is most often reminiscent of the Qawwali manner of singing of the Sufi tradition. Such emphasis on the aural (rather than textual) dimension may be seen in the prison scene with Baltar and the captured Six ("Pegasus" 2.10). Baltar's agony at the view of the tortured body (and perhaps soul) of Gina, the captive Six, is encapsulated in the spiritually oriented musical component of the scene.

Symphonic music makes several rare—but very important—appearances in the soundtrack. Observes McCreary:

> When Rymer returned to direct the season [one] finales . . . he again wanted a score that would stand out . . . and this time it meant bringing the orchestra back. In setting *Passacaglia* against the opening montage of *Kobol's Last Gleaming Part I*, it suddenly felt fresh and new.[11] (McCreary 2/4/2007)

Thus, in contrast to Hollywood-like practices, whereby the use of symphonic music conveyed the dominant culture's ideological agenda, McCreary's sparse symphonic sounds are used specifically for the manipulation of the audience's ability to create musical significations. Rather than forming a stereotypical mood-creating, aurally unobtrusive, nondiegetic matrix, symphonic music is now meant to startle. In a similar vein, when nondiegetic solo piano music first appeared in "Torn" (3.06), it accompanied all scenes with the Cylons on the basestar, and carried the same startling effect of familiarity. At first hearing, it resembled the *Adagio sostenuto* of the first movement of Beethoven's "Moonlight" Sonata (Opus 27, No. 2) and, indeed, it was identified in the closed captioning as Beethoven. Very soon, however, it was evident that the music was a newly composed piece and the similarities to Beethoven's Sonata extended only as far as the *adagio* (slow) tempo, and the triplet-based outline of the melody. McCreary's "Battlestar Sonatica" (an obvious pun on Beethoven's work) is a freestanding composition that even follows the formal structure of a classical sonata.[12]

In general, however, music in *BSG* foregrounds current musical trends (themselves not completely free from politico-ideological structures) that tend to popularize ethnic sounds and emphasize cross-cultural practices. The explosion of interest in world music in the past two decades has resonated with parallel tendencies in all facets of American music industry. Record companies promote the music of non-Western artists as aggressively as they do Yo-Yo Ma's Beethoven recordings, while in academic institutions (also reflections of socioeconomic agendas) the study of ethnomusicology has become a staple of standard undergraduate music curriculum. In that respect, it might not be extraordinary at all that the series' sound would reflect the same idiosyncratic fusion of traditional and world music as that represented in the eclectic tendencies of the recording industry.

Overt engagement with contemporary American culture, however, may be found not only in the music's ethnic nuances, but also in musical allusions. A rare instance of intertextuality appears at the end of "Scar" (2.15). After a fierce dogfight, where Starbuck has allowed Kat to kill the Cylon Raider Scar, Starbuck works out her tightly concealed feelings for Anders in a boxing practice with Helo. In this otherwise intense scene (Helo engages in a forceful series of punches), we get a rare glimpse into the heroine's emotional side: she might actually be in love. At that moment the mellow, sentimental sound of an acoustic guitar gradually acquires a specific melodic profile, and we are stunned to realize that Stanley Myers's famous Cavatina from the *Deer Hunter* (1978) makes a nondiegetic appearance at the conclusion of the scene. In addition to its brutally realistic depiction of the Vietnam War, *The Deer Hunter* provides fascinatingly empathetic portraits of the men who found themselves in that predicament. Starbuck here is allowed to shed her wartime, pilot-hero persona, and this moment of rare emotional explosion is appropriately celebrated in a most unusual musical fashion—with a pun on a film that has become symbolic of wartime American culture. When the rest of the soundtrack assiduously avoids any such culture- and time-specific musical significations, composer and producer seem to exploit the perceivers' collective memory in order to intensify the sentimental character of the scene.

Operating under a similar premise, the music from the Season Three finale specifically targets the collective memory of the perceiver, thus reversing three seasons of significant absence of musical or cultural encoding. In "Crossroads, Part 1" (3.19), mysterious music catches Colonel Tigh's ear as he tries to tune in on an old radio at Joe's bar. The music, unrecognizable through the radio's static, also attracts the attention of Anders. Later at the bar, both Tory Foster and Anders hear the music over the radio, but nobody else seems to be able to hear it. The mysterious music becomes an obsession with Tigh: when he hears it again in the courtroom, he orders for the music to be turned off; and the episode concludes with Tigh, obviously disturbed by the maddening insistence of the music, trying to locate its source inside the ship. In "Crossroads, Part 2" (3.20), the mysterious music intensifies and develops into an important part of the plot. Anders and Tory become distracted again by the music. Tyrol turns out to be the fourth person who can hear the music, as he awakes from his sleep and proceeds to decipher its source and melodic profile. When Anders overhears Tyrol humming the strange music, framed in a way that suggests superhuman senses, he realizes it is the same music he has been hearing:

Tyrol: You hear *that* song?
Anders: Yeah, it's freaking me out. I hear it everywhere but I
          can't—but I can't really hear it, you know what I mean?
Tyrol: Yeah, it's like you can grab just a part of the melody and
          then it goes away, like it's something from childhood . . .
Anders: Childhood . . .

At the same time, Tigh anxiously discusses it with a dismissive Adama:

Tigh: I'm telling you, Bill, they put the music in the ship. I can
          hear it.
Adama: I believe you. I'll look into it.
Tigh: You'll look into it? You'll look into it? I am here telling
          you there is Cylon sabotage aboard our ship!
Adama: Sabotage. With music?
          Tigh: I know, I know. I can't quite understand it myself.
          There's too much confusion.
Adama: I promise I'll look into it.

Later, when the fleet has jumped to the Ionian nebula and is under Cylon attack, all ships experience a power outage, and one is tempted to connect this event to the sabotage reference from before—but, to echo Adama, with music?

For Tigh, locating the source becomes an obsession. With ear glued to the ship, he continues to hear the original mysterious music, but this time Tyrol also seems to hear it (apparently in his head). In a dazed manner, he voices, "There must be some way out of here." The scene cuts to Tigh, who proceeds to complete the phrase with "said the joker to the thief." Another abrupt cut takes us to Anders, who recites, "There's too much confusion here," and the fourth cut takes as to Tory's conclusion of "I can't get no relief." The four are seen being pulled toward each other, as if a secret switch inside their heads has been activated simultaneously. The perceiver thus far had heard only inconsequential sitar riffs of the song, with no particular musical significance. It is not until the music triggers a textual response from the characters (as they separately recite lines from a song) that the perceiver might become aware of the song reference.

As the music gradually intensifies and appropriates rock elements, it becomes nondiegetic in nature—that is, it functions as background music for the action that follows. Electric guitars, sitars, and percussion now occupy the sonic landscape, as an invisible energy compels the four characters to gather in the same space. First Tory and then all together hum the opening melody of the mysterious tune, possibly in an attempt to identify it. They don't, but the perceivers do: it is Bob Dylan's "All Along the Watchtower," and for the first time it has made a concrete aural appearance.[13] It is quickly understood that seeking its source (as Tigh has

done in a dramatic fashion) is less important than experiencing the space
it occupies. The mysterious nature of their convergence at that location
begins to unravel. "We are Cylons," Tyrol asserts, "and we have been from
the start." With the Cylon attack underway, they debate and deny their
newly realized identity in favor of their duties toward the Colonial Fleet.
"I'm an officer in the Colonial Fleet," Tigh defiantly proclaims. "Whatever else I am, whatever else it means, that's the man I want to be. And if
I die today, that's the man I'll be." Without a pause, the massive sound
of an electric guitar signals the opening in McCreary's own version of the
song. What started as a magnetic garble audible only to four characters
(and to the perceiver) has now evolved into a nondiegetic panorama of
storming energy.

The song here assumes the role of another protagonist. If indeed the
four are Cylons, the discovery of their identity through sound and music
indicates a level of communication that has not been explored in the plot
thus far. Now the significance of the music is transferred from the narrative characters to the perceiver, and from that point on, the music's
ideological premise also rests on its associations to the audience. For if
the song is meant to ground the narrative in a historical and cultural
continuum in a way that the series had eschewed thus far, one may wonder why we haven't had more such instances of musical allusions before.
According to his online commentary, McCreary was first informed of the
song's inclusion by Moore:

> I have to admit that my first thought was that Ron might be going
> crazy. . . . Do we want a performer who can sing and play guitar
> exactly like Dylan? or Hendrix? . . . I learned that the idea was not
> that Bob Dylan necessarily exists in the characters' universe, but
> that an artist on one of the Colonies may have recorded a song with
> the exact same melody and lyrics. Perhaps this unknown performer
> and Dylan pulled inspiration from a common, ethereal source.
> Therefore, I was told to make no musical references to any
> "Earthly" versions, Hendrix, Dylan or any others. The arrange-
> ment needed to sound like a pop song that belonged in the
> *Galactica* universe, not our own. (3/25/2007)

Producer and composer seem to be asking of us the impossible: to
strip the song of all its musical and cultural codes, to resist reading in the
music any attempt to historicize the narrative. They are asking us to listen

to it as pure sound, as if for the first time, irrespective of any previous encoding—intertextuality is turned on its head. The televisual narrative has appropriated a culturally, historically, and musically specific song, whose aesthetic substance is readily identifiable to the perceiver, and whose diegetic profile in relation to the plot is yet to be determined. Usually it is the narrative characters who are deaf to the music—they are not supposed to be able to listen to nondiegetic sounds; here it is the perceiver who is impelled to be deaf.[14] Thus, while the musical discourse demands active awareness of the plot's aural dimension, the perceiver is encouraged to remain deaf to the music's allusion to a popular song.

Bob Dylan's 1967 song "All Along the Watchtower" becomes a signifier of American musical heritage, whose specific cultural codes cannot possibly be lost on the perceiver. Besides it being one of the most easily identifiable songs from the sixties, the song also partakes of a specific cultural ethos, saturated in the then vibrant idiom of rock music:

"There must be some way out of here," said the joker to the thief,
"There's too much confusion, I can't get no relief.
Businessmen, they drink my wine, plowmen dig my earth,
None of them along the line know what any of it is worth."
     "No reason to get excited," the thief, he kindly spoke,
"There are many here among us who feel that life is but a joke.
But you and I, we've been through that, and this is not our fate,
So let us not talk falsely now, the hour is getting late."
     All along the watchtower, princes kept the view
While all the women came and went, barefoot servants, too.
Outside in the distance a wildcat did growl,
Two riders were approaching, the wind began to howl.

Many will likely recall Jimi Hendrix's version of "All Along the Watchtower," included in his *Electric Ladyland* album of 1968. McCreary's version, like Hendrix's before, relies on dense electric guitar and percussion sounds—elements that, in Albin Zak's description of Hendrix's song texture, similarly intensify "an impression of disorientation ('too much confusion') and claustrophobia ('there must be some kind of way out of here')" (634). As George Lipsitz argues, many popular songs have "a long history in the collective memory of the audience," for "rock-and-roll music embodies a dialogic process of active remembering" (113). The perceiver engages in dialogue with the song, as much as

McCreary engaged in a dialogical process with the previous two versions when making his own arrangement.[15] They may claim otherwise, but composer and producer foreground the music in a manner that cannot but enhance the narrative by aurally invoking the past—that is, our past.

The song itself also conveys pastness: the four characters share this musical memory in time (at least two of them agree that they remember it from childhood) and, similarly, American audiences will recognize it as the product of shared cultural and musical memory.[16] In the sixties, Dylan was the "voice of his generation," and the perceiver is encouraged to contemplate also the social forces that shaped that period's musical aesthetics, such as war and protest, unrest and propaganda—that is, a world not unlike our post-9/11 present. Hendrix's version, in particular, "was heard far away in Vietnam, where GIs felt they knew exactly what the song was about" (Marqusee 238). Today its evocation may simply be a reflection of nostalgia.[17]

Less a protest song than an introspective statement, "All Along the Watchtower" reflects Dylan's considerable engagement with the Bible. Between the release of *Blonde on Blonde* in March 1966 and *John Wesley Harding* in December 1967,[18] Dylan's song aesthetics were transformed from the rock opulence of electric guitars to his previously explored ascetic directness. Dylan the person went through a transformation as well, precipitated by his retreat to Woodstock, his marriage and the birth of his first son, and his motorcycle accident of July 1966 (Zak 619)—the latter being an event responsible for his shift to the biblically inspired lyrics that characterize many of his songs after 1966.[19] Dylan's biblical source for "All Along the Watchtower" is Isaiah 21:5–9:

5. Prepare the table, watch in the watchtower, eat, drink: arise, ye princes, and anoint the shield.

6. For thus hath the LORD said unto me, Go, set a watchman, let him declare what he seeth.

7. And he saw a chariot with a couple of horsemen, a chariot of asses, and a chariot of camels; and he hearkened diligently with much heed:

8. And he cried, A lion: My lord, I stand continually upon the watchtower in the daytime, and I am set in my ward whole nights:

9. And, behold, here cometh a chariot of men, with a couple of horsemen. And he answered and said, Babylon is fallen, is fallen;

and all the graven images of her gods he hath broken unto the ground. (King James Version)

The polysemic nature of Dylan's lyrics has invited numerous speculations and interpretations over the years, especially of the two archetypal characters of the joker and the thief.[20] Because of its function at the season's cliffhanger, the song immediately claims the perceivers' attention, without necessarily revealing its meaning. Whether the cryptic lyrics constitute a commentary on the narrative may or may not be revealed in Season Four. Rather than drawing tentative and, possibly, erroneous parallels between the song's meaning and visual narrative in *BSG*, I focus on the narrative space that the *absence* of the song occupies in the final episode. The song's nondiegetic vocals (sung by the composer's brother, Brendan) are first introduced at the exact moment when Vipers launch a counterattack on the Cylons. Interestingly, the last strophe of Dylan's song is omitted; McCreary's version ends with repetitions of the opening line of the third stanza: "All along the watchtower." The action implied in the rest of the song instead takes place on-screen: the "two riders" of the song's last line, an ominous allusion to the two biblical horsemen, are visually supplanted by Starbuck and Apollo, two contemporary riders piloting their Vipers. The sequence that unfolds, however, seems to both support and subvert the despondent message of the song's narrative: at this moment of crisis and impending doom, similar to the apocalyptic images implied in the Bible and echoed in Dylan's lyrics, Starbuck returns (in one sense or another) with the promise of finding Earth.

As the last episode concludes with Starbuck's triumphant return from Earth, the music emits a threatening sonic cloud that reaches an explosive urgency. With the electric guitar riffs à la Hendrix, it culminates in a visual shot of planet Earth and, more specifically, North America. When asked to comment on that final shot, Moore has simply asserted that *BSG* "is an American show," and admitted that "sadly, if another continent were shown, for example Africa, some viewers probably wouldn't recognize it as Earth."[21] I am not sure if this tongue-in-cheek comment is meant to resound as an overarching criticism (or endorsement) of specifically American cultural elements in the series, or whether the use of an all-American song in the finale indicates self-indulgence on the producers' part. After all, the quintessence of rock music resonates with today's audiences not only because of its fixity in time (the sixties) but also in space (North America).

If music is meant to have a signifying role, then one has to wonder whether the musical or verbal diegesis has the last word in *BSG*. In places where the music underscores the visual narrative, the soundtrack succeeds in paralleling the novel features of the series. It is only when one aspect (either musical or verbal) tends to subvert the other, as in the Season Three finale, that a film theorist might be inclined to "mysticize music," to use Abbate's words, to privilege the musical aspect of the narrative, and thus view it as an agent that "overrides or alters the plot being acted out in the verbal and visual domains" ("Round Table" 20). In the case of *BSG*, however, I am inclined to read the reverse: that it is the *essence* of the music used that is altered and redefined rather than the plot. Rock music, as Simon Frith has argued, "rests on an ideology of the peer group as both the ideal and reality of rock communion" (213). It is not the music that underscores the scene's narrative, but rather the diachronic element of the plot that imposes new status on the music. Wherever the story may lead us in Season Four, the aural dimension of Dylan's song has been redefined forever because of its renewed communion with contemporary audiences through *BSG*.

Notes

This essay is dedicated to my sister, Anthee Papanikolaou, film aficionado and science-fiction enthusiast, who first introduced me to *BSG* in the summer of 2006. I would like to thank Bear McCreary for taking the time to read this essay and for his kind endorsement. Many thanks to Robert Fallon, my colleague at BGSU, for helpful discussion in preparation of this essay.

1. In this essay two terms associated with film music criticism will be used throughout. Diegetic (or phenomenal) is actual music, whose source is implied by either script or action and can be heard by the characters; nondiegetic (or noumenal) is background music meant to be heard only by the spectator. Another function of this dichotomy, specifically as it pertains to sound, is unique in *BSG*. Normally, battle sounds would be regarded as diegetic sounds—the narrative characters create them and hear them as part of the action. In this particular case, those sounds occur in the vacuum of space, where no sound is perceivable to those who perform or witness them. Thus, diegetic sounds in *BSG* may occasionally appropriate a nondiegetic function—a duality that is rather uniquely applicable to this type of cinematic genre.

2. McCreary admits that Michael Rymer, the director of the miniseries, "deserves the credit for first eliminating the orchestra. . . . [H]e knew he wanted something that would totally stand out from the traditional orchestral science-fiction score" (2/4/2007).

3. As an homage to the original series, McCreary reworked the famous fanfare theme into the "Colonial Anthem." In "Final Cut" (2.08), McCreary's version is heard when D'Anna Biers, until then known as a civilian reporter, shows the video documentary she filmed on *Galactica* to the Cylons on Caprica. The triumphant nature of the music, which on the Cylons' screen seems to match the resilience shown by the *Galactica* crew, takes on an ironic twist when we realize that D'Anna is herself a Cylon.

4. Film music criticism has found it difficult to determine one term that adequately fuses the visual and aural aspects of a film, and that combines the dual role of the spectator as viewer and listener. I embrace Anahid Kassabian's preference for the term *perceiver* and use it in place of "viewer" or "listener" because "it does not privilege one sense over others, and because it is slightly more active in tone than 'spectator' or 'auditor'" (173n1).

5. In "The Eye of Jupiter" (3.11), McCreary used those two instruments to create a "haunting" aural landscape for Tyrol's discovery of the temple (12/15/2006).

6. See McCreary's informative commentary on the "Balinese-inspired" theme of the Temple of Five in "Rapture" (3.12) (1/26/2007).

7. They prominently introduce the Celtic theme that initially appears in "The Hand of God" (1.10); its reorchestrated version recurs during Apollo and Adama's farewell in "Exodus, Part 1" (3.03), and at the conclusion of "Exodus, Part 2" (3.04).

8. McCreary also had the ahistorical aspect of the plot in mind when he decided to saturate the nondiegetic fabric of the soundtrack with instruments "as ancient as possible," such as the human voice, percussion, and the duduk (9/28/2006).

9. Duduks have been featured prominently before in film, as in Peter Gabriel's soundtrack for Martin Scorsese's *The Last Temptation of Christ* (see my essay in *Scandalizing Jesus?*). An important difference between the two composers' approaches to the use of world music lies in the fact that Gabriel tends to mix recordings of traditional music from around the world with electronic sounds, while McCreary chooses to compose his own musical themes using the actual sounds of non-Western instruments for production purposes only.

10. The 9/8 rhythmic-motivic idea was first introduced by Gibbs in the 2003 miniseries, and was subsequently retained as a signature idea.

11. A passacaglia epitomizes music of the Baroque period. At its most fundamental, it consists of a series of melodic variations over a repeated basso ostinato pattern (see Silbiger). The strict compositional process may not be immediately recognizable by the perceiver, but its formal austerity must account for the "freshness" that McCreary and Rymer envisioned in that scene.

12. According to McCreary, it was Ronald D. Moore who originally "wanted to try scoring Baltar's experiences on the Cylon basestar with unsettlingly familiar classical piano music. His initial idea was Beethoven's Moonlight Sonata" (3/11/2007). McCreary claims it to be "a musical representation of Baltar's fear" (11/3/2006).

13. Closed-captioning identifies it as "All Along the Watchtower" at exactly that moment.

14. I borrow the theoretical framework on the "deafness" of the narrative characters from Abbate's discussion of a similar premise in operatic music (*Unsung Voices* 125–26).

15. McCreary's arrangement opens with guitarist Steve Bartek's "twangy Middle Eastern guitars, builds with his haunting electric sitar, and breaks into pounding, distorted guitar riffs" (3/25/2007).

16. Even those who may not be old enough to have a memory of Dylan's or Hendrix's versions, will recognize it through its reincarnations by artists as diverse as U2, Prince, and the Dave Matthews Band. It is telling that, immediately after the airing of "Crossroads, Part 1" (3.19) on March 18, 2006, online forums exploded with commentaries on the song, in spite of the fact that it had not yet been identified on the show nor had it been performed in its entirety. For example, on TV.com's forum, the exchange ranged from an appreciation of the song's iconic status, to questions about the version used (both Dylan's and Hendrix's versions were mentioned), to its symbolism in the series <http://www.tv.com/battlestar-galactica-2003/show/23557/what-is-the-song-that-tigh-hears-spoiler-warning-for-crossroad-part-2/topic/11046-689820/msgs.html?page=0>.

17. Nostalgia may even be detected in the object of the radio itself. Its old-fashioned presence and function (it emits a static as Tigh tries to tune into the song) also evoke pastness.

18. Michael Gray recently described Dylan's *John Wesley Harding*, the album where "All Along the Watchtower" first appeared, as "a most serious, darkly visionary exploration of the myths and extinct strengths of America" (349).

19. In 1968 Dylan's mother described how in his house in Woodstock, he would constantly refer to "a huge Bible [he kept] open on a stand in the middle of his study" (Heylin 285).

20. Useful commentary on the song's lyrics may be found in Cartwright, De Somogyi (7–10), and Gilmour.

21. According to Moore, Sci-Fi Channel offered to purchase the rights to Jimi Hendrix's version of "All Along the Watchtower," but "he [Moore] turned it down saying that he couldn't justify the Battlestar Universe having that version of the song" <http://en.wikipedia.org/wiki/Crossroads_%28Battlestar_Galactica%29>.

18

"All This Has Happened Before": Repetition, Reimagination, and Eternal Return

Jim Casey

A passage from the Sacred Scrolls, spoken by humans and Cylons alike reads, "All this has happened before, and all of it will happen again" (1.08). On the surface, the line may appear to be nothing more than a clever metatextual moment, alluding to the provenance of the 2003 "reimagining" of *Battlestar Galactica* as a reworking of an earlier series by the same name. *BSG* has happened before, in 1978. In fact, *BSG* has happened several times. The original *BSG* was revived two years later as *Galactica 1980*; a continuation of original, called *Battlestar Galactica: The Second Coming*, was developed by Richard Hatch in 1999; and a Fox Studios and USA Television project was offered to director Bryan Singer and producer Tom DeSanto in 2001.[1] Even the original story has happened before, in Exodus. Glen A. Larson's original series replaced the Israelites' quest for the Promised Land with the Colonials' search for Earth, and supplanted the Twelve Tribes of Israel with the Twelve Tribes of Man. But the quotation also draws attention to the repetitions and reiterations inherent in the serialized art form (particularly serialized television). *BSG* has happened before, and, during the season, happens every week. Not only does each show begin with the familiar apparatus comprised of music, titles, and the opening sequence, but most episodes also offer a quick synopsis of what has happened before: "Previously on *Battlestar*

Galactica . . ." Notice, however, that, although each of these elements has happened before, each is altered with every new incarnation.

The title music for Season One in the United States was an original instrumental by Bear McCreary called "Two Funerals," and was written specifically for "Act of Contrition" (1.04); beginning with Season Two, U.S. audiences have heard the U.K. title music, featuring the Gayatri Mantra, during the opening sequence. Similarly, the opening text has varied season to season. The original introduction reads,

> The Cylons were created by Man.
> They Rebelled.
> They Evolved.
> They Look and Feel Human.
> Some are programmed to think they are Human.
> There are many copies.
> And they have a Plan.

For Season Two, the fourth and fifth lines were dropped and the second and third lines flipped: "They Evolved. / They Rebelled." For Season Three, the transposed lines were returned to their original order: "They Rebelled. / They Evolved." Often, the titles include a survivor count; these numbers fluctuate episode to episode.[2] Finally, the episode recaps are often not the same as the earlier events they purportedly relate. Not only are they compressed and then juxtaposed to other relevant events, but they often depict things that never actually happened. No one says, "Cally shot Sharon!" in the episodes preceding "Home, Part 2" (2.07), for example, and Admiral Adama never announces that he will give command of the *Pegasus* over to Chief Engineer Garner prior to "The Captain's Hand" (2.17).

"All this has happened before, and all of it will happen again" is first uttered by the *Gemenon Traveler* copy of Leoben Conoy, when he is being interrogated by Starbuck (1.08). In subsequent episodes, various human and Cylon characters speak the words, including President Roslin (1.12) and Baltar's virtual Six (1.10). In addition to honoring the original series and reflecting the structural components of serialized TV, the quoted scripture encapsulates *BSG*'s approach to the formal and thematic concerns of reference, return, and redemption.

Reference, Appropriation, and Homage

The new series not only co-opts the earlier version of the storyline, but appropriates themes and plots from a variety of science-fiction classics. For example, the Cylons' attack on and destruction of Caprica (M.01) is very similar to the storyline of the *Terminator* franchise, in which machines designed by humans rebel and attack their creators by hacking into the humans' defense-system mainframe. The Cylon attack devastates the human political structure, so that the presidential succession falls to the secretary of education (M.01), just as it does in Pat Frank's *Alas, Babylon*. Unlike the clanking, mechanistic Cylons of the original series,[3] however, the new Cylons have become advanced enough to "look and feel human," similar to the andys of Philip K. Dick's *Do Androids Dream of Electric Sheep?* or the replicants of *Blade Runner* (1982). The seductive Cylon Six recalls the Nexus-6 models (from both the novel and the film) as well as Number Six from Patrick McGoohan's 1967 *The Prisoner*, and possibly *Star Trek Voyager*'s Seven of Nine. The human-looking Cylons often have implanted memories, as in the anime classic, *Ghost in the Shell* (1995), with several characters who are unaware that they are not human. The Cylons have data-encoded identities, similar in many respects to the cyber-realities of *The Matrix* (1999) or William Gibson's *Neuromancer*, and are "resurrected" if they should die, like the various characters of Philip José Farmer's *Riverworld* series. In an attempt to rescue her daughter, *BSG*'s Sharon Agathon takes what the *Riverworld* novels refer to as the "suicide express" in order to move her consciousness to a body-copy on the Cylon Base Ship (3.12).[4] Even the mysterious virtual Six who accompanies Baltar may have been commandeered from another source. When she tells Baltar, "I'm you. I'm your subconscious frakking with your mind" (2.07), she suggests a scenario similar to Chuck Palahniuk's *Fight Club* or Philip K. Dick's *A Scanner Darkly*.

BSG consciously alludes to the earlier series: schematics of the old Cylon Centurion models are seen among the paperwork at the Armistice Station and a life-sized model appears in the museum aboard *Galactica* (M.01); one of the Centurion models replies to Aaron Doral with the original series' Cylon catchphrase "By your command" (M.02); Stu Phillips's theme music for the old series is played during *Galactica's* decommissioning ceremony (M.01) and as background music for the documentary/news segment created by D'Anna Biers (2.08); and the first words of the Sacred Scrolls, "Life here began out there" (M.02), echo a line from the credits of the 1978 *Battlestar Galactica*. But the new series actively references other works as well. My title's quotation, for example, ostensibly taken from the Sacred Scrolls, is also the first line of Disney's animated *Peter Pan* (1953): "All of this has happened before and it will all happen again."

Ronald D. Moore, writer and executive producer of *BSG*, began his career writing for *Star Trek: The Next Generation* and worked on both *Star Trek: Deep Space Nine* and *Star Trek: Voyager*, so many of the allusions are either nods to *Star Trek* or set in direct opposition to the conventions of that universe. For example, when Tough Guy and Carousel accidentally jump their Raptor inside the solid rock of a mountain (2.19), the incident resembles a *Star Trek* transporter accident. Surprisingly, however, very few of these moments are parodic, or even ironic. One notable exception occurs when Brother Cavil, discovered as a Cylon, utters the clichéd refrain of extraterrestrial first contact, "Take me to your leader" (2.20). In general, *BSG*'s references to other works act not as comic relief, but rather as straight homage, to set the tone, or to develop character.

Many of the homages are fleeting, such as the quick glimpses of the Starship *Enterprise* (M.02, in the final shot of the Colonial Fleet) or the *Firefly* transport ship (M.01, when Laura Roslin is diagnosed with cancer). Some of the borrowed elements are tenuous, as with *Colonial One*'s vague stylistic connection to Kubrick's *2001: A Space Odyssey* (1968). Some of the references are ambiguous, such as the phrase "end of line," derived from the line-code formulations of the Master Control Program in *Tron* (1982) and surfacing in both the cryptic gibberish of the Cylon Hybrid (3.06) and Three's seemingly symbolic dream, in which she is cornered and shot by armed marines on the *Galactica*, next to a hatch labeled End of Line (3.08). But most of the homages are precise visual quotes. When Apollo points his gun at the face of Tom Zarek and asks him, "How about it, Tom. You still have a death wish?" (1.03), the body language and proxemics of the players reproduce the famous image of Clint Eastwood and the bank robber in *Dirty Harry* (1971). Similarly, an ejection sequence (1.04) mirrors the emergency ejection in *The Right Stuff* (1983), and Starbuck's bouncing ball (2.06) is taken from *The Great Escape* (1963).

Yet even when the visuals are not exactly the same, the spirit of the original adds resonance. The connection between Starbuck and Leoben is conveyed by the tableau of the two characters standing on opposite sides of a barrier with their hands pressed palm to palm on the window that separates them (1.08), just as Spock and Kirk do in *Star Trek II: The Wrath of Khan* (1982). Similarly, the surreal paranoia of *The Twilight Zone's* "Nightmare at 20,000 Feet," starring William Shatner as a passenger who believes he sees a gremlin on the wing of his plane, informs the fatigue-induced hallucinations mentioned by Starbuck in her admonition to her pilots, "Remember, we're all flying solo on this mission. So that means there'll be nobody there to bitch slap you if you start to get tired or start seeing little toasters on your wing" (3.10); the shock and despair that conclude Ambrose Bierce's "An Occurrence at Owl Creek Bridge" (or Robert Enrico's short film) prefigure Baltar's suicide attempt and the subsequent vision of himself downloaded (3.13); and the frightening preternatural speed of the replicant Pris at the end of *Blade Runner* intensifies Six's menace when she sprints around Starbuck at the Delphi Museum, moving much too fast for the pilot to shoot her (1.13).

Often, the suggestion of imminent threat in *BSG* is much more subtle, such as when Helo comments that "a storm is coming" (3.19), echoing the conclusion of *The Terminator* (1984).[5] When Adama cuts himself shaving (1.01 and 3.20), the seemingly trivial event foreshadows later calamities, just as it does when John Baxter cuts himself shaving in *Don't Look Now* (1973). These evocative moments often have little narrative purpose; instead, they are used to set the tone of a scene. When *Galactica* is boarded by Centurions and has her computers infected with a Cylon virus (2.02), the darkened corridors promote anxiety and fear partly because they are reminiscent of the *Alien* films. Similarly, there are no direct visual analogues to Helo and Sharon wandering through empty Caprica City (1.03), but their environment suggests the eerie isolation of various other empty cities, such as those in Stephen King's *The Stand*, *Night of the Comet* (1984), *28 Days Later* (2002), or any of the films based on Richard Matheson's 1954 novel *I Am Legend* (*The Last Man on Earth* [1964], *The Omega Man* [1971], and *I Am Legend* [2007]).

BSG also patterns specific instants after current and historical events in order to create particular effects or moods, modeling scenes and shots after events such as the attack on Pearl Harbor (M.01), the bombing of Hiroshima (M.01), the swearing in of Lyndon B. Johnson (M.02), the ordinance accident on the USS *Forrestal* on July 29, 1967 (1.04), the famous handshake between Rabin and Arafat during the Oslo Accords (1.11), the Kent State and Boston Massacres (2.04), the shooting of Lee Harvey Oswald by Jack Ruby (2.04), the Nazis' march into Paris (2.20), Alexander Haig's declaration that "I'm in control here" after Reagan had been shot (2.06), Mario Savio's Free Speech Movement oration at Berkeley in 1964 (2.20), and numerous references to post-9/11 America. Often, these allusions offer useful insights into characters. We instantly know something about Apollo when he says, "Let's be careful out there" (1.01), like Sergeant Phil Esterhaus of *Hill Street Blues*; or Baltar's virtual Six when she tells him, "Don't make me angry, Gaius. You wouldn't like me when I'm angry" (1.06), just like David Banner from *The Incredible Hulk*; or President Adar when Roslin recounts his determination to "Stay the course" (1.02). It is possible that even Boomer's assertion that she is from Troy (1.08) might be an allusion to Homeric myth, since she is a Trojan Horse of sorts. Similarly, Roslin's suggestion to Baltar after the last presidential debate, "Why don't you go frak yourself" (2.19), echoes the suggestion made by Vice President Dick Cheney to Senator Patrick Leahy and reveals Roslin's anger and distress.

Repetition and Eternal Return

The cyclical conception of time that the Sacred Scrolls advocate resembles Friedrich Nietzsche's concept of eternal return (or eternal recurrence), which was first propounded in aphorism 341 of *The Gay Science:*

> What if some day or night a demon were to steal into your loneliest loneliness and say to you: "This life as you now live it and have lived it you will have to live once again and innumerable times again; and there will be nothing new in it, but every pain and every joy and every thought and every sigh and everything unspeakably small or great in your life must return to you." (194)

For the Colonial citizens, this concept of recurrent time represents one of the most fundamental tenets of their religious beliefs. As Roslin tells Starbuck, "If you believe in the gods then you believe in the cycle of time, that we are all playing our parts in a story that is told again and again throughout eternity" (1.12). For Roslin, her part in the story seems to parallel that of Moses. The vision of the twelve snakes, induced by Roslin's consumption of Chamalla extract, leads the priestess Elosha to identify the president as an avatar of the scripture's great leader, who, although dying of a wasting disease, guides humankind to the Promised Land. However, according to the Book of Pythia, one of the Sacred Scrolls that serve as scripture for the Colonial religion, the great leader "would not live to enter the new land" (1.10). The reincarnation of the Moses-figure is not the only repetition here. The oracle Pythia is prefigured by the Pythia who presided over the Oracle at Delphi and the two and ten snakes of Roslin's vision recur in the episode not only in the prophecy, but also in the twelve Vipers that help defeat the Cylons (1.10).

This fluidity seems integral to the nature of *BSG*'s time-cycle. As Leoben explains to Starbuck, "Each of us plays a role [in the eternal story]. Each time a different role. Maybe the last time I was the interrogator and you were the prisoner. The players change, the story remains the same" (1.08). All this has happened before and will happen again, but in different contexts. Like the end-words of a sestina, the recurring elements of the series continue to appear, but the surrounding situation or apparatus has changed. These iterations are clever mirror images, like the "toaster" Helo sees reflected in a toaster on Caprica (1.05). As Leoben indicates, the players often change, but the situations remain the same. Of these repetitions, some are positive, such as when new lapel insignia are presented to Catman (2.06), Adama (2.12), Apollo (2.17), and Seelix (3.16); some are negative, such as when Sharon (1.12), Tigh (2.08), Cain (2.12), Apollo (2.14), and Baltar (3.04) all have guns pointed at their heads and urge their antagonists to just "Do it." But perhaps the most dramatic and thematically relevant situation is the repeated question of Cylon identity. Adama (1.08), Ellen Tigh (1.09), Baltar (1.07), Tyrol (2.04), Gaeta (3.05), and Jammer (3.05) are all suspected or accused of being Cylons or Cylon collaborators. Boomer (1.02), Tyrol (2.19), and Baltar (3.06) all believe that they may be Cylons. In Season One, Boomer discovers that she is (1.13), and at the end of Season Three, Tigh, Chief, Anders, and Tory Foster all discover that they are too (3.20).

True to Leoben's description, many of these reiterations feature complete role-reversals, as the whirligig of time brings in his revenges: just as the Cylons have pursued the genocide of the human race, the humans consider wiping out the Cylons through the use of a virus (3.07); just as Doral the Cylon blows himself up with explosives onboard *Galactica* (1.06), Duck the human becomes a suicide bomber on New Caprica (3.01); just as the Cylons use a virus to paralyze the Colonial Vipers (M.01), the humans use a virus (sent by Sharon) to shut down the Cylon Raiders (2.09); and finally, brilliantly, just as Baltar sees a virtual Six in his head, Caprica Six sees Baltar in hers—her virtual Baltar even scripts her lines for her, just as Six does for him (2.18).[6] But these repeated circumstances do more than just provide ironic turnabout. Like the repeated briefings, mission planning sessions, card games, flight deck preparations, and so on, the inverted conflicts reveal the essentially cyclical nature of time. This is particularly evident during the funeral intercuts in "Act of Contrition" (1.04), when the episode moves between the services for Zak Adama and the memorial for the thirteen Viper pilots. Ceremonies of life, such as baptisms, marriages, and funerals, emphasize the way living repeats itself in myriad ways. Mircea Eliade suggests that such rituals provide the opportunity to move beyond the quotidian and into consecrated time. He argues that primitive rites, including marriages and funerals, allow "the abolition of time through the imitation of archetypes and the repetition of paradigmatic gestures," converting "profane time" into sacred time (35). Thus, repetition takes on a sanctifying and redemptive function for both time and humanity.

Redemption through Eternal Return

The show and its creators repeatedly suggest the possibility that humanity is an essentially flawed race. As Cally notes, the Cylons could defeat the Colonials simply by sitting back and allowing humanity's own self-destructive tendencies to tear the race apart (3.18). This thematic concern is voiced at the very beginning of the series when, during his unrehearsed speech at *Galactica*'s decommissioning ceremony, Adama asks,

> Why are we as a people worth saving? We still commit murder because of greed, spite, jealousy. And we still visit all of our sins upon our children. We refuse to accept the responsibility for anything that we've done. Like we did with the Cylons. We decided to play God, create life. When that life turned against us, we comforted ourselves in the knowledge that it really wasn't our fault, not really. You cannot play God then wash your hands of the things that you've created. Sooner or later, the day comes when you can't hide from the things that you've done anymore. (M.01)

Leoben echoes this sentiment when Adama encounters him at the Ragnar Anchorage munitions station (M.02), and Sharon later tells the commander, "You said humanity never asked itself why it deserved to survive. Maybe you don't" (2.12). The human race may have avoided extinction, but as Adama tells Starbuck, "It's not enough to survive. One has to be worthy of surviving" (2.12). As a race, we have visited "all of our sins upon our children," but within the context of the series, our children include the Cylons. As a Six leading troops on Caprica observes, "We're the children of humanity. That makes them our parents, in a sense" (1.03). Like many science-fiction cautionary tales, *BSG* refigures the ethical mistakes of Mary Shelley's Frankenstein, who played God, created life, and then tried to wash his hands of his creature, his child. Fortunately for humankind, personal redemption may be attained through the fulfillment of God's will.

This is particularly apparent in the very flawed characters of Baltar and Starbuck, each of whom has been singled out to play a major role in God's design. The babbling Cylon Hybrid seems to refer to Baltar as "the Chosen One" (3.11), and Six repeatedly urges him to follow God's "path" by embracing his own "destiny" (2.06): "Life has a melody, Gaius. A rhythm of notes that become your existence once played in harmony with God's plan. It's time to do your part and realize your destiny" (1.13). Although few specifics have been revealed regarding God's "plan" for him (1.01), Baltar has been offered the opportunity for redemption through his service as "an instrument of God" (1.10). Similarly, Starbuck must accept her own role as an agent of God's will. Leoben tells her that she has a "path" and a "destiny" when she interrogates him (1.08), and many of his words are repeated by the oracle, Yolanda Brenn (3.17). Socrata Thrace tells her daughter that she is "special" (3.17), and Sharon affirms, "You're special. . . . You have a destiny" (2.05).

Intimations of the nature of Starbuck's destiny may be found in the recurring image of the mandala. Multiple mandalas appear in the Temple of the Five (3.11), and when the algae-planet's star goes nova, revealing itself to be the Eye of Jupiter, the atmospheric effect looks like a mandala. The Eye of Jupiter directs the fleet to a supernova in the Ionian system, which also displays the features of a mandala (3.12). As Helo points out, the mandalas of the Temple bear a striking resemblance to the image painted on the wall of Starbuck's Caprica apartment (3.12). Starbuck admits that she doodled the symbol often as a child, and we see an example of her childhood art in "Maelstrom" (3.17). Later, while on patrol during a refueling operation, Starbuck again sees the mandala in the form of a storm system on the nearby gas giant (3.17).[7] Other mandalas appear in the dripped candle-wax Starbuck sees in the memorial corridor, and perhaps even in the figurine of Aurora (3.17).[8]

Mandalas are common in Dharmic religions. They may be representative of various things, but the Dalai Lama and other spiritual leaders describe the mandala as symbolic of the myriad aspects of both the universe and the lone individual. By contemplating the mandala, a person may become more aware of the interconnectedness of the micro- and the macrocosmic, ultimately cultivating a realization of the spiritual force within herself. For Starbuck, this dawning realization allows for the possibility of transformation that has always been present for her in some way. The first mandala we see, in Starbuck's apartment, is surrounded by text concerning individual transformation:

> methodically
> Smoking my
> cigarette
> with every breath
> I breathe
> out the day.
> with every delicious
> sip
> i drink away the night
> stroking my hair to
> the beat of his heart
> watching a
> Boy turn
> into a
> Man. (2.02)

Plummeting into the crushing storm-mandala of the gas giant, Starbuck has a vision in which she speaks to an entity who looks like Leoben but may not be.[9] Not-Leoben tells Starbuck that she wants to "cross over" but has always been afraid, "afraid of the unknown. Death" (3.17). Yet, as Three has observed earlier in the series, "There's something beautiful, miraculous, between life and death" (3.08), and Not-Leoben declares his willingness to guide Starbuck to "discover what hovers in the space between life and death" (3.17). Like the Ghost of Christmas Past, Not-Leoben allows Starbuck to travel back in time so she can witness her mother's death.[10] After she has confronted the moment and enjoyed a reconciliation of sorts with her mother, Not-Leoben says, "See? There's nothing terrible about death. When you finally face it, it's beautiful. You're free now to become who you really are" (3.17).

This potential for self-actualization brings us back to Nietzsche's theory of eternal return. In the aphorism, the demon claims that everything will recur "in the same succession and sequence." This seems to imply circularity without change, a condition that probably would "transform and possibly crush you" (*Gay Science* 194). But eternal return offers the possibility of affirmation. And as Lawrence Hatab describes it, the process of Nietzschean *Becoming* seems strangely analogous to what may have occurred during and after Starbuck's dive into the nihilating mandala:

> The self-ascending "mystical" leap into a nihilating ground, the holistic process which unfolds but dissolves individuation, the Dionysian abandonment into the whole; then follows the Apollonian transparent forming of this formlessness, which is *creation*, since there is no "substance"; this is characterized as *power*, the only way to express self-emergence; power begets *joy*, as this is a *self*-emergence; joy leads to the holistic *affirmation* of this self-emerging process, and this vision of affirmation is necessarily enformed as *eternal recurrence of the same*. (128)

After first discovering the storm-mandala, but before her descent into it, Starbuck comments to Apollo that despite all they have been through, they are right back where they started (3.17). She only escapes the seemingly futile circle of repetition by fully accepting her destiny through a declarative gesture that mirrors the "*Amor fati*" of Nietzsche's aphorism 276 (*Gay Science* 157). She tells Apollo, "Lee, I'll see you on the other side" (3.17), and plunges into the unknown, as her Viper apparently explodes.

Discussing the original series, James Iaccino argues that the humans possess the potential for a darkness as great as that of the Cylon threat. The same may be said for *BSG*. For the humans of *BSG*'s various incarnations, the possibility always exists, as Iaccino says, to

> convert the inner destroyer to the more worthwhile creator that can fashion new worlds and societies out of devastation. All it takes is the realization that a shadow "full of sin" lies within each of us. By acknowledging our evilness, we are one step closer to discovering that "wellspring of grace" which also emanates from the shadow and to which we can devote the rest of our lives actualizing. (73)[11]

Danielle Chapelle notes that when read within the context of psycho-analysis, Nietzsche's ideas apply to both "the history of the individual" and "the history of metaphysics." Eternal return offers the possibility of "redemptive transformation" and triumph over individual and "collective historical repression" (11). As her reappearance in "Crossroads, Part 2" (3.20) suggests, Starbuck's "death" at the gas giant is actually a redemptive transformation. Sharon has already told Starbuck that, through the process of resurrection, "Death becomes a learning experience" (2.15); Starbuck's death allows her to see Earth, and, possibly, her true self. Not-Leoben guides her to this moment of self-realization, and there may be other guides. Before she descends into the storm, she tells Apollo, "They're waiting for me" (3.17). As her ship explodes, we see an image of her younger self bathed in the glowing white light associated with the Final Five. This moment may also be another homage, alluding to the scene in *Jacob's Ladder* (1990) when Jacob Singer accepts his fate and ascends into the white light of heaven with his son, Gabe.

If this is so,[12] then another moment in the film becomes relevant to this discussion. Before he has come to terms with his own death, Jacob speaks with the cherubic Louis, who explains the theories of medieval mystic, Meister Eckhart. Louis tells Jake,

> He said the only thing that burns in Hell is the part of you that won't let go of your life; your memories, your attachments. They burn 'em all away. But they're not punishing you, he said. They're freeing your soul. . . . So the way he sees it, if you're frightened of dying and you're holding on, you'll see devils tearing your life away. But if you've made your peace then the devils are really angels freeing you from the earth.

Like Starbuck, Jacob fears death. When he finally lets go of the world and faces that fear, the demons that have been tormenting him through-out the film turn into angels. Similarly, the Cylons are seen as demonic— Elosha associates the "lower demon" of the scriptures with Sharon (2.06)—but Not-Leoben seems almost angelic. He tells Starbuck, "I'm here to prepare you to pass through the next door. To discover what hovers in the space between life and death" (3.17). Likewise, the virtual Six explains to Baltar, "I'm an angel of God sent here to protect you. To guide you. To love you" (2.07).[13] When he is accused of treason, Baltar prays to God, and Six, who had disappeared, returns to comfort him. "All will be well," she says (2.07), echoing perhaps the words of medieval mystic, Julian of Norwich: "Sinne is behovely, but alle shalle be wele, and alle shalle be wele, and alle maner of thinge shalle be wele" (209). Julian's comforting theology states that God "oned" us to himself (307). This idea of being part of God appears in both Nietzschean and Cylon philosophy. Nietzsche argues, "Around the hero everything becomes a tragedy, around the demi-god everything becomes a satyr-play; and around God everything becomes—what? perhaps 'world'" (*Beyond* 97, apothegm 150). As Joan Stambaugh observes, "This passage suggests the image of a center of power from which the world, so to speak, radiates. It seeks to describe the 'ring of rings' in its aspect of power and what follows from that power" (100). Like the center of a mandala, God occupies a position of power from which everything radiates. But if all the world radiates from God, then God radiates through all the world, including humans. Similarly, Leoben asserts, "We're all God, Starbuck. All of us. I see the love that binds all living things together" (1.08). And because we are a part of God, we exist outside time, rather than swimming in the stream. Eternal return allows us to recognize this situation and the godhead within us. This imbues *BSG*, which has consistently been accused of being too dark, with a tremendous sense of hope. Starbuck, like all of humanity, is "a screwup" (1.12), but she appears emerging over the horizon at the end of Season Three like Aurora, bringing "a fresh start" (3.17) and a new day. As she tells Apollo, "It's going to be okay" (3.20). All shall be well.

Notes

1. *BSG: The Second Coming* was a 4½-minute theatrical trailer, and the Singer/DeSanto project never came to fruition, due to Fox Studios' withdrawal and Singer's commitment to *X-Men 2*.

2. There are occasionally problems with these numbers. For example, there have often been single-digit losses after major combat operations and there was only one life lost between 2.13 and 2.14, despite the fact that the earlier episode shows several bodies vented into space when the *Daru Mozu* is sabotaged.

3. In the original *BSG* the first Cylons were a reptilian race that, according to Apollo "died off thousands of yahrens ago, leaving behind a race of super-machines. But we still call [the machines] Cylons" ("Saga of a Star World"). Andromus the humanoid Cylon was introduced in "The Night the Cylons Landed, Part I," in *Galactica 1980*, but the other Cylons were all metallic robots.

4. Gina notes that "suicide is a sin" (2.12). Technically, Sharon does not commit suicide (she has her husband kill her), nor does Three in a later episode (a Centurion shoots her in "Hero" 3.08). In contrast, Brother Cavil does kill himself (3.03).

5. When the Cylons find the humans on New Caprica, Six declares to Baltar, "Judgment Day" (2.20), possibly alluding to *Terminator 2: Judgment Day* (1991).

6. Cleverly, Six's theme is played with the melody line reversed whenever the virtual Baltar appears.

7. This may connect back to the Temple of the Five, since the eye of the real planet Jupiter is an enormous storm system.

8. Aurora refers to both the Goddess of the Dawn and an astrological event. Although usually appearing as a striated curtain, an aurora may look like a corona of divergent rays (a mandala) when directly above the observer.

9. After viewing her mother's death, Starbuck says, "You're not Leoben" and he replies, "I never said I was" (3.17). Given the mendacity of the Leoben model, and the possible equivocation of his response, this does not necessarily indicate the he is not Leoben, but Starbuck's evaluation is probably correct.

10. This power over temporal space may or may not connect to the corporeal Leoben's claim to exist outside the normal flow of time: "A part of me swims in the stream. But in truth, I'm standing on the shore. The current never takes me downstream" (1.08).

11. Iaccino sees the Cylons as an archetypal shadow destroyer, associated with Jung's god of storm and frenzy, Wotan. According to Jung, Wotan unleashes the dark passions of the unconscious (179–93).

12. It seems quite possible, since *BSG* has other homages to the film, such as when Six suddenly advances on Baltar in "Bastille Day" (1.03). The moment mirrors a shot in *Jacob's Ladder* when Jezebel gets in Jake's face. In both *BSG* and the film, make-up, false teeth, and the suddenness of the threat all help to produce the frightening impression of demonic possession.

13. In Three's visions, the glowing images of the Final Five look strikingly similar to the Beings of Light from the original series (introduced in "War of the Gods"), who were called "angels" by "less developed races."

Bibliography

Abbate, Carolyn. "15th Congress of the International Musicological Society, Round Table: Musical Analysis: Systematic versus Historical Models." *Acta Musicologica* 63 (1991): 20–22.

———. *Unsung Voices: Opera and Musical Narrative in the Nineteenth Century.* Princeton, NJ: Princeton University Press, 1991.

Adam, Alison. *Artificial Knowing: Gender and the Thinking Machine.* New York: Routledge, 1998.

Agamben, Giorgio. *Homo Sacer: Sovereign Power and Bare Life.* Translated by Daniel Heller-Roazen. Stanford, CA: Stanford University Press, 1995.

———. *State of Exception.* Translated by Kevin Attell. Chicago: University of Chicago Press, 2005.

Anders, Lou. "The Natural and the Unnatural: Verisimilitude in *Battlestar Galactica.*" In *So Say We All: An Unauthorized Collection of Thoughts and Opinions on* Battlestar Galactica, edited by Richard Hatch, 83–94. Dallas: Benbella Books, 2006.

Anderson, Warwick. *The Cultivation of Whiteness: Science, Health, and Racial Destiny in Australia.* New York: Basic Books, 2003.

Ankai. "Chain-Smoking & Apologies: Podcasts." January 31, 2007. Television Without Pity. <http://forums.televisionwithoutpity.com/index.php?showtopic=3149128 &st=105>.

Appiah, Kwame Anthony. *The Ethics of Identity.* Princeton, NJ: Princeton University Press, 2004.

Attebery, Brian. *Decoding Gender in Science Fiction.* New York: Routledge, 2002.

Atwood, Margaret. *The Handmaid's Tale.* Boston: Houghton Mifflin, 1986.

Aurthur, Kate. "It's One Tough Universe in 'Galactica.'" *The News & Observer.* April 17, 2007. <www.newsobserver.com/105/v-print/story/508520.html/>.

Bacon-Smith, Camille. *Enterprising Women: Television Fandom and the Creation of Popular Myth.* Philadelphia: University of Pennsylvania Press, 1992.

Bakhtin, Mikhail. *Rabelais and His World.* Translated by Helene Iswolsky. Cambridge, MA: MIT Press, 1968.

Bassom, David, *Battlestar Galactica: The Official Companion.* London: Titan Books, 2005.

———. *Battlestar Galactica: The Official Companion Season Two.* London: Titan Books, 2006.

"Battlestar Galactica." *Scifi.com.* <www.scifi.com/battlestar>.

BattlestarGalactica.com. May 21, 2006. <http://www.battlestargalactica.com/index.htm>.

Battlestar Galactica Episode Guide. September 23, 2005. <http://www.saltyrain.com/ epguides/battlestar2.html>.

Battlestar Wiki. Anne Cofell Saunders. <"http://en.battlestarwiki.org/wiki/Anne_Cofell_ Saunders">.

Battlestar Wiki. Tom Zarek. <http://en.battlestarwiki.org/wiki/Tom_Zarek.>.

Baudrillard, Jean. *The Spirit of Terrorism and Requiem for the Twin Towers.* Translated by Chris Turner. New York: Verso, 2002.

BBC. "Timeline: Iraq after Saddam." BBC News. March 20, 2007. <http://news.bbc.co.uk/2/hi/ middle_east/4192189.stm>.

Bederman, Gail. *Manliness and Civilization: A Cultural History of Gender and Race in the United States, 1880–1917.* Chicago: University of Chicago Press, 1995.

Bell, James John. "An Army of One God: Monotheism Versus Paganism in the *Galactica* Mythos." In *So Say We All: An Unauthorized Collection of Thoughts and Opinions on* Battlestar Galactica, edited by Richard Hatch, 233–55. Dallas: Benbella Books, 2006.

Benedict, Dirk. "Starbuck: Lost in Castration." *Dirk Benedict Central.* Archived Articles. May 2005. <http://www.dirkbenedictcentral.com/home/articles-archive.php>.

Benjamin, Walter. "The Work of Art in the Age of Its Technological Reproducibility: Second Version." In *Selected Writings Volume 3: 1935–1938,* edited by Howard Eiland and Michael W. Jennings, 101–33. Cambridge, MA: Harvard University Press, 2002.

Bhabha, Homi K. *The Location of Culture.* New York: Routledge, 1994.

Blanchot, Maurice. *The Writing of the Disaster.* (1980) Translated by Ann Smock. Lincoln: University of Nebraska Press, 1995.

Bloch, Ernst. *A Philosophy of the Future.* Translated by John Cumming. New York: Herder and Herder, 1970.

Bobo, Lawrence. "Whites' Opposition to Busing: Symbolic Racism or Realistic Group Conflict?" *Journal of Personality and Social Psychology* 45 (1983): 1196–210.

Bourgeois Nerd. "Chain-Smoking & Apologies: Podcasts." January 30, 2007. Television Without Pity. <http://forums.televisionwithoutpity.com/index. php? showtopic=3149128&st=90>.

Boykoff, Maxwell T., and Jules M. Boykoff. "Balance as Bias: Global Warming and the US Prestige Press." *Global Environmental Change* 14 (2004): 125–36.

Brecht, Bertolt. "A Short Organum for Theatre." In *Brecht on Theatre: The Development of an Aesthetic,* edited and translated by John Willett, 179–208. New York: Hill and Wang, 1964.

Bresnick, Adam. "Prospoetic Compulsion: Reading the Uncanny in Freud and Hoffman." *The Germanic Review* 71, no. 2 (1996): 114–32.

Brooker, Will. *Using the Force: Creativity, Community and Star Wars Fans.* New York: Continuum, 2002.

Browne, Nick. "The Political Economy of the Television (Super) Text." *Quarterly Review of Film Studies* 9, no. 3 (1984): 174–82.

Brummett, Barry. "Burke's Representative Anecdote as a Method in Media Criticism." *Critical Studies in Mass Communication* 1 (1984): 161–76.

———. "Electric Literature as Equipment for Living: Haunted House Films." *Critical Studies in Mass Communication* 9 (1985): 247–61.

Bryant, Donald C. "Rhetoric: Its Functions and Its Scope." In *Rhetoric: A Tradition in Transition,* edited by Walter R. Fisher, 196–230. East Lansing: Michigan State University Press, 1974.

Buck-Morss, Susan. *Thinking Past Terror: Islamism and Critical Theory on the Left.* 2003. Reprint, New York: Verso, 2006.

Bukatman, Scott. *Terminal Identity: The Virtual Subject in Post-Modern Science Fiction.* Durham, NC: Duke University Press, 1993.

Burke, Kenneth. *Counter-Statement.* 2nd ed. Los Altos, CA: Hermes Publications, 1953.

———. *A Grammar of Motives.* Berkeley: University of California Press, 1969.

———. *Language as Symbolic Action: Essays of Life, Literature, and Method.* Berkeley: University of California Press, 1968.

———. *Permanence and Change: An Anatomy of Purpose.* Rev. ed. Los Altos, CA: Hermes Publications, 1954.

———. *The Philosophy of Literary Form: Studies in Symbolic Action.* Baton Rouge: Louisiana State University Press, 1941.

———. *A Rhetoric of Motives.* Berkeley: University of California Press, 1969.

Bush, George W. "Address to a Joint Session of Congress and the America People." United States Capitol, Washington, D.C. September 20, 2001. <http://www.whitehouse.gov/news/releases/2001/09/20010920-8.html>.

Butler, Judith. *Precarious Life.* London: Verso, 2004.

Cartwright, Bert. *The Bible in the Lyrics of Bob Dylan.* Bury, Lancashire: Wanted Man, 1985.

"Cast Members Talk About Their Roles." January 31, 2007. <http://www.battlestargalactica.com/outside_docs/bg_outdoc0025.htm>.

Chapelle, Danielle. *Nietzsche and Psychoanalysis.* Albany: SUNY Press, 1993.

Christopher, Renny. "Little Miss Tough Chick of the Universe: *Farscape*'s Inverted Sexual Dynamics." In *Action Chicks: New Images of Tough Women in Popular Culture*, edited by Sherrie A. Inness, 257–81. New York: Palgrave Macmillan, 2004.

ClashTV. "Greg Pak on Galactica, Hulk and More." *Illusion: The Pulp Culture Channel.* <http://www.illusiontv.com/gregpak.php>.

Clifton, Jacob. "Burdens: A Proof. The Stoic Value of the Cylon Threat." In *So Say We All So Say We All: An Unauthorized Collection of Thoughts and Opinions on* Battlestar Galactica, edited by Richard Hatch, 145–60. Dallas: Benbella Books, 2006.

Clover, Carol. *Men, Women and Chainsaws: Gender in the Modern Horror Film.* London: British Film Institute, 1992.

Clover, Joshua. *The Matrix.* London: British Film Institute, 2004.

Cochrane, Kira. "For Your Entertainment." *Guardian G2.* May 1, 2007. <http://film.guardian.co.uk/news/story/0,,2069287,00.html>.

"Code Sigma 957." April 29, 2006. <http://sigma957.suddenlaunch. com/>.

Condit, Celeste. "The Rhetorical Limits of Polysemy." *Critical Studies in Mass Communication* 6 (1989): 103–22.

Cooke, Miriam. "WO-man, Retelling the War Myth." In *Gendering War Talk*, edited by Miriam Cooke and Angela Woollacott, 177–204. Princeton, NJ: Princeton University Press, 1993.

Cooke, Miriam, and Angela Woollacott, eds. *Gendering War Talk.* Princeton, NJ: Princeton University Press, 1993.

Cox, Dan. "Articles and Interviews: Information on an upcoming *Battlestar Galactica* Revival." *Analytical Episode Guide to Battlestar Galactica.* September 2005. <http://www.battlestarpegasus.com/features/articles_interviews/archive/2002/article_revivalJL.html>.

Creeber, Glen. *Serial Television: Big Drama on the Small Screen.* London: British Film Institute, 2004.

Curl, Joseph. "Bush Calls for Global Cooperation." *The Washington Times*, December 2, 2004. <http://washingtontimes.com/national/20041202-122549-7793r.htm>.

Dahlen, Chris. "A.V. Club Interviews: Ronald D. Moore." *The Onion.* April 17, 2007. <http://www.avclub.com/content/node/60737>.

Danner, Mark. "Torture and Truth: America, Abu Ghraib, and the War on Terror." New York: New York Review of Books, 2004.

Dean, Tim. "Art as Symptom: Žižek and the Ethics of Psychoanalytic Criticism." *diacritics* 32, no. 2 (2002): 21–41.

Delany, Samuel R. "Some Presumptuous Approaches to Science Fiction." In *Speculations on Speculation: Theories of Science Fiction*, edited by James Gunn and Matthew Candelaria, 289–300. Lanham, MD: Rowman & Littlefield, 2005.

Derrida, Jacques. "Différance." In *Literary Theory: An Anthology*, edited by Julie Rivkin and Michael Ryan, 278–99. Malden, MA: Blackwell, 1998.

De Somogyi, Nick. *Jokermen and Thieves: Bob Dylan and the Ballad Tradition*. Bury, Lancashire: Wanted Man, 1986.

Dinello, Daniel. *Technophobia: Science Fiction Visions of Posthuman Technology*. Austin: University of Texas Press, 2005.

Doane, Mary Ann. *Femme Fatales: Feminism, Film Theory, Psychoanalysis*. New York: Routledge, 1991.

Doctorow, Cory. "The Rapture of the Geeks: Funny Hats, Transcendent Wisdom, and the Singularity." *Whole Earth* (Spring 2003): 38–39.

Dolar, Mladen. "'I Shall Be With You on Your Wedding Night': Lacan and the Uncanny." *October* 58 (1991): 5–23.

"Do You Want 'Freedom Fries' With That?" *CBS News*. March 11, 2003. <http://www.cbsnews.com/stories/2003/03/11/politics/main543555.shtml>.

Dryden, Linda. "*She*: Gothic Reverberations in *Star Trek: First Contact*." In *Postfeminist Gothic: Critical Interventions in Contemporary Culture*, edited by Benjamin A. Brabon and Stéphanie Genz, 154–69. Basingstoke, Hampshire: Palgrave Macmillan, 2007.

DuBois, W. E. Burghardt. *The Souls of Black Folk: Essays and Sketches*. New York: Bantam Classic, 1989.

Dyer, Richard. *Stars*. London: British Film Institute, 1979.

Dyson, Michael. *Come Hell or High Water: Hurricane Katrina and the Color of Disaster*. New York: Basic, 2006.

Edwards, Gavin. "Intergalactic Terror: 'Battlestar Galactica' Tackles Terrorism Like No Other Show." *Rolling Stone*, January 17, 2006. <http://www.rollingstone.com/news/story/9183391/intergalactic_terror>.

Eick, David. "Podcast Commentary: Final Cut." <http://media.scifi.com/battlestar/downloads/podcast/mp3/208/bsg_ep208_FULL.mp3.>.

Eliade, Mircea. *Cosmos and History: The Myth of the Eternal Return*. Translated by Willard R. Trask. New York: Harper & Row, 1959.

Ewen, Elizabeth, and Stuart Ewen. *Typecasting: On the Arts and Sciences of Human Inequality*. New York: Seven Stories Press, 2006.

Fiske, John. "The Cultural Economy of Fandom." In *The Adoring Audience: Fan Culture and Popular Media*, edited by Lisa A. Lewis, 30–49. New York: Routledge, 1992.

———. *Understanding Popular Culture*. Boston: Unwin and Hyman, 1989.

Foucault, Michel. *Discipline and Punish: The Birth of the Prison*. Translated by Alan Sheridan. New York: Vintage-Random House, 1995.

———. *"Society Must Be Defended": Lectures at the Collège de France 1975–1976*. Translated by David Macey. New York: Picador, 2003.

Freedman, Eric. "Television, Horror and Everyday Life in *Buffy the Vampire Slayer*." In *The Contemporary Television Series*, edited by Michael Hammond and Lucy Mazdon, 159–80. Edinburgh: Edinburgh University Press, 2005.

Freud, Sigmund. "The Aetiology of Hysteria." (1896) Vol. 3. *The Standard Edition of the Complete Psychological Works of Sigmund Freud*, edited and translated by James Strachey, 89–221. London: Hogarth Press, 1953–74.

———. *Civilization and Its Discontents*. (1930) Translated by James Strachey. New York: W. W. Norton, 1961.

———. "Fetishism." (1927) Vol. 21. *The Standard Edition of the Complete Psychological Works of Sigmund Freud*, edited and translated by James Strachey, 149–57. London: Hogarth Press, 1953–74.

———. *Inhibitions, Symptoms and Anxiety*. (1925) Edited by James Strachey. Translated by Alix Strachey. London: Hogarth Press, 1971.

———. *The Interpretation of Dreams*. (1900–1942) Edited and translated by James Strachey. New York: Avon Books, 1998.

———. "The Uncanny." (1919) In *Penguin Freud Library 14: Art and Literature*, edited by Albert Dickson, 335–76. London: Penguin, 1990.

Frith, Simon. *Music for Pleasure: Essays in the Sociology of Pop*. New York: Routledge, 1988.

Fuss, Diana. *Essentially Speaking: Feminism, Nature and Difference*. New York: Routledge, 1989.

"Galactica Politica—Battlestar Galactica as Social Commentary." *Newsvine.com*. April 14, 2007. <http://galactica-politica.newsvine. com>.

Garff, Joakim. *Søren Kierkegaard: A Biography*. Translated by Bruce H. Kirmmse. Princeton, NJ: Princeton University Press, 2005.

Geertz, Clifford. *The Interpretation of Cultures*. New York: Basic Books, 1973.

Gilmour, Michael J. *Tangled Up in the Bible: Bob Dylan and Scripture*. New York: Continuum, 2004.

Goldwater, Barry. "Daisy." <http://www.pbs.org/30secondcandidate/timeline/years/1964b.html>.

Good, I. J. "Speculations Concerning the First Ultraintelligent Machine." Vol. 6. *Advances in Computers*, edited by Franz L. Alt and Morris Rubinoff, 31–88. San Diego: Academic Press, 1965.

Gorbman, Claudia. *Unheard Melodies: Narrative Film Music*. Bloomington: Indiana University Press, 1987.

Gordon, Joan. "Yin and Yang Duke it Out." In *Storming the Reality Studio: A Casebook of Cyberpunk and Postmodern Fiction*, edited by Larry McCaffery, 196–202. Durham, NC: Duke University Press, 1991.

Govan, Sandra Y. "The Insistent Presence of Black Folk in the Novels of Samuel R. Delany." *Black American Literature Forum* 18, no. 2 (1984): 43–48.

Gray, Michael. *The Bob Dylan Encyclopedia*. New York: Continuum, 2006.

Green, Ronald M. *Kierkegaard and Kant: The Hidden Debt*. Albany: SUNY Press, 1992.

Greene, Eric. "The Mirror Frakked: Reflections on *Battlestar Galactica*." In *So Say We All: An Unauthorized Collection of Thoughts and Opinions on* Battlestar Galactica, edited by Richard Hatch, 5–22. Dallas: Benbella Books, 2006.

Grossberg, Lawrence. "On Postmodernism and Articulation: An Interview with Stuart Hall" (1986). In *Stuart Hall: Critical Dialogues in Cultural Studies*, edited by David Morley and Kuan-Hsing Chen, 131–50. London: Routledge, 1996.

Hale, Grace Elizabeth. *Making Whiteness: The Culture of Segregation in the South, 1890–1940*. New York: Vintage Books, 1998.

Hall, Stuart. "Who Needs 'Identity'?" In *Identity: A Reader*, edited by Paul du Gay, Jessica Evans, and Peter Redman, 15–30. Thousand Oaks, CA: Sage Publications, 2001.

Haraway, Donna. *Simians, Cyborgs, and Women: The Reinvention of Nature*. New York: Routledge, 1991.

"Harry checks out the 1st two nights of the *Battlestar Galactica* miniseries." *Ain't It Cool News*. November 13, 2003. <http://www.aint-it-cool-news.com/display.cgi?id =16490>.

Hartman, Chester, and Gregory Squires. *There Is No Such Thing as a Natural Disaster: Race, Class, and Hurricane Katrina*. New York: Routledge, 2006.

Hartman, Geoffrey. "Memory.com: Tele-Suffering and Testimony in the Dot Com Era." *Raritan* 19, no. 3 (Winter 2000): 1–18. Reprinted as "Tele-Suffering and Testimony" in *The Geoffrey Hartman Reader*, edited by Geoffrey Hartman and Daniel T. O'Hara, 432–45. Edinburgh: Edinburgh University Press, 2004.

———. "Trauma Within the Limits of Literature." *European Journal of English Studies* 7, no. 3 (2003): 257–74.

Hatab, Lawrence J. *Nietzsche and Eternal Recurrence: The Redemption of Time and Becoming*. Washington, D.C.: University Press of America, 1978.

Havrilesky, Heather. "Darkness Becomes Them: When the Future of Humankind Rests in the Hands of God-Fearing Robots, Terrorism is Our Only Hope." *Salon.com.* October 6, 2006. <http://www.salon.com/ent/tv/review/2006/10/06/battlestar/print.html>.

Hayles, N. Katherine. *My Mother Was a Computer: Digital Subjects and Literary Texts.* Chicago: University of Chicago Press, 2005.

Heath, Stephen. "Translator's Note." In Roland Barthes, *Image Music Text,* translated by Stephen Heath. New York: Hill and Wang, 1977.

Heffernan, Virginia. "In *Galactica,* It's Politics as Usual. Or Is It?" *New York Times,* October 26, 2006. <http://travel2.nytimes.com/2006/10/26/arts/television/26batt.html>.

Herbert, Melissa S. *Camouflage Isn't Only for Combat: Gender, Sexuality, and Women in the Military.* New York: New York University Press, 1998.

Herdman, John. *Voice Without Restraint: A Study of Bob Dylan's Lyrics and Their Background.* New York: Delilah Books, 1982.

Heylin, Clinton. *Bob Dylan: Behind the Shades Revisited.* New York: Harper Entertainment, 2003.

Hills, Matt. *Fan Cultures.* New York: Routledge, 2002.

———. *The Pleasures of Horror.* London: Continuum, 2005.

Hontz, Jenny. "Webisodes: A Battle Against the Empire." *Newsweek,* October 23, 2006.

hooks, bell. *Reel to Real: Race, Sex, and Class at the Movies.* New York: Routledge, 1996.

Houston, Julia. "Galactica, Pt 1." Interview with James Callis. October 5, 2006. *About.com: Sci Fi/Fantasy.* <http://scifi.about.com/od/bgsonscifi/a/callis1_2.htm>.

Huizinga, Johan. *Homo Ludens: A Study of the Play Element in Culture.* Boston: Beacon Press, 1955.

Iaccino, James F. *Jungian Reflections within the Cinema: A Psychological Analysis of Sci-Fi and Fantasy Archetypes.* Westport, CT: Praeger, 1998.

Inhofe, James. "Transcript of Senator Inhofe's Remarks at the 05/11/2004 Senate Armed Services Hearing on Iraqi Prisoner Treatment (Panel 1)." Senate.gov. May 11, 2004. <http://inhofe.senate.gov/pressapp/record.cfm?id=221389>.

Inness, Sherrie. *Tough Girls: Women Warriors and Wonder Women in Popular Culture.* Philadelphia: University of Pennsylvania Press, 1999.

Irigaray, Luce. *This Sex Which Is Not One.* Translated by Catherine Porter and Carolyn Burke. Ithaca, NY: Cornell University Press, 1985.

Jacobs, Jason. *Body Trauma TV: The New Hospital Drama.* London: British Film Institute, 2003.

Jacobson, Matthew Frye. *Whiteness of a Different Color: European Immigrants and the Alchemy of Race.* Cambridge, MA: Harvard University Press, 1999.

Jameson, Fredric. "Reification and Utopia in Mass Culture." *Social Text* 1 (1979): 130–48.

Jardin, Xeni. "Fans Battle TV Over *Galactica.*" *Wired.com.* August 6, 2003. <http://www.wired.com/news/games/0,2101,59906,00.html>.

Jenkins, Henry. *Convergence Culture: Where Old and New Media Collide.* New York: New York University Press, 2006.

———. *Textual Poachers: Television Fans and Participatory Culture.* New York: Routledge, 1992.

Jentsch, Ernst. "On the Psychology of the Uncanny" (1906). Translated by Roy Sellars. *Angelaki: Journal of Theoretical Humanities* 2, no. 1 (1995): 7–16.

Johnson-Smith, Jan. *American Science Fiction TV.* London: I. B. Tauris, 2004.

Joy, Bill. "Why the Future Doesn't Need Us." *Wired* 8, no. 4 (April 2000). <http://www.wired.com/wired/archive/8.04/joy.html>.

Julian of Norwich. *The Writings of Julian of Norwich: A Vision Showed to a Devout Woman and a Revelation of Love.* Edited by Nicholas Watson and Jacqueline Jenkins. University Park: Pennsylvania State University Press, 2006.

Jung, Carl G. *Civilization in Transition.* Edited and translated by Gerhard Adler and R. F. C. Hull. Vol. 10. *The Collected Works.* Princeton, NJ: Princeton University Press, 1990.

Kakoudaki, Despina. "Spectacles of History: Race Relations, Melodrama, and the Science Fiction/ Disaster Film." *Camera Obscura 50* 17, no. 2 (2002): 109–52.

Kant, Immanuel. *Religion Within the Limits of Reason Alone.* Translated by Theodore M. Greene and Hoyt H. Hudson. New York: Harper & Row, 1960.

Kassabian, Anahid. *Hearing Film: Tracking Identifications in Contemporary Hollywood Film Music.* New York: Routledge, 2001.

Kember, Sarah. *Cyberfeminism and Artificial Life.* New York: Routledge, 2003.

Kennedy, Randall. *Interracial Intimacies: Sex, Marriage, Identity, and Adoption.* New York: Random House, 2003.

Kinder, Donald R., and Lynn Sanders. *Divided by Color: Racial Politics and Democratic Ideals.* Chicago: University of Chicago Press, 1994.

King, Geoff, and Tanya Krzywinska. *Science Fiction Cinema: From Outerspace to Cyber-space.* London: Wallflower, 2000.

Kierkegaard, Søren. *Concluding Unscientific Postscript.* Translated by Howard V. Hong and Edna H. Hong. Princeton, NJ: Princeton University Press, 1992.

———. *Either/Or, Part I.* Translated by Howard V. Hong and Edna H. Hong. Princeton, NJ: Princeton University Press, 1987.

———. *Either/Or, Part II.* Translated by Howard V. Hong and Edna H. Hong. Princeton, NJ: Princeton University Press, 1987.

———. *The Point of View.* Translated by Howard V. Hong and Edna H. Hong. Princeton, NJ: Princeton University Press, 1998.

———. *The Sickness Unto Death.* Translated by Howard V. Hong and Edna H. Hong. Princeton, NJ: Princeton University Press, 1980.

———. *The Two Ages.* Translated by Howard V. Hong and Edna H. Hong. Princeton, NJ: Princeton University Press, 1978.

Kociemba, David. "'Actually, It Explains a Lot': Reading the Opening Title Sequences of *Buffy the Vampire Slayer.*" *Slayage: The Online International Journal of Buffy Studies* 22 (6.2), November 2006.

Kuhn, Thomas S. *The Structure of Scientific Revolutions.* 3rd ed. Chicago: University of Chicago Press, 1996.

Lacan, Jacques. *The Four Fundamental Concepts of Psychoanalysis: The Seminar of Jacque Lacan, Book XI.* (1973). Edited by Jacques-Alain Miller. Translated by Alan Sheridan. Repr., New York: W. W. Norton, 1988.

Laclau, Ernesto. *Politics and Ideology in Marxist Theory.* New York: Verso, 1977.

Landon, Brooks. *Science Fiction After 1900: From the Steam Man to the Stars.* New York: Routledge, 2002.

Leaver, Tama. "The Battlestar Galactica Webisodes and the Tyranny of Digital Distance." *Ponderance,* September 11, 2006. <http://ponderance.blogspot.com/2006/09/battlestar-galactica-webisodes-tyranny.html>.

Lee, Patrick. "Moore Talks *Galactica* Finale," *Sci Fi Wire,* March 13, 2006. <http://www.scifi.com/scifiwire/index.php?category=0&id=34886>.

Leonard, Elisabeth Anne. *Into Darkness Peering: Race and Color in the Fantastic.* Westport, CT: Greenwood Press, 1997.

Levey, Noam N. "Political Winds Shift on Prairie." *Los Angeles Times,* April 16, 2007: A1 and A12.

Levinas, Emmanuel. *Time and the Other.* (1979) Translated by Richard A. Cohen. Pittsburgh: Duquesne University Press, 1987.

Linville, Susan E. "'The *Mother* of All Battles': *Courage Under Fire* and the Gender-Integrated Military." *Cinema Journal* 39, no. 2 (2000): 100–120.

Lipsitz, George. *Time Passages: Collective Memory and American Popular Culture.* Minneapolis: University of Minnesota Press, 1990.

Littlejohn, Janice Rhoshalle. "A Sleeker *Battlestar Galactica* Returns." *Space.com*. December 4, 2003. <http://www.space.com/entertainment/galactica_new_031204. html>.

Lorenzen, Michael. "Battlestar Galactica and Mormonism." <www.michaellorenzen.com/ galactica.html>.

Lury, Karen. *Interpreting Television*. London: Hodder Arnold, 2005.

MacLean, Nancy. *Behind the Mask of Chivalry*. Oxford: Oxford University Press, 1994.

Marqusee, Mike. *Chimes of Freedom: The Politics of Bob Dylan's Art*. New York: New Press, 2003.

Martel, Ned. "The Cylons Are Back and Humanity Is in Deep Trouble." *New York Times*, December 8, 2003, E10.

Martin, Andre, and Patrice Petro, eds. *Rethinking Global Security: Media, Popular Culture, and the "War on Terror."* Piscataway, NJ: Rutgers University Press, 2006.

Martin, Dan. "The Final Frontier." *The Guardian*, January 13, 2007.

Marx, Karl. "On James Mill." In *Karl Marx: Selected Writings*, edited by David McLellan, 114–23. Oxford: Oxford University Press, 1977.

Mason, Dave. "Rebellious Starbuck in for Another Rough Ride." Scripps Howard News Service. January 4, 2006.

McCarty, William. "Brandon Jerwa on New Battlestar Galactica: Season Zero." *Newsarama.com*. May 22, 2007. <http://forum.newsarama.com/ showthread.php?t =113605>.

McCreary, Bear. <http://www.bearmccreary.com>.

McLemee, Scott. "Fear of a Monotheistic Cyborg Planet." *Out of the Crooked Timber*. <http:// crookedtimber.org/2006/10/06/fear-of-a-monotheistic-cyborg-planet>.

Miller, Jason Lee. "Ron Moore on Podcasting and Battlestar Galactica." *Webpronews.com*. October 5, 2006. <http://www.webpronews.com/insiderreports/2006/10/05/ron-moore-on-podcasting-and- battlestar-galactica>.

Miller, Laura. "The Man Behind 'Battlestar Galactica.'" *Salon.com*. March 24, 2007. <www.salon.com/ent/feature/2007/03/24/battlestar/print.html>.

———. "Space Balls: While Politicians Spent a Campaign Season Avoiding the Big Issues, TV's Bravest Series Has Been Facing Them in Thrilling Fashion." *Salon.com*. November 10, 2006. <http://www.salon.com/ent/tv/review/2006/11/10/battlestar/print.html>.

Miller, Mark Crispin. *Cruel and Unusual: Bush/Cheney's New World Order*. New York: W. W. Norton, 2004.

Miller, Susanna. *The Psychology of Play*. New York: Jason Aronson, 1974.

Minh-ha, Trinh T. "No Master Territories." In *The Post-Colonial Studies Reader*, edited by Bill Ashcroft, Gareth Griffiths, and Helen Triffin, 215–18. New York: Routledge, 1995.

Mittell, Jason. "Narrative Complexity in Contemporary American Television." *The Velvet Light Trap* 58 (Fall 2006): 29–40.

Mooney, Chris. "Blinded by Science: How Balanced Coverage Lets the Scientific Fringe Hijack Reality." *Columbia Journalism Review* (November–December 2004): 26–35.

Moore, Ronald D. "Galactica Interview." February 20, 2004. BBC Cult. <http://www.bbc.co.uk/ cult/news/cult/2004/02/20/9599.shtml>.

———. "Naturalistic Science Fiction or Taking the Opera out of Space Opera." <http:// galacticasitrep.blogspot.com/2006_03_01_archive.html>.

———. "Podcast Commentary: Precipice." Battlestar Wiki. April 19, 2007. <http:// en.battlestarwiki.org/wiki/Podcast:Precipice>.

———. "Podcast Commentary: Resurrection Ship, Part 1." *Scifi.com*. January 6, 2006. <http://media.scifi.com/battlestar/downloads/podcast/mp3/211/bsg_ep211_ FULL.mp3>.

———. "Podcast Commentary: Torn." Battlestar Wiki. February 6, 2007. <http:// en.battlestarwiki.org/wiki/Podcast:Torn>.

———. "RDM on Technobabble." September 6, 2006. Battlestar Wiki. June 6, 2007. <http:// en.battlestarwiki.org/wiki/Technobabble>.

———. "20 Answers, My responses Be Here" #18. March 27, 2007. Sci Fi Forums. <http://forums.scifi.com/index.php?s=6e8523ebeffc5ca742c318ae9ebfd1ea&showtopic=2270103&view=findpost&p=3041869>.

Moravec, Hans P. *Mind Children: The Future of Robot and Human Intelligence.* Cambridge, MA: Harvard University Press, 1988.

Morris, Tee. "Identity Crisis: The Failure of the Mini-series, the Success of the Series." In *So Say We All: An Unauthorized Collection of Thoughts and Opinions on* Battlestar Galactica, edited by Richard Hatch, 113–22. Dallas: Benbella Books, 2006.

Nakayama, Thomas. "Show/Down Time: "Race," Gender, Sexuality, and Popular Culture." *Critical Studies in Mass Communication* 11 (1994): 162–79.

The National Security Strategy of the United States of America. September 2002. <http://www.whitehouse.gov/nsc/nss.html>.

The National Security Strategy of the United States of America. March 2006. <http://www.whitehouse.gov/nsc/nss/2006/>.

Nguyen, Hanh. "The Luck of Starbuck: For the Gutsy *Battlestar Galactica* Pilot, It's Mostly Bad." *Ottawa Citizen*, April 22, 2006.

Nietzsche, Friedrich. [*Beyond Good and Evil*] *The Complete Works of Friedrich Nietzsche.* New York: Russell and Russell, 1964.

———. *The Gay Science.* Edited by Bernard Williams. Translated by Josafine Nauckhoff and Adrian Del Caro. Cambridge Texts in the History of Philosophy. Cambridge: Cambridge University Press, 2001.

Nishime, LeiLani. "The Mulatto Cyborg: Imagining a Multiracial Future." *Cinema Journal* 44 (Winter 2005): 34–49.

Oates, Joyce Carol. *On Boxing.* Garden City, NY: Dolphin/Doubleday, 1987.

Omi, Michael, and Howard Winant. *Racial Formation in the United States: From the 1960s through the 1980s.* New York: Routledge, 1986.

Oreskes, Naomi. "The Scientific Consensus on Climate Change." *Science.* 306.5702 (December 3, 2004): 1686.

Ott, Brian L. "Set Your Cathode Rays to Stun(ning)." *Flow: A Critical Forum on Television and Media Culture* 1, no. 10 (February 18, 2005). <http://jot.communication.utexas.edu/flow/>.

———. *The Small Screen: How Television Equips Us to Live in the Information Age.* Malden, MA: Blackwell Publishing, 2007.

Ott, Brian L., and Eric Aoki. "Counter-Imagination as Interpretive Practice: Futuristic Fantasy and *The Fifth Element.*" *Women's Studies in Communication* 27, no. 2 (2004): 149–76.

———. "Popular Imagination and Identity Politics: Reading the Future in *Star Trek: The Next Generation.*" *Western Journal of Communication* 65, no. 4 (2001): 392–415.

Owen, Rob. "Executive Producer Ron Moore Discusses Thrilling 'Galactica' Cliffhanger." *Pittsburgh Post-Gazette*, March 26, 2007. <http://www.postgazette.com/pg/07085/770732-352.stm>.

———. "Jettison Expectations. *Battlestar Galactica* Is Serious Drama, Not Kiddie Sci-fi." *Pittsburgh Post-Gazette,* July 10, 2005.

P., Ken. "An Interview with Ron Moore." *IGN.com.* December 4, 2003. <http://movies.ign.com/articles/444/444306p1.html>.

Papanikolaou, Eftychia. "Identity and Ethnicity in Peter Gabriel's Sound Track for *The Last Temptation of Christ.*" In *Scandalizing Jesus?: Kazantzakis's* The Last Temptation of Christ *Fifty Years On*, edited by Darren J. N. Middleton, 217–28. New York: Continuum, 2005.

Peirse, Alison. "Postfeminism Without Limits? *Charmed,* Horror and Sartorial Style." In *Investigating* Charmed: The Magic Power of TV, edited by Karin Beeler and Stan Beeler, 112–26. London: I. B. Tauris, 2007.

Penley, Constance. *NASA/TREK: Popular Science and Sex in America.* London: Verso, 1997.

Peterson, Kim. "Reborn *Galactica* Can Do Battle with the Best of Sci-fi." *The Seattle Times*, April 28, 2006.

Pinedo, Isabel. "The Wet Death and the Uncanny." *Paradoxa: Studies in World Literary Genres* Special Issue: "The Return of the Uncanny" 3, nos. 3–4 (1997): 407–16.

Poe, Edgar Allen. *Selected Tales by Edgar Allen Poe.* London: Penguin, 1994.

Postman, Neil. *Amusing Ourselves to Death: Public Discourse in the Age of Show Business.* New York: Viking Penguin, 1985.

Powell, Anna. "'The Face Is a Horror Story': The Affective Face of Horror." *Pli* 16 (2005): 56–78.

Raghavan, Sudarsan. "4 Years After Hussein's Fall, Regret in Iraq." *Washingtonpost.com.* April 9, 2007. <http://www.washingtonpost.com/wpdyn/content/article/2007/04/08/AR2007040801058_pf.html>.

Ramazani, Vaheed. "The Mother of All Things: War, Reason and the Gendering of Pain." *Cultural Critique* 54 (2003): 26–66.

"A Rare Glimpse Inside Bush's Cabinet." *CBS News.* November 17, 2007. <http://www.cbsnews.com/stories/2002/11/17/60minutes/main529657.shtml>.

Roediger, David. *The Wages of Whiteness: Race and the Making of the American Working Class.* New York: Verso, 1999.

———. *Working Toward Whiteness: How America's Immigrants Become White. The Strange Journey from Ellis Island to the Suburbs.* New York: Basic, 2005.

Rose, David. *Guantanamo: The War on Human Rights.* New York: New Press, 2004.

Roth, Lane. "Ambiguity of Visual Design and Meaning in TV's *Battlestar Galactica.*" *Extrapolation* 24, no. 1 (1983): 80–87.

Rubin, Gayle. "The Traffic in Women: Notes on the 'Political Economy' of Sex." In *Toward an Anthropology of Women,* edited by Rayna R. Reiter, 157–210. New York: Monthly Review, 1975.

Rubio, Steven. "Legitimate Authority: Debating the Finer Points." In *So Say We All: An Unauthorized Collection of Thoughts and Opinions on* Battlestar Galactica, edited by Richard Hatch, 123–34. Dallas: Benbella Books, 2006.

"Rumsfeld: 'Worst Still To Come.'" CBS/AP. May 7, 2004. <http://www.cbsnews.com/stories/2004/05/10/iraq/main616338.shtml>.

Rutledge, Gregory E. "Futurist Fiction and Fantasy: The "Racial Establishment." *Callaloo* 24 (Winter 2001): 236–52.

Sakata, Hiromi Lorraine. "Devotional Music [in Pakistan]." In *The Garland Encyclopedia of World Music.* Vol. 5: "South Asia: The Indian Subcontinent." Edited by Alison Arnold, 751–61. New York: Garland, 2000.

Salter, Michael A. "Play in Ritual: An Ethnohistorical Overview of Native North America." In *Play and Culture,* edited by Helen B. Schwartzman, 70–82. West Point, NY: Leisure Press, 1980.

Sandvoss, Cornel. *Fans.* Cambridge: Polity Press, 2005.

Sardar, Ziauddin, and Sean Cubitt, eds. *Aliens R Us: The Other in Science Fiction Cinema.* London: Pluto Press, 2002.

Scarry, Elaine. *The Body in Pain.* New York: Oxford University Press, 1985.

Scherer, Michael, and Benjamin, Mark. "Electrical Wires." *The Abu Ghraib Files. Salon.com.* March 14, 2006.<http://www.salon.com/news/abu_ghraib/2006/03/14/chapter_4/index.html>.

———. "Standard Operating Procedure." *The Abu Ghraib Files. Salon.com.* March 14, 2006. <http://www.salon.com/news/abu_ghraib/2006/03/14/ chapter_1/index.html>.

Scholes, Robert. *Structural Fabulation: An Essay on Fiction of the Future.* Notre Dame, IN: University of Notre Dame Press, 1975.

Shaviro, Steven. *Connected, or What It Means to Live in the Network Society.* Minneapolis, MN: University of Minnesota Press, 2003.

Silbiger, Alexander. "Passacaglia." *Grove Music Online.* Edited by Laura Macy. <http://www.grovemusic.com>.

Solaro, Erin. *Women in the Line of Fire: What You Should Know about Women in the Military*. Emeryville, CA: Seal Press, 2006.

Soler, Colette. "Literature as Symptom." In *Critical Essays on Jacques Lacan*, edited by Ellie Ragland, 70–75. New York: G. K. Hall, 1999.

Sontag, Susan. "The Imagination of Disaster." In *Liquid Metal: The Science Fiction Film Reader*, edited by Sean Redmond, 40–47. London: Wallflower, 2004.

Spivak, Gayatri Chakravorty. "Can the Subaltern Speak?" In *The Post-Colonial Studies Reader*, edited by Bill Ashcroft, Gareth Griffiths, and Helen Triffin, 24–28. New York: Routledge, 1995.

Stambaugh, Joan. *Nietzsche's Thought of Eternal Return*. Baltimore: Johns Hopkins University Press, 1972.

Starr, Charlie W. "*Galactica*'s Gods, or, How I Learned to Stop Worrying and Love the Cylon God." In *So Say We All: An Unauthorized Collection of Thoughts and Opinions on* Battlestar Galactica, edited by Richard Hatch, 95–111. Dallas: Benbella Books, 2006.

Steiner, Linda. "Oppositional Decoding as an Act of Resistance." *Critical Studies in Mass Communication* 5 (1988): 1–15.

Sterling, Bruce. "Old Genies in New Bottles: How to Prevent a Singularity from Happening." *Whole Earth* (Spring 2003): 14–19.

Stillshimpy. "Chain-Smoking & Apologies: Podcasts." March 6, 2007. Television Without Pity. <http://forums.televisionwithoutpity.com/index.php?showtopic= 3149128&st=210>.

———. "Chain-Smoking & Apologies: Podcasts." December 9, 2006. Television Without Pity. <http://forums.televisionwithoutpity.com/index.php?showtopic=3149128&st=45>.

Stover, Matthew Woodring. "The Gods Suck." In *So Say We All: An Unauthorized Collection of Thoughts and Opinions on* Battlestar Galactica, edited by Richard Hatch, 23–34. Dallas: Benbella Books, 2006.

Strachan, Alex. "Battlestar Galactica: It May Sound Silly or Pretentious. It Isn't. It's Just Good." *The Montreal Gazette*, January 14, 2006, D9.

———. "Battlestar Hype Justified After All." *The Star Phoenix* (Saskatoon, Saskatchewan), July 9, 2005, E8.

Sutton-Smith, Brian. *The Ambiguity of Play*. Cambridge, MA: Harvard University Press, 1997.

Sutton-Smith, Brian, and Diana Kelly-Byrne. "The Idealization of Play." In *Play in Animals and Humans*, edited by Peter K. Smith, 305–21. New York: Basil Blackwell, 1984.

Tabbi, Joseph. *Postmodern Sublime: Technology and American Writing from Mailer to Cyberpunk*. Ithaca, NY: Cornell University Press, 1995.

Tait, Sue. "Autoptic Vision and the Necrophilic Imaginary in *CSI*." *International Journal of Cultural Studies* 9, no. 1 (2006): 45–62.

Taylor, Charles. *The Ethics of Authenticity*. Cambridge, MA: Harvard University Press, 1991.

———. *Sources of the Self: The Making of the Modern Identity*. Cambridge, MA: Harvard University Press, 1989.

Telotte, J. P. *A Distant Technology: Science Fiction Film and the Machine Age*. Hanover, NH: Wesleyan University Press, 1999.

Theweleit, Klaus. "The Bomb's Womb and the Genders of War." In *Gendering War Talk*, edited by Miriam Cooke and Angela Woollacott, 283–315. Princeton, NJ: Princeton University Press, 1993.

Tilly, Steve. "Galactica Not Your Father's Sci-fi." *The Ottawa Sun*, October 6, 2006.

———. "Women Rule *Battlestar*." *Toronto Sun*, January 8, 2006.

Tracy, R. N. Captain USN (Ret). Personal Interview. June 7, 2007.

Troutt, David. *After the Storm: Black Intellectuals Explore the Meaning of Hurricane Katrina*. New York: New Press, 2006.

Uniform Code of Military Justice (UCMJ). *Military-Network.com*. <http://www.military-network.com/main_ucmj/main_ucmj.htm>.

Van DeBurg, William. *Hoodlums: Black Villains and Social Bandits in American Life.* Chicago: University of Chicago Press, 2004.

Vinge, Vernor. "First Word." *Omni* (January 1983): 10.

———. "Technological Singularity." *Whole Earth Review* 81 (Winter 1993): 88–95.

———. 2003. "Technological Singularity." Annotated reprint. <http://www.wholeearthmag. com/ArticleBin/111-3.pdf>.

Virilio, Paul. *Ground Zero.* Translated by Chris Turner. New York: Verso, 2002.

Waldby, Catherine. "Biomedicine, Tissue Transfer and Intercorporeality." *Feminist Theory* 3, no. 3 (2002): 239–54.

Werts, Diane. "Fanfiction Booms as Modern Folklore." *Newsday.com.* April 29, 2005. <http:// whedon.info/article.php3?id_article=9409>.

West, Cornel. *Democracy Matters: Winning the Fight Against Imperialism.* New York: Penguin, 2004.

Wheatley, Helen. *Gothic Television.* Manchester: Manchester University Press, 2007.

Williams, Raymond. *Television: Technology and Cultural Form.* New York: Routledge, 2003.

Winant, Howard. *The World Is a Ghetto.* New York: Basic Books, 2001.

Wisteria. "Chain-Smoking & Apologies: Podcasts." December 8, 2006. Television Without Pity. <http://forums.televisionwithoutpity.com/index.php?showtopic=3149128>.

Wolmark, Jenny. *Aliens and Others: Science Fiction, Feminism and Post-modernism.* New York: Harverster Wheatsheaf, 1994.

Wood, Aylish. *Technoscience in Contemporary American Film: Beyond Science Fiction.* Manchester: Manchester University Press, 2002.

Wood, Robin. "Return of the Repressed." *Film Comment,* July 14,1978, 24–32.

Yingling, Paul. "A Failure in Generalship." *Armed Forces Journal,* May 2007. <http:// www.armedforcesjournal.com/2007/05/2635198>.

Young, Marilyn. "Permanent War." *positions* 13, no. 1 (2005): 177–93.

Young, Robert, cinematographer. *The Eskimo: Fight for Life.* Dir. Asen Balikci. 1970. Issued as part of *Netsilik Eskimo 1.* National Film Board of Canada. VHS. 1972.

———. *Nothing but a Man.* Dir. Michel Roemer. 1964. New Video NYC. DVD. 2004.

Zak, Albin J., III. "Bob Dylan and Jimi Hendrix: Juxtaposition and Transformation 'All Along the Watchtower.'" *Journal of the American Musicological Society* 57 (2004): 599–644.

Episode List (2003–2007)

Episode	U.S. Air Date	Title
Miniseries		
M.01	8 Dec. 03	Battlestar Galactica (2003 miniseries)—Part 1
M.02	10 Dec. 03	Battlestar Galactica (2003 miniseries)—Part 2
Season 1		
1.01	14 Jan 05	33
1.02	14 Jan 05	Water
1.03	21 Jan 05	Bastille Day
1.04	28 Jan 05	Act of Contrition
1.05	04 Feb 05	You Can't Go Home Again
1.06	11 Feb 05	Litmus
1.07	18 Feb 05	Six Degrees of Separation
1.08	25 Feb 05	Flesh and Bone
1.09	04 Mar 05	Tigh Me Up, Tigh Me Down
1.10	11 Mar 05	The Hand of God
1.11	18 Mar 05	Colonial Day

Episode	U.S. Air Date	Title
1.12	25 Mar 05	Kobol's Last Gleaming, Part 1
1.13	01 Apr 05	Kobol's Last Gleaming, Part 2
Season 2		
2.01	15 Jul 05	Scattered
2.02	22 Jul 05	Valley of Darkness
2.03	29 Jul 05	Fragged
2.04	05 Aug 05	Resistance
2.05	12 Aug 05	The Farm
2.06	19 Aug 05	Home, Part 1
2.07	26 Aug 05	Home, Part 2
2.08	09 Sep 05	Final Cut
2.09	16 Sep 05	Flight of the Phoenix
2.10	23 Sep 05	Pegasus
2.11	06 Jan 06	Resurrection Ship, Part 1
2.12	13 Jan 06	Resurrection Ship, Part 2
2.13	20 Jan 06	Epiphanies
2.14	27 Jan 06	Black Market
2.15	03 Feb 06	Scar
2.16	10 Feb 06	Sacrifice
2.17	17 Feb 06	The Captain's Hand
2.18	24 Feb 06	Downloaded
2.19	03 Mar 06	Lay Down Your Burdens, Part 1
2.20	10 Mar 06	Lay Down Your Burdens, Part 2
Webisodes		
W.01–10	05 Sep to 05 Oct 06	Battlestar Galactica: The Resistance
Season 3		
3.01	06 Oct 06	Occupation
3.02	06 Oct 06	Precipice
3.03	13 Oct 06	Exodus, Part 1
3.04	20 Oct 06	Exodus, Part 2
3.05	27 Oct 06	Collaborators

Episode	U.S. Air Date	Title
3.06	03 Nov 06	Torn
3.07	10 Nov 06	A Measure of Salvation
3.08	17 Nov 06	Hero
3.09	01 Dec 06	Unfinished Business
3.10	08 Dec 06	The Passage
3.11	15 Dec 06	The Eye of Jupiter
3.12	21 Jan 07	Rapture
3.13	28 Jan 07	Taking a Break from All Your Worries
3.14	11 Feb 07	The Woman King
3.15	18 Feb 07	A Day in the Life
3.16	25 Feb 07	Dirty Hands
3.17	04 Mar 07	Maelstrom
3.18	11 Mar 07	The Son Also Rises
3.19	18 Mar 07	Crossroads, Part 1
3.20	25 Mar 07	Crossroads, Part 2

Notes on Contributors

Jim Casey is a Visiting Professor at Allegheny College. Although primarily a Shakespeare scholar, he has somehow convinced people that he has something intelligent to say about comics, anime, film, and science fiction.

Christopher Deis is a doctoral candidate and instructor at the University of Chicago. When not dreaming of an alternate reality where he, Tory, and Six live in bliss, Christopher researches race, American politics, and the politics of popular culture.

Chris Dzialo is a PhD student in the Film and Media Studies Department at the University of California, Santa Barbara. He wishes he were a Cylon so that he could see the face of his still-hazy dissertation aboard the Resurrection Ship.

Matthew Gumpert is an Associate Professor of American Culture and Literature at Kadir Has University, Turkey, specializing in classical influences on modern culture. His book *Grafting Helen: The Abduction of the Classical Past* was published by the University of Wisconsin Press (2001).

Erika Johnson-Lewis is a PhD candidate at Florida State University where she's secretly converting all of her students into *BSG* fans. She is also working on her dissertation.

Elizabeth Johnston teaches at Monroe Community College in Rochester, New York. She studies the eighteenth century, and has published on topics as diverse as fashion in the Middle East, female rivalry on reality television, and the nineteenth-century reception of Elizabeth Barrett Browning.

Lorna Jowett is a Senior Lecturer in American Studies and Media at the University of Northampton, U.K., where she teaches some of her favorite things, including science fiction and television (sometimes both at once).

Carla Kungl is an Associate Professor of English at Shippensburg University, where she teaches technical writing, developmental writing, and British literature and culture. Her first book, *Creating the Fictional Female Detective* (McFarland), was released in 2006.

Tama Leaver is currently a lecturer at the University of Western Australia. He writes about digital culture, science fiction, film, television, blogging, podcasting, and what he calls "participatory pedagogies," most which can be found at www.tamaleaver.net.

C. W. Marshall is an Associate Professor of Greek and Roman Theatre at the University of British Columbia, in Vancouver, where he borrows books from the Cylon base on Caprica.

An Associate Professor in the Department of English at the University of British Columbia, **Kevin McNeilly** teaches and writes about cultural studies, improvised music, and contemporary poetry.

Robert W. Moore is a freelance scholar and single father in Chicago, Illinois, whose daughter Elizabeth made him realize that young girls need action heroes with whom they can identify as much as boys do, and who inspired his research into the rise of heroic female characters on television.

Rikk Mulligan is a PhD candidate in the American Studies program at Michigan State University, in East Lansing (not Ann Arbor), where he fends off requests for web development in favor of wading through the gutters of genre fiction and popular culture.

Brian L. Ott is an Associate Professor of Media Studies at Colorado State University. He is author of *The Small Screen: How Television Equips Us to Live in the Information Age* (Blackwell).

Eftychia Papanikolaou is Assistant Professor of Musicology at Bowling Green State University in Ohio. *Galactica*'s universe provided a blissful break from her research on the interconnections of music, religion, and politics in the long nineteenth century.

Alison Peirse lectures in Media and Popular Culture at Leeds Metropolitan University, U.K. Her research interests are horror film and cult television, in particular aesthetics, the body, and violence on-screen. She has articles forthcoming on *Charmed*, *Nip/Tuck*, and *Dog Soldiers*.

Tiffany Potter teaches English at the University of British Columbia. While secretly researching popular culture, she is technically a specialist in eighteenth-century British and American literature, publishing on theater, libertinism, sexuality, and early writing on indigenous women.

Suzanne Scott is a PhD candidate in Critical Studies at the University of Southern California School of Cinematic Arts, writing her dissertation on new media narratives and Harry Potter fan culture. Her "Scholar Callsign" program has yet to be endorsed by the academy.

Carl Silvio is an Assistant Professor of English at Monroe Community College in Rochester, New York. He is the coeditor of *Culture Identities and Technologies in the* Star Wars *Films: Essays on the Two Trilogies* (McFarland).

Kevin J. Wetmore Jr. is a Professor of Theatre at Loyola Marymount University. In addition to being an actor and director, he is also the author of several books, including *The Empire Triumphant: Race, Religion and Rebellion in the* Star Wars *Films* (McFarland).

Matthew Wheeland is a journalist based in Berkeley, California. He writes primarily on business, the environment, and technology, and his articles have appeared in a variety of print and online publications.

INDEX